THE

Tea Council's

GUIDE TO THE

Best Tea Places in England

THE LITTLE BOOKROOM

NEW YORK

No. 9, The Courtyard, Gowan Avenue, London SW6 6RH. Every effort has been made to ensure the accuracy of this publication. However, the publishers do not hold themselves responsible for inaccuracies or omissions. The contents are believed to be correct at the time of going to press, but changes may have occurred since that time. Seventh edition, reprinted 2001. Acknowledgements: The Pump Room, Bath; Bruce Richardson, Elmwood Inn; Tai Tai Tea House; South Warwickshire Tourism; Lewes District Council; Harrogate International Centre; Scottish Tourist Board; Staffordshire Moorlands District Council; Wales Tourist Board; Norwich City Council; North Norfolk District Council; Devon County Council; City University, London: Richard Bailey. Library of Congress Cataloging-in-Publication Data. The best tea places in England / Tea Council Ltd. of UK.-- 7th ed., reprinted. p. cm. Originally published: 2001. Includes index. ISBN 1-892145-16-2 (paperback) 1. Tearooms--Great Britain--Guidebooks. 2. Afternoon teas--Great Britain. 3. Tea. I. Tea Council. TX907.5.B7 B49 2001 647.9541--dc21 2002004107

COMPILED BY MELANIE ADAMS & JANE PETTIGREW
DESIGN BY LOUISE FILI LTD

 5 St. Lukes Place New York N.Y. 10014 (212)691-3321 fax (212) 691-2011
editorial@littlebookroom.com

Contents

FOREWORD *p.* 4

THE TEA GUILD *p.* 5

GUILD AWARDS *p.* 6

TEA PLACES IN ENGLAND

South West Region *p.* 9

South East Region *p.* 37

London Region *p.* 55

East Region *p.* 77

Middle England Region *p.* 95

North East Region *p.* 119

North West Region *p.* 143

TEA PLACES IN WALES *p.* 161

TEA PLACES IN SCOTLAND *p.* 173

TEA ROOMS AROUND THE WORLD *p.* 189

350 YEARS OF TEA IN BRITAIN *p.* 203

WHAT IS TEA? *p.* 211

SOME OF THE WORLD'S BEST TEAS *p.* 217

BUYING, STORING AND BREWING TEA *p.* 224

INDEX OF BEST TEA PLACES *p.* 227

Foreword

Even though the modern world in which we find ourselves seems to be dominated by a fast-food, self-service, "buy now, pay later" mentality, I am proud to say that Britain has resisted the invasion of "coffee culture" and has preserved tea as her favourite drink. Indeed, as a nation, we still drink 165 million cups of tea every single day.

Tea has always played a vital part in our culture and daily lives but has recently enjoyed a reappraisal by consumers, both young and old that has led to a resurgence of interest in tea's diversity and its ability to be the perfect drink for any mood or occasion.

Tea is now also recognised as a sophisticated connoisseur's drink, much like wine, as it is both commonplace and chic to hold business meetings in refined surroundings over tea rather than lunch.

This is the seventh edition of the Tea Guild's *Best Tea Places* guide, and this year we have produced an informative guidebook that deserves pride of place on any tea-lover's book shelf. As well as spanning tea's colourful 350-year history, the guide also includes useful tips on how best to buy, store and brew your own tea.

Membership in the Tea Guild is only granted to establishments that are able to offer a wide range of high-quality teas and food, served in a relaxing or reviving atmosphere — which is why this guide lists some of the very best tea venues in the country, with prices to suit all pockets.

So, whether you are travelling for business or pleasure, the *Best Tea Places* guide should be the first item that you pack. Simply do not leave home without it. If on your travels you happen upon a quaint rural tea shop or a stylish urban tea lounge that is not already a member of the Guild, please let us know and we will set the tea-tasting team on the trail.

Enjoy your tea,
William Gorman
Executive Director

The Tea Guild

Although tea is our national drink and is served in thousands of outlets across Britain every day, an independent study commissioned by The Tea Council in 1995 concluded that very few of those outlets were serving tea to the high standards that The Tea Council believed desirable.

In accordance with these findings, The Tea Council decided that recognition should be given to establishments that do meet high standards in both preparing and serving tea. Acknowledgement was given in the form of an invitation to become members of the unique and prestigious Tea Guild. As the reputation of the Guild grew, other establishments were encouraged to aspire to these high standards also.

Before joining, all establishments must first be approved by incognito inspectors appointed by The Tea Council, and once a shop or tea lounge has become a member, The Tea Council keeps a watching brief on members throughout the year to ensure that standards of excellence are maintained.

Interest in the Guild has grown to such a level that it now includes 98 outlets all over Britain. They range from traditional tea shops set in country cottages, converted railway stations and museums, elegant tearooms in listed buildings in rural and town centre settings, grand lounges in stylish hotels, and — the most recent to join — modern tea bars that offer a more contemporary approach and aim to attract customers away from the high street coffee bars.

We believe that each member tea place featured in this book offers customers a relaxing and reviving experience at a price that offers value for money. The Tea Guild endorses high standards of tea making and serving, home baking, cleanliness and hygiene, staff efficiency and attitude and aims to guide members of the tea-drinking public from within Britain and abroad to the very best tea venues.

To make the guide more interesting, it now features a new section on traditional regional tea-time foods, and suggestions for things to see and do across the regions. We have also increased the international section to help readers find a good cup of tea when travelling abroad. More information about the Guild is available on the Tea Council's web site at www.tea.co.uk.

Guild Awards

Each year, the Tea Council awards its ultimate tea accolade, Top Tea Place of the Year, to the tea shop or tearoom that it considers has reached the highest possible standards of brewing and serving tea. The search for the best in Britain begins in April of each year and continues through May The competition is extremely tough, but one establishment eventually shines through and the prize, a beautiful stained-glass window, is awarded to the winning tea place in June. The winner in 2001 was Trenance Cottage Tearoom & Gardens, in Newquay, Cornwall, owned by Bob and Judy Poole. The Pooles bought it in 1986 when it was virtually derelict and have lovingly repaired the 200-year-old Georgian villa, restoring it to its earlier charm. The tearoom, which looks over the beautiful Trenance Gardens, is a perfect setting for tea.

Awards of Excellence also went to another 11 outstanding tearooms: Bird on the Rock Tearoom in Shropshire; Lewis's Tea-Rooms in Dulverton; the Bridge Tea Rooms in Bradford-on-Avon; Margaret's in Baconsthorpe; Greystones 17th Century Tea Room in Leek, (Winner in 2000); Shepherds Tea Rooms in Chichester; the Marshmallow in Morton-in-Marsh; Kind Kyttock's Kitchen in Fife; Ollerton Mill Tea Shop in Newark and Norwich Tea & Coffee Shop in Norwich.

The award of Top London Afternoon Tea is also given each year to the best of London's tea venues. This award was devised in order to redress the imbalance of Top Tea Place, which makes it inherently difficult to judge country tea shops against the tea lounges of lavish luxury hotels. The award reflects the lengthy, calm and leisurely afternoon teas that these establishments are renowned for. The Dorchester Hotel, where the Promenade serves spectacular teas in a haven of tranquillity and elegance, and the equally serene Lounge at the Four Seasons, are just two of the previous winners of the coveted London award.

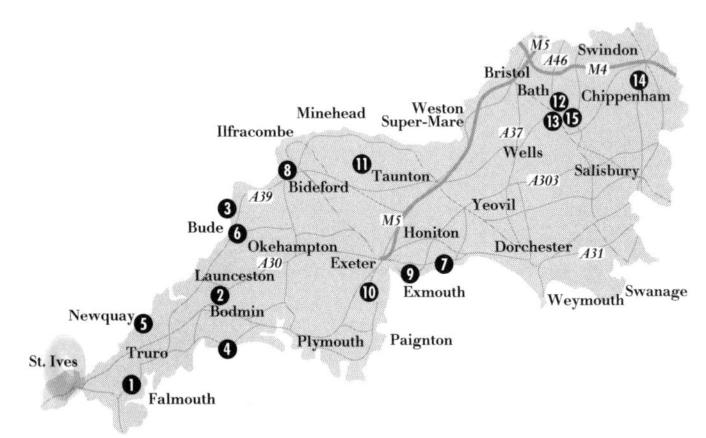
M5
Swindon
A46
M4
Bristol
14
Bath
12
Chippenham
Minehead
Weston
Super-Mare
13
15
Ilfracombe
A37
Wells
8
11
Taunton
Salisbury
A303
Bideford
A39
3
Yeovil
M5
Bude
6
Honiton
Okehampton
Dorchester
A31
A30
Exeter
7
9
Launceston
10
Exmouth
2
Swanage
Weymouth
Newquay
5
Bodmin
Plymouth
Paignton
4
Truro
St. Ives
1
Falmouth

The South West

Cornwall

❶ CHARLOTTE'S TEA-HOUSE *p.* 10

❷ MAD HATTER'S *p.* 11

❸ THE OLD RECTORY FARM TEAROOMS *p.* 12

❹ THE PLANTATION CAFÉ *p.* 13

❺ TRENANCE COTTAGE TEA ROOM & GARDENS *p.* 14

Devon

❻ COURT BARN COUNTRY HOUSE HOTEL *p.* 15

❼ THE CLOCK TOWER TEAROOMS *p.* 16

❽ THE COMMODORE HOTEL *p.* 17

❾ THE COSY TEAPOT *p.* 18

❿ TILLY'S TEA ROOM *p.* 19

Somerset

⓫ LEWIS'S TEA-ROOMS *p.* 20

⓬ SALLY LUNN'S HOUSE & MUSEUM *p.* 21

⓭ THE PUMP ROOM *p.* 22

Wiltshire

⓮ POLLY TEA ROOMS *p.* 23

⓯ THE BRIDGE TEA ROOMS *p.* 24

Charlotte's Tea-House

COINAGE HALL
NO. 1 BOSCAWEN STREET
TRURO, CORNWALL TR1 2QU
TEL: 01872 263706
OWNERS: JOAN & MIKE POLLARD

The Coinage Hall is in the centre of Truro, opposite the Hall for Cornwall, directly behind the bronze War Memorial. Charlotte's is on the first floor.

OPEN ALL YEAR.
MONDAY–SATURDAY, 10AM–5PM;
CLOSED SUNDAY.

The Coinage Hall in Truro has a history that goes back to 1302 and the halcyon days of Cornish tin mining, but the present Grade II-listed building was built in 1848 and recently was lovingly restored by the previous owners. Charlotte's Tea-House, on the first floor of the building, is the realisation of their dream of creating a sanctuary of Victorian tranquility just a few steps from the city's busy streets. The ambience is enhanced by crystal chandeliers and period furniture, homemade cakes served on silver-plated cake stands, and waitresses in period costume.

The emphasis is on quality and every care is taken to provide the best. Charlotte's was voted the top teahouse in Cornwall in the *Annual West Country Cooking Guide to Eating Out 2000/2001*. Everything on the menu is made on the premises and there is always a tempting display of cakes. Light lunches include potato toasties, omelettes and salads, and there are cream teas and Charlotte's speciality high teas — all made to order. Visitors can browse in the antique and collectors' showrooms or visit the wonderful selection of Italian drapes on the same floor as the tearoom.

House Blend, Assam, Earl Grey, Darjeeling, Ceylon, Jasmine, Lapsang Souchong, Yunnan, Decaffeinated, Blackcurrant, Ginseng and Vanilla, Lemon and Ginger, Peppermint, Elderflower, Strawberry and Rose, Elderflower and Lemon.

Mad Hatter's

28 CHURCH STREET, LAUNCESTON
CORNWALL PL15 8AR
TEL: 01566 777188
OWNER: HELEN TEW

Launceston is just off the A30 in North Cornwall. Mad Hatter's is in the centre of the town, 30 yards from the town square, opposite W. H. Smith.

OPEN IN SUMMER: MONDAY–SATURDAY, 9:30AM–5:30PM; SUNDAY, 11AM–4:30PM. OPEN IN WINTER: MONDAY, TUESDAY, THURSDAY–SATURDAY, 10:30AM–PM; WEDNESDAY, 10:30AM–2PM; CLOSED SUNDAY. OPENING TIMES VARY; PLEASE TELEPHONE TO CONFIRM.

Helen Tew doesn't believe that quality and high standards have to be at the expense of entertainment, and admits that being "as mad as a hatter" helped in creating this very idiosyncratic tearoom, where Lewis Carroll's characters are everywhere. Helen offers a wonderfully humorous menu that includes Mad Hatter's Platters of cheese, tuna or smoked ham with bread and pickles, Alice's Scrumptious Sandwiches, March Hare's Marvellous Cakes and Mad Hatter's Specials. A new range of very popular toasted sandwiches includes a Mouldy Old Dough (stilton and mushroom) and even Call the Paramedics! (raspberry jam, chocolate chips and bananas served with clotted cream).

But the favourite item has to be the Indecisive Cake Taster whereby those tempted by several of the homemade, calorie-laden gateaux can sample any three or, in desperation, ask the waitress to choose for them. Also featured — a special selection of delicious bread and cakes suitable for those on a special diet, including gluten-free, fat-free and sugar-free items.

Assam, Ceylon, China, Darjeeling, Earl Grey, English Breakfast, Jasmine, Kenya, Lapsang Souchong, Mad Hatter's Special Blend (lightly spiced). Scented teas and herbal infusions also are available.

The Old Rectory Farm Tearooms

RECTORY FARM
MORWENSTOW, NEAR BUDE
CORNWALL EX23 9SR
TEL: 01288 331251
OWNERS: R. B. SAVAGE & V. K. METTERS
MANAGER: J. A. SAVAGE
2000 TEA COUNCIL AWARD OF EXCELLENCE

From the A39, from Bideford to Bude, turn off at the sign to Morwenstow. Follow signs to the village and church. The tearoom is next to the church.

OPEN EASTER–OCTOBER:
MONDAY–SUNDAY, 11AM–6PM.

Rectory Farm has a long, long history and is mentioned in a document dated 1296, when it belonged to the monks of St. John of Bridgwater. The main hall of the house, with its heavy oak beams and ancient stone flagged floor, is now the tearoom, which has been run by the same family for over 50 years. It was the current owner who set it up when she realised that a lot of people were passing her door on their walks along the coastal footpath that runs right past the front door. She recognised the potential for a busy tearoom and created a warm, traditional interior with Victorian furniture and chintz curtains, and today there is a steady stream of customers right through the summer season. As well as enjoying high quality lunches, teas and dinners, you can buy local jams, chutneys and other produce from the little shop area.

Visitors come from all over the world to see the Church of St. John the Baptist, made famous by Parson Hawker, an eccentric who introduced the Harvest Festival to British churches and wrote the famous Cornish anthem "Trelawney." Rectory Farm, which is next door, gives them a chance to also enjoy a really good traditional English tea.

India, Earl Grey, Lapsang Souchong, Gunpowder, Keemun, Assam, Jasmine, various herbals.

The Plantation Café

THE COOMBES, POLPERRO
CORNWALL PL13 2RG
TEL: 01503 272223
E-MAIL: LINDA@COX4.FSBUSINESS.CO.UK
OWNERS: MRS. ANNE SMITH & MISS LINDA COX

Park in the main car park and walk to the Plantation Café, which is on the right-hand side of the main road, halfway between the car park and the harbour.

OPEN ALL YEAR:
SUNDAY–FRIDAY, 11AM–5:30PM;
IN PEAK SEASON, 11AM–9:30PM;
CLOSED SATURDAY.

The Plantation Café history dates back to the last century, when a Polperro man went off to North America adventuring and made a fortune on the plantations. He returned to his home village and with some of the money built the black and white house beside the river that is the tearoom today.

The tropical tea garden running alongside the River Pol has won awards for its beauty and colour. Its features include palm trees, hanging baskets, floral tubs, a water fountain, an old cartwheel, a working mangle and a butter churn. In the spring, families of ducklings on the river delight visitors, making it a perfect haven to relax under the umbrellas on a sunny day.

Inside the Victorian tearoom, with its old beams and bow window, the walls are decorated with novelty teapots, plates, jugs and biscuit barrels. A real fireplace (lit in autumn and spring) has a copper canopy decorated with copper and brass pots, pans and kettles.

Specialities include homemade cakes, soups, lemonade and traditional Cornish cream teas. A variety of home-cooked specials feature old favourites, modern Mediterranean dishes, local fish specialities and a good choice of unique vegetarian dishes. Plantation Café has a varied children's menu and dogs are also made very welcome.

Assam, Broken Orange Pekoe, Ceylon, Darjeeling, Decaffeinated, Earl Grey, Green Gunpowder, Jasmine, Camomile, and a wide range of fruit tisanes.

Trenance Cottage Tea Room & Gardens

TRENANCE COTTAGE
TRENANCE LANE, NEWQUAY
CORNWALL TR7 2HX
TEL/FAX: 01637 872034
WEB SITE: WWW.TRENANCE-COTTAGE.CO.UK
E-MAIL: ROBERT@TRENANCE-COTTAGE.CO.UK
PROPRIETORS: BOB & JUDY POOLE
2001 TEA COUNCIL TOP TEA PLACE OF THE YEAR

From the town centre, proceed down Edgcumbe Avenue past Waterworld/zoo, under the viaduct, past Trenance Gardens and Heritage Cottages into Trevemper Road with rose gardens and boating lakes on the right. Trenance Cottage lies directly opposite the lakes. The Newquay Shuttle train stops opposite during the season.

OPEN ALL YEAR FOR ACCOMMODATION.
TEAROOM OPEN MARCH–NOVEMBER,
10:30AM–5PM, DAILY. IN WINTER,
TIMES VARY, SO PLEASE TELEPHONE.

A visit to Trenance Cottage means taking a step back in time through a wonderful wisteria arch at the entrance to the Georgian villa where Judy and Bob Poole have re-created the tearoom that existed here well before the Second World War. The building was virtually derelict when the couple bought it in 1986, but they have chopped away the tree roots that were growing from unlikely parts of the house, repaired the roof, and generally renovated and restored it to its earlier charm. Like so many people, they had grown tired of plastic cups, tea bags and poor quality food, and decided to go into business themselves in order to offer something rather better. The tearoom seats up to 30 visitors while the terraced gardens can accommodate 80 visitors. Serving morning coffee, light lunches, homemade cakes and scones, the menu features a variety of Cornish produce — crab, cheeses, pasties, smoked mackerel, saffron buns, freshly made ice cream, spring water and, of course, clotted cream. Many of the local products are offered for sale and make ideal presents. For those wishing to stay, there are three bedrooms offering a high standard of accommodation.

Tearoom Blend, Assam, Darjeeling, Earl Grey, English Breakfast, Lapsang Souchong, China Green, Decaffeinated, other speciality teas. Herbal infusions also are offered.

Court Barn Country House Hotel

CLAWTON, HOLSWORTHY
DEVON EX22 6PS
TEL: 01409 271219
FAX: 01409 271309
OWNERS: SUSAN & ROBERT WOOD
AA 1987 & '89 TEA COUNCIL AWARD OF EXCELLENCE
EGON RONAY RECOMMENDED
AA ROSETTE

Clawton is 2.5 miles south of Holsworthy off the A388 (from Bude to Launceston). Court Barn is next to Clawton's 12th-century church.

OPEN ALL YEAR EXCEPT THE FIRST WEEK OF JANUARY. MONDAY–SUNDAY, 10AM–5:30PM. BOOKINGS PREFERRED FOR LUNCH.

Court Barn is a charming Victorian house, rebuilt in 1853 from a 16th-century manor house known as Court Baron. The hotel stands in five acres of beautiful, tranquil formal gardens, hidden amongst the rolling Devon countryside and close to the spectacular National Trust and English Heritage coastline.

The house is filled with antiques, paintings and decorative objects. Fresh flowers fill the elegant dining rooms and lounges creating a warm, friendly atmosphere. On balmy summer days, the garden makes an idyllic setting for a special Devon clotted cream tea with one of the 45 teas on the menu. For the more energetic, there is croquet, lawn tennis and badminton, or gentle strolls around the garden.

The menu is crammed with wonderful home-baked sweets and savouries, soups and pâtés, vegetarian dishes, sandwiches and cakes such as marsala and almond, honey and cherry, chocolate and walnut. Home cooking at its best.

House Blends (India/Ceylon, India/Kenya), Indian, Darjeeling, Darjeeling and Ceylon, Assam, Kenya, Lapsang Souchong, Earl Grey, Pure China Oolong, Keemun, Rose Pouchong, Gunpowder, English Breakfast. Fruit-flavored teas and herbal infusions also are offered.

The Clock Tower Tearooms

CONNAUGHT GARDENS
PEAK HILL ROAD, SIDMOUTH
DEVON EX10 8RZ
TEL: 01395 512477
OWNERS: STEWART & JUNE FRASER

From the town centre, proceed to the seafront and turn right. Take the road up a slight incline following signs to Manor Road car park. Connaught Gardens is directly opposite the car park and the tearooms are in the clock tower, at the top of Jacobs Ladder.

OPEN ALL YEAR EXCEPT CHRISTMAS DAY.
MONDAY–SUNDAY INCLUSIVE, 10AM–5PM.
LONGER HOURS IN SUMMER.

Previously in a state of ruin, the Clock Tower has been lovingly restored by the Frasers and now offers an unusual and charming venue for lunch or tea. It stands on the remains of ancient lime kilns and once served as a boathouse, but today the castellated building, with its Gothic-style windows, has been brought back to life. The old stone walls cascade with plants and flowers, and visitors who choose a table outside in the beautiful gardens can relish amazing views of the sea and the stunning coastline. Inside, there are low beams decorated with amazing wood carvings by a local artist, and the polished wooden floors and warm tones of the wooden furniture create a relaxed, friendly, welcoming atmosphere.

The selection of hot and cold drinks (including Ovaltine and hot chocolate) and the range of sandwiches and toasties, jacket potatoes, pizzas, ploughmans, full lunches and tea-time traditionals, make this a good place in both the cold of winter and the blazing heat of summer. There are scones with clotted cream and jam, toasted teacakes and a selection of cakes and gateaux for those with a sweet tooth.

House Blend, Assam, Darjeeling, Earl Grey.

The Commodore Hotel

MARINE PARADE, INSTOW
NORTH DEVON EX39 4JN
TEL: 01271 860347
FAX: 01271 861233
OWNER: BRUCE WOOLAWAY
1997 TEA COUNCIL TOP TEA PLACE OF THE YEAR

From the M5 take Exit 27 for the North Devon link road. Take the turning to Instow signposted just before Torridge Bridge. Follow signs for Instow seafront and these will bring you to Marine Parade.

OPEN TO NON-RESIDENTS ALL YEAR, 7:30AM–9:30PM. AFTERNOON TEA IS SERVED FROM 3–6PM.

Originally a Georgian gentleman's residence, this waterside hotel sits elegantly overlooking the mouth of the rivers Taw and Torridge in one of North Devon's prettiest locations. The Woolaways, a local Devon family, have owned the hotel since 1969, and they have created a stylish, welcoming environment where views of the palm trees, sweeping lawns that slope gently down to the sandy shore and the constantly changing waterfront scenery, make it a perfect place for afternoon tea. In summer months, relax on the terrace and watch the yachts scudding by with billowing sails, and in the chillier winter months take shelter from the sea breezes in the comfortable lounge.

The hotel's marine setting is echoed in the menu, where a good range of seafoods is offered for lunchtime savouries and in open sandwiches. And since this is the home of clotted cream, don't miss the cream tea, or treat yourself to one of the many teas and cakes that are served every afternoon.

Assam, Darjeeling, Lapsang Souchong, Earl Grey, Traditional PG Tips. Flavored teas and herbal infusions also are offered.

The Cosy Teapot

13 FORE STREET
BUDLEIGH SALTERTON
DEVON EX9 6NH
TEL: 01395 444016
OWNERS: MARGARET & JOHN FAIRHURST,
BETTY & RICHARD PUGSLEY

Budleigh Salterton is 11 miles from Junction 30 off the M5, and four miles east of Exmouth. The Cosy Teapot is situated at the lower end of the main street, on the left-hand side, going towards the seafront.

OPEN MARCH 1–OCTOBER 31, MONDAY–SATURDAY, 10AM–5PM; NOVEMBER 1–FEBRUARY 28, OPENING TIMES VARY. PLEASE RING FOR DETAILS.

This delightful Victorian-style tearoom is housed in what was once — in about 1880 — the library and later a shoe mender's shop. To reach it, you have to cross a small bridge that crosses the Budleigh Brook, which babbles over a pebbly bed right past the door. Once inside, visitors from all over the world enjoy a traditional English tearoom with friendly waiters and waitresses who serve the tea in fine Royal Albert china on tables covered with lace tablecloths and decorated with vases of fresh flowers.

Two sisters, Margaret and Betty, assisted by their husbands, John and Richard, pride themselves on their menu, the great majority of which they make themselves. The Devonshire cream tea is naturally very popular, but you might like to try their variation — the Cosy Teacake Special, which is served with teacakes instead of the usual scones. There is always a splendid selection of homemade cakes (fruit cakes, chocolate, coffee and Victoria sponges, for example), flapjacks and shortbreads, as well as fruit pies and crumbles served with clotted cream or custard. At lunchtime, the menu offers salads, homemade soups and freshly prepared sandwiches. One of the specialities is locally caught crab — subject, of course, to availability.

Assam, Darjeeling, Ceylon, Earl Grey, Lady Grey, Lapsang Souchong, English Breakfast, Afternoon Blend, Camomile, Peppermint, Lemon and Ginger, Blackcurrant.

Tilly's Tea Room

2 PIERMONT PLACE
DAWLISH, DEVON EX7 9PQ
TEL: 01626 889999
FAX: 01626 889999
E-MAIL: TERRI@TILLYSTEAROOM.FREESERVE.CO.UK
OWNERS: WILLIAM & TERRI MAGGS

Tilly's is located 100 yards from the seafront, opposite the tourist information centre.

OPEN ALL YEAR.
WEDNESDAY–SATURDAY, 10AM–4:30PM.
SUNDAY NOON–5PM.

Until 50 years ago, Dawlish was famous for growing violets, which until then had been very fashionable, particularly with the royal family. It is said that at the height of the violet season, the perfume drifted across the town. Now, to add to its credits, Dawlish boasts this fine traditional tearoom, just a three-minute stroll from the seafront.

William and Terri opened Tilly's Tea Room because they felt there was a distinct lack of "proper" tearooms in the area between Exeter and Torquay and out towards Dartmoor. They wanted to create a traditional atmosphere of calm and comfort, where the wonderful aroma of fresh tea and coffee and homemade cakes tempted customers inside to enjoy a friendly welcome and top-quality food. So, having bought a rundown restaurant in an attractive Victorian building, they set about restoring and redecorating it in period style. The décor is one of nostalgia enhanced by a rather eclectic collection of old photographs, pictures, farming tools and advertising signs. Pretty table settings include fresh flowers, and tea is served in fine bone china cups and saucers.

Earl Grey, Assam, Darjeeling, Lapsang Souchong, Green Tea, Redbush, Camomile, Peppermint, Apple and Ginger, Hawthorne and Limeflower.

Lewis's Tea-Rooms

13 THE HIGH STREET
DULVERTON, SOMERSET TA22 9HB
TEL: 01398 323850
OWNERS: DAVE & KATHIE FULLER
2001 TEA COUNCIL AWARD OF EXCELLENCE

Dulverton is on the A3223 that runs from northwest to southeast across Exmoor. It is 14 miles north of Tiverton and 25 miles south of Minehead.

OPEN ALL YEAR, SPRING AND SUMMER, SEVEN DAYS A WEEK: 10AM–5PM. WINTER TIMES VARY, PLEASE TELEPHONE TO CONFIRM.

"The quintessential British tearoom" is how one of the many delighted customers described Lewis's in the visitors' book, and this is exactly what the owners had hoped to create. This bright, spacious tearoom, set in the high street of this attractive Exmoor town, was originally two rooms and has two fires that burn brightly in the winter months. Decorated with pottery, paintings, brush ducks and small antiques (many for sale) and an abundance of dried-flower gifts and arrangements, also for sale, this primrose-painted room, with its wooden floor, pretty tablecloths and fresh flowers, is instantly welcoming. On sunny days, the small, flower-filled courtyard offers extra seating. Also on display in the tearoom is hand-painted, blue-and-white or lemon-and-white Lewis Chintz china by local artist Pauline Clements, available exclusively at Lewis's.

Visitors are encouraged by the friendly staff to enjoy a pot of loose-leaf tea or a freshly brewed cafetiere of coffee in an unhurried atmosphere to a background of soothing classical music. As well as the irresistible selection of home-made cakes prominently displayed on the centre table, there is a large choice of cream teas varied according to taste and appetite. Full English breakfasts are also available, alongside a tempting selection of rarebits — firm favourites with the customers — and traditional puddings.

Assam, Darjeeling, Ceylon, Orange Pekoe, English Breakfast, Afternoon Blend, Earl Grey, Lapsang Souchong, Keemun, Gunpowder, Jasmine, Decaffeinated Ceylon, Lemon, Summer Pudding, Apple Crumble, Passion Flower, various fruit-flavoured, various herbal infusions.

Sally Lunn's House & Museum

4 NORTH PARADE PASSAGE
BATH BA1 1NX
TEL: 01225 461634
FAX: 01225 811800
E-MAIL: CORSHAM@AOL.COM
WEB SITE: WWW.SALLYLUNNS.CO.UK
OWNERS: JONATHAN OVERTON & JULIAN ABRAHAM

Sally Lunn's is in the heart of the city of Bath, two minutes' stroll from the Abbey and Roman Baths. Follow the street signs or ask for directions.

OPEN ALL YEAR.
MONDAY–SATURDAY, 10AM–11PM;
SUNDAY, 11AM–11PM.
MUSEUM: MONDAY–SATURDAY 10AM–6PM;
SUNDAY 11AM–6PM.

In 1680, a young refugee by the name of Solange Luyon arrived in Bath from France and took work with a local baker. Sally Lunn, as the locals called her, showed him how to make French brioches, and the bakery became famous for the bun that took her name and which the Georgian gentry were served at public breakfasts and afternoon teas. Today, the old bakery (the oldest house in Bath) is a tea shop that still makes and serves the generous round Sally Lunn buns to the original recipe, and they are delicious served as a sweet treat or as part of a savoury snack.

Half Sally Lunns are served with or as the base for most of the items on the menu. They are toasted and topped with Welsh rarebits, with smoked salmon, pâté and scrambled eggs, or with jam, lemon curd, fruit compote and clotted cream. High tea includes a bun topped with smoked salmon or sliced eggs, mayonnaise and cucumber, followed by a toasted, buttered half Sally Lunn topped with generous pots of jam and clotted cream.

House Blend, Earl Grey, Darjeeling Moondakotte, Ceylon Mooloya, Assam Thanai, Lapsang Souchong, other blends and specialist teas.

The Pump Room

STALL STREET
BATH BA1 1LZ
TEL: 01225 444477
FAX: 01225 447979
OPERATOR: MILBURNS RESTAURANTS LTD,
FOR BATH & NORTH EAST SOMERSET COUNCIL

The Pump Room is located in the heart of the city of Bath, adjacent to the Roman Baths, just 50 yards from the Abbey.

OPEN ALL YEAR EXCEPT CHRISTMAS DAY AND BOXING DAY. APRIL–SEPTEMBER, 9AM–6PM; AUGUST, 9:30AM–10PM; OCTOBER–MARCH: MONDAY–SATURDAY, 9:30AM–5PM; SUNDAY 10:30AM–5PM. CLOSING TIMES MAY VARY SLIGHTLY (LAST ADMISSION 30 MINUTES BEFORE CLOSING).

The historic Pump Room was built by Thomas Baldwin and John Palmer between 1790 and 1795. It overlooks the King's Bath and visitors may taste the spa waters from Britain's only geothermal spring in the Pump Room's Spa Fountain.

This magnificent room has been a favourite meeting place since the late 18th century, when fashionable society gathered there to socialise and take the waters. Today the room serves as a restaurant that offers elevenses, a selection of excellent hot and cold lunchtime dishes, and a full afternoon tea menu. As well as the traditional Pump Room tea, there is a champagne tea with smoked salmon sandwiches, scones with strawberry jam and clotted cream, and half a bottle of champagne; a Tompion tea (named after the imposing Tompion clock, made by the famous clockmaker Thomas Tompion), with a selection of finger sandwiches and home-made scones with jam and cream; and high tea, which includes cheddar and stilton crostinis and a selection of cakes and pastries. Throughout the day, music is provided by a Pump Room trio or a pianist, who continue a 300-year-old tradition of music making in these elegant surroundings.

Assam, Ceylon, Darjeeling, Earl Grey, English Breakfast, Lapsang Souchong. Herbal infusions are also available.

Polly Tea Rooms

26–27 HIGH STREET, MARLBOROUGH
WILTSHIRE SN8 1LW
TEL: 01672 512146
OWNER: JULIAN WEST
AA 1985 TEA COUNCIL TOP TEA PLACE OF THE YEAR
EGON RONAY RECOMMENDED

Marlborough is on the A4.
Polly's is halfway along the high street.

OPEN ALL YEAR. MONDAY–FRIDAY, 8:30AM–6PM;
SATURDAY, 8AM–7PM; SUNDAY, 9AM–7PM.

Polly Tea Rooms is probably one of the most important tourist attractions in Marlborough, and everyone who has tea here says how wonderful it is. The shop is in a very fine bow-windowed 17th-century building that was originally a house; there has been a tea shop here for more than 50 years. As you walk through to the large beamed tearoom, you are bound to be tempted by the mouthwatering array of chocolates and pastries on the counter just inside the entrance. Everything is made on the premises by local pastry chefs, and you'll find it hard to decide what to choose from the long list of possibilities — macaroons, rum truffles, date slice, lemon and redcurrant cheesecake, muesli scones, Danish pastries and lots more.

Once you have made your decision, sit back and enjoy the traditional setting with its pretty flowered china, pine dressers, lace tablecloths and neatly uniformed girls who are busy all day serving tourists, schoolboys from nearby Marlborough College and their parents, and local customers who find this the perfect place to sit and relax.

Indian, Earl Grey, Lapsang Souchong.
Fruit infusion is also offered.

The Bridge Tea Rooms

24A BRIDGE STREET
BRADFORD-ON-AVON
WILTSHIRE BA15 1BY
TEL: 01225 865537
OWNER: FRANCINE WHALE

1994–97, 1999, 2000, 2001
TEA COUNCIL AWARD OF EXCELLENCE
1998 TEA COUNCIL TOP TEA PLACE OF THE YEAR
EGON RONAY RECOMMENDED

Turn immediately left after going over the bridge and park in the town car park. Walk out of the car park and the tearooms are situated just across the narrow street in front of you.

OPEN ALL YEAR EXCEPT CHRISTMAS DAY AND BOXING DAY. MONDAY–FRIDAY, 9:30AM–5PM; SATURDAY, 9:30AM–5:30PM; SUNDAY, 10:30AM–5:30PM.

Although the building that houses the Bridge Tea Rooms was constructed in 1675, the interior has been themed in Victorian style with aspidistras, 19th-century china and memorabilia, including busts of Queen Victoria herself and sepia photographs of local views and past relatives of the owner, Francine Whale. The waitresses' costumes recall the early days of London's first tearooms, when white frilly aprons were worn over black dresses and white mobcaps covered curls and topknots. The ambience and service are delightful and the food is excellent.

A full afternoon tea includes sandwiches, a crumpet, a scone with thick Devon clotted cream and jam, and a cake. But if you just want a cup of tea and something sweet, there is a wide choice of really luscious cakes and patisserie that come fresh from the oven. Try a slice of carrot, banana and walnut cake, or choose one of the roulades — Belgian chocolate, fresh strawberry, lemon, hazelnut, pineapple or coconut.

House Blend, Earl Grey, Darjeeling FOP, First Flush Darjeeling, Assam, Lapsang Souchong, Ceylon, BOP, Ceylon Orange Pekoe, Kenya, Pelham Blend, Jasmine, various fruit-flavoured teas.

Tea-Time Traditions from the South West

CORNWALL, DEVON, GLOUCESTERSHIRE, SOMERSET, WILTSHIRE

Cornwall is perhaps best known for its rich clotted cream, which turns scones and Cornish splits into sheer indulgence, and makes irresistible ice cream. Early recipes for "clouted" cream instructed dairy maids to allow fresh milk, with its very high fat content, to stand for up to 24 hours and then to heat it very gently until it "simpreth and bubbeleth a little." After cooling, the thick crusty layer of clotted cream is skimmed off and served with cakes, pies and splits — soft white yeasted buns that are also found under the same name in north Devon and as Chudleighs in the south of the county.

Saffron first arrived in England during the 14th century and quickly became a very popular flavouring in both savoury and sweet dishes. Saffron fields were soon established in Essex in order to produce our own cheaper stocks of the spice, but the industry died out in the early 15th century and supplies were once again imported from the East through the Cornish ports. Originally baked for festive occasions, saffron cakes, breads and buns are still made in Cornwall.

Biscuits were always made in the past for traditional fairs and sold in little bags or packages by travelling merchants. Most were a plain, rather short mixture with dried fruits, ginger, or other spices and flavourings. Cornish fairings are typical crisp ginger biscuits, still popular today.

Devon's clotted cream is thicker and more creamy in colour than Cornwall's version, and is traditionally served with scones or splits and strawberry jam. It also used to be added to the local pork and leek pies, and was an ingredient of Devon flats — rather like scones but drier and more biscuity. When it comes to eating at Sally Lunn's from Bath, it is whipped cream that is used to fill the large, soft, slightly sweet bread rounds that some say take their name from the French for "sun and moon" (*soleil et lune*) — round and golden like the sun on top and pale on the bottom like the moon. It is more probable that they are named after the girl who baked them — Solange Luyon.

Bath is also well known for its Bath buns, which were traditionally flavoured with caraway seeds but today usually contain currants or candied peel and are topped with crushed sugar.

Anywhere in Britain where lace was once made, St. Catherine's Day has always been celebrated with Cattern cakes or St. Catherine's cakes. Like many feast-day cakes, they were originally made with plain dough enriched with more expensive ingredients such as dried fruits, cream, spices, caraway seeds, almonds, eggs and sugar. The Devonshire versions of the cakes are spicy and contain ground almonds, currants and raisins.

The apple orchards of Gloucestershire and Somerset provided fruit for pies, shortbreads and cakes. Gloucester shortcake is sandwiched together with a layer of apples that has been cooked with brown sugar. At the beginning of Lent, Gloucestershire pancakes vary from those made in the rest of the country in that they are made with suet and are almost like fritters. Lardy cakes are another Gloucestershire and Wiltshire speciality and, like so many of our favourite tea-time treats, are irresistible — even though you know (as you find yourself standing at the shop counter to buy a big one for tea) that they are full of ingredients you really shouldn't eat. But oh, that soft, sweet, fruity dough! Well worth a trip to the West Country.

For a hot savoury for high tea, Gloucestershire created its own version of Welsh rarebit by baking together cheese, butter, ale and breadcrumbs and then serving the bubbling mixture on toast. A similar adaptation from Somerset is made with layers of grated cheese and sliced onions topped with buttered breadcrumbs.

Things to See and Do in the South West

CORNWALL, DEVON, BATH & SOMERSET, WILTSHIRE

Cornwall

The city of Truro, at the heart of which you will find Charlotte's Tea-House, developed as a navigable port and centre for the tin and copper trades. It became the hub of fashionable life in the 17th and 18th centuries, and many of the buildings from that period remain, including houses in Lemon Street, Boscawen Street and Walsingham Place. Truro Cathedral, built between 1880 and 1910, is the most significant feature of the town. It has fine Victorian stained glass, 14th-century statues, a reredos carved from Bath stone, and various interesting pieces of modern art. The Royal Cornwall Museum has a permanent display on the history of Cornwall from the Stone Age to the present day, as well as a collection of more than 10,000 minerals, ceramics, and fine and decorative art. South of the town is Trelissick Garden, a National Trust property, one of Cornwall's finest woodland gardens overlooking the River Fal. The 500 acres of ground are considered a plantsman's delight and contain a large collection of hydrangeas, camellias, rhododendrons, and exotic plants that thrive in the mild Cornish climate, and the Cornish Apple Orchard contains a definitive collection of Cornish apple varieties.

Launceston, a historic walled hill-fortress town, is home to Mad Hatter's tearoom. Set between Dartmoor and Bodmin Moor, it is known as the gateway to Cornwall and was once the county's ancient capital. The ruined keep of its castle overlooks the River Tamar, and other medieval reminders are the remains of the St. Augustinian priory, built in 1136; the 12th-century Church of St. Thomas's and St. Mary Magdalene Church, famous for its ornate carvings on the outside walls. It was also once a thriving market town, and although the cattle market closed in 1991, the pannier market continues. Mad Hatter's is centrally placed in the town and is within walking distance of some of the finest historic buildings, including the castle, Southgate Arch (the only remaining gateway of the three original entrances to the old walled town), the Town Hall (a Gothic-style building dating from 1887), and the Georgian houses of Castle Street just around the corner. John Betjamin once said of Castle Street, "This street is the most perfect collection of 18th-century town houses in Cornwall." The Lawrence House Museum is part of one of these houses, and the displays in the various rooms document local history, connections with the Napoleonic wars, the coming of the railway and memorabilia from the Methodist movement. Southwest from the town, on the road to Bodmin Moor, the hamlet of Trewint has very close associations with John Wesley's Methodists. Wesley Cottage tells how Wesley was entertained here in the home of Digory, a stonemason, in 1744, and how an extension was built to the house especially for Wesley's use whenever he was in the district. Five miles northwest of Launceston, the Tamar Otter Sanctuary at North Petherwin is the only place in the West Country breeding British otters and re-introducing the young animals to the wild. The Launceston Steam railway links the town to Newmills, carrying passengers in either open or closed Victorian carriages, depending on the weather.

The Plantation Café is in the heart of Polperro, a fishing village of picturesque cottages that nestle in the sheltered harbour and cling to the steep and craggy hillsides rising on all sides. Between the cottages are small shops and converted sail lofts that now house artists' and craftspeople's studios and showrooms. Once this was the centre for pilchard fishing and smuggling when brandy casks, bales of tobacco and chests of tea were illicitly brought ashore. Visit the Museum of Smuggling to find out more. Horse-drawn trolley wagons carry visitors through the narrow streets to and from the village centre, and fishing trips and pleasure cruises offer spectacular views of the coastline from the water. Walkers can take the South West Coast Path to enjoy the countryside and coastal views from dry land. Nearby, Looe was once also famous for pilchards and smuggling, and is today Cornwall's second most important fishing port. You can hire a motorboat or stroll along Banjo Pier, wander through the narrow streets and visit the Old Guildhall Museum. At West Looe, the high-tech Discovery Centre tells the secrets of the local flora and fauna. Along the coast at St. Austell, the new Eden Project has already been called the "Eighth Wonder of the World." Set inside a 50-metre crater overlooking St. Austell Bay, two gigantic conservatories are home to the plants, fruits and flowers of the Mediterranean, South Africa and California.

Trenance Cottage Tea Room and Gardens are on the north coast of Cornwall at Newquay, often known as the Cornish Riviera. The town has long stretches of golden beach, smugglers' caves, rock pools, soaring cliffs, and sports and leisure facilities for everyone. The harbour was once busy with sailing schooners and ketches involved in the export of china clay. Construction of the new quay was started in 1439 and gave the town its name. Huer's Hut at Towan Headland was originally used during the fishing season by the "huer" or lookout, who watched for the shoals of fish. The island of Trevelgue Head at Porth was a prehistoric camp and ancient village. At Crantock, the Gannel Estuary is an excellent area for birdwatching, windsurfing and trawling for shrimps. Trenance Cottage Tea Room is close to the zoo and Waterworld, both of which offer plenty of fun for children, and in Trenance Gardens, with its brilliant show of flowers and subtropical plants, you can walk, take a trip on the boating lake or visit the Heritage Cottages — Victorian houses set out as they would have been in the 19th century and including an arts and crafts shop. Just inland from Newquay, Trerice is famous for its rare perennials, and the gold and purple colours in the Front Court set against the Elizabethan stone walls of the 16th-century manor house. Inside the house there are some fine plaster ceilings and fireplaces.

Morwenstow is home to the Old Rectory Farm Tearooms and is a village famous for its Victorian vicar and hymn writer, Robert Stephen Hawker, who began the Harvest Festival tradition as we know it today. The fascinating churchyard of St. John the Baptist Church contains memorials to the sailors who perished on the wild and dangerous coast, and the smugglers, wreckers and dissenters to whom Hawker was minister. Walkers can follow the coastal path that links Morwenstow to Bude, once a busy port and now a main coastal resort with interesting little shops, sandy beaches, rock pools, a surfing centre and Bude Canal (opened in 1825), where you can fish, canoe and stroll. Bude is also host each year to an August jazz festival, which attracts international artists and includes more than 150 events, including New Orleans-style street parades. Bude Castle was once the country home of Sir Goldsworthy Gurney, a Cornish inventor whose concrete raft technique enabled man to build on sand. Inland from Bude are some lovely villages, including Kilkhampton, Poughill and Week St. Mary, each with its church and country inn, and Stratton, where the Battle of Stratton is re-enacted each year in May.

Devon

The Clock Tower Tearooms in Sidmouth are surrounded by breathtaking views of amazing coastal countryside and the charms of this timeless seaside resort. John Betjamin once said of the town, "If it were not for the sea, Sidmouth would be a tropic forest." Visitors never cease to enjoy the softly curving, south-facing bay, the long stretch of golden sands, the dramatic red cliffs, the floral displays that splash the streets and gardens with blazing colours, and the unique appeal of the town itself with its elegant Regency architecture. It offers attractions for everyone — the water for sailing enthusiasts; sports facilities for those who like bowls, cricket, fishing, golf, pony trekking, swimming, tennis and more; paths and tracks for those who enjoy exploring and walking; the annual festival of music, dance and colour; and the beauty of the nearby villages of Salcombe Regis, Sidbury and Sidford, amongst the most unspoilt of English villages. A stroll around Sidmouth reveals much of the town's history through all the blue plaques on the walls of historic buildings, including the pre-Reformation Old Ship Inn, the stylish Fortfield Terrace, the parish church restored in the 19th century, the Sidmouth Museum Heritage Centre, and, on Salcombe Hill, an observatory built by the famous astronomer Sir Norman Lockyer.

Tilly's Tea Room is also on Devon's south coast at Dawlish, a part-Georgian, part-Victorian coastal town that was opened up to holidaymakers when Isambard Kingdom Brunel introduced the railway here. At its centre is an attractive park with an avenue of chestnut trees, flowerbeds filled with colour, palms, cacti, all sorts of exotic plants, black swans, waterfowl and a waterfall that tumbles right down to the sea. The town sits on the edge of wonderful rolling countryside and, on the coastal side, impressive cliffs. A little to the east, Dawlish Warren offers sandy beaches that slope very gently into the sea, with plenty of opportunities for walking along the South West Coast Path, which runs in one direction to Dawlish and

Teignmouth, and in the other to Exmouth, Exeter and East Devon. The family beach area is safe for children and has a range of play areas and shops. Throughout the summer there are events, concerts, play parties, an open-air market and a very impressive fireworks spectacular.

Instow's Commodore Hotel on the North Devon coast is set in an area of wonderful natural beauty that remains largely untouched by modern influences and retains its local traditions, romance and colour. Instow itself offers all the charm and relaxing attractions of its waterside location, and nearby are Tapely Park, the Bideford Station and Signal Box Museum, Barnstaple's North Devon Museum and the North Devon Farm Park and Heritage Centre. All along this stretch of coast are golden beaches (some of which have won awards, like the one at Woolacombe, recently voted one of the world's top-10 beaches), small coves and hidden bays, steep cliffs and sheltered harbours. For ramblers, the South West Coast Path (the South West Way) is Britain's longest footpath, running more than 600 miles from Somerset to Dorset; the Two Moors Way runs from South Devon to Lynton in North Devon, linking the two national parks of Exmoor and Dartmoor; and the 180-mile Tarka Trail follows a figure-eight path centring on Barnstaple, and takes walkers through peaceful countryside, wooded valleys, rugged moorland and along the coast. One section of the trail offers 25 miles of traffic-free, flat cycling along a disused railway line.

The Cosy Teapot is close to Budleigh Salterton's seafront. The town, formerly Salterton or Salterne, derives its name from the manufacture of salt in large salt pans that were situated at the lower part of the River Otter. The salt making and distribution were controlled by the monks of the priory of Otterton.

The town has always resisted the temptation to become a popular holiday resort and has remained a small, charming, self-contained residential seaside town. Sir Walter Raleigh was born close by, at Hayes Burton, a mile or two inland, and his home, the nearby church where he worshipped and the old thatched vicarage where he taught, have remained virtually unchanged. Down on the seafront, by the old sea wall, the artist Millais composed one of his masterpieces, *The Boyhood of Raleigh*, before finishing the work in his London studio. Opposite the famous wall is the thatched

Fairlynch Museum, which has a permanent exhibition on local history, costume and lace, and also has a smugglers' cellar. Not far from the town, other attractions include the picture-postcard town of Otterton with its working mill that grinds corn and sells the flour; the gardens and arboretum at Bicton College, with its extensive camellia collection; and Bicton Park Botanical Gardens, which offer 18th-century tranquillity with an Italian garden, terraced lawns, fountains, lakes, an orangery, a 19th-century palm house, a tropical house with exotic jungle plants and a countryside museum with traction engines.

Court Barn Country House Hotel at Holsworthy is on the border of North Devon and Cornwall, and close to Bude Bay. The town is mentioned in the *Domesday Book* and is described as a port, meaning a secure market place for trade. Today it is still a busy place, particularly on Wednesdays, when the pannier market takes place in the square, and the cattle market, fascinating for anyone not used to rural life, is held in Underlane. Every third Friday of the month there is also a farmers' market in the square. Hoslworthy Museum is housed in a 17th-century manor house, which was acquired in 1724 by the Bishop of Exeter for use as a parsonage. The museum specialises in history and archaeology, and holds local archives, photographs and china. The original kitchen has its cobbled floor and a large open fireplace with all the domestic items that would have been in use in the 1600s. Stanhope Park is a large public space with children's play area, and a mile and a half out of town, the Simpson Barton nature trail follows a disused railway track and has a badger's sett, newly planted areas of alder, cherry, oak and ash trees, fish ponds, a wildlife pond, lakes and a moor field with a great variety of wild flowers. Nearby, the Tamar lakes are an important area for birds where waders rest on their migration routes, and there are also facilities for canoeing, windsurfing and sailing, and plenty of footpaths.

Bath and Somerset

The Georgian city of Bath is the home of two Guild teashops — the Pump Room at the Roman Baths and Sally Lunn's House and Museum.

The area of the town around Abbey Green and York Street is one of the oldest quarters and has plenty of small speciality shops selling everything from Russian crafts to lace and lacquerwares. In the midtown area, the Roman Baths and Abbey are surrounded by little alleyways and lanes packed with boutiques. Near Pulteney Bridge, the Guildhall market has been a popular spot for centuries for the sale of fresh flowers and local cheeses, silver and leatherwares. Bath is one of the West Country's most important centres for antiques, and there are more than 70 dealers, secondhand shops and reclamation centres. Museums include the Roman Baths and Pump Room, No. 1 Royal Crescent (a fine 18th-century house redecorated and furnished by the Bath Preservation Trust), the Museum of Costume & Assembly Rooms, the Holbourne Museum of Art (with a superb collection of 17th- and 18th-century paintings, silver, porcelain and sculpture), the Bath Industrial Heritage Museum (in a reconstructed Victorian engineering factory) and the Jane Austen Centre (newly opened in 1999 in a Georgian town house in Queen Square). Outside Bath, the American Museum at Claverton Manor documents American life in the 17th–19th centuries. At Lansdown, Beckford's Tower and Museum is a neoclassical Italianate tower built by William Beckford in 1827 as a study and retreat; it has an elegant belvedere, a spiral stone staircase and a collection illustrating Beckford's life. South of Bath, medieval Farleigh Hungerford Castle is set in the gently rolling valley of the River Frome, and has medieval wall paintings, a crypt and a chapel, and throughout the year is the scene of re-enactments of historical and military events.

Dulverton, home to Lewis's Tea-Rooms, is on the very edge of Exmoor National Park and is therefore an excellent centre from which to explore the area. It is a small, friendly town in the Barle Valley, surrounded by steep wooded hills and with good access to the nearby countryside and a number of waymarked footpath walks that start here. The Exmoor National Park Authority has its office here, and the Park's Visitor Centre is in Fore Street, so this really is the ideal spot to gather information about the stunning scenery, the dramatic coastline, historic buildings, facilities for walking, horse-riding, fishing and other sporting activities. Exmoor is one of the most beautiful protected parts of Britain, and has more than

700 miles of footpaths and bridleways, more than 100 different types of heather, the unique and rare Exmoor ponies, and lots of local special events all year round — the October Dulverton Carnival, for example, and Discovery Walks, farmers' markets, antique and collectors' fairs, summer galas, deer-spotting tours, flower shows and archaeology walks.

Wiltshire

Bradford-on-Avon, home to the Bridge Tea Rooms, has a long history dating back to the Iron Age. There are buildings in the town today representing every period, from Saxon times to the present day. The "broad ford on the river," after which the town is named, was the site of a battle fought by King Cenwealh of Wessex in 652. The 18th- and 19th-century wealth of the town was the result of a thriving woollen industry, and from the 1850s to the early 1990s, the rubber industry became the most important industrial activity. The Saxon Church of St. Laurence has over the ages been used as a charnel house, a school and dwellings until it was rediscovered in the 19th century. Westbury House was the home of the wealthy woollen manufacturer Joseph Phelps, and St. Margaret's Hall was once a dyehouse. There is a tithe barn from the 14th century that belonged to the Abbey of Shaftsbury and has a cruck roof, an old threshing floor and a shop in the restored granary. The 14th-century Packhorse Bridge leads across the railway line into Barton Orchard, and here in the quiet lane the tall narrow houses were probably weavers' cottages. Other places of interest in Bradford include Abbey Mill, the last of the mills to be built in the town in 1857; medieval Trinity Church, with its 18th-century font and interesting brasses and memorials; the Hall Almshouses from 1700; St. Mary Tory, a tiny chapel with an adjoining hospice used by pilgrims; and Coppice Hill which leads to the ruined shell of a former 1818 Wesleyan Chapel.

Polly Tea Rooms in Marlborough's high street is at the heart of a town with a rich history and is ideally placed for visits to the surrounding Wiltshire countryside. The town was always an important staging post on the main road from London to Bath and Bristol, and close by there are attractive villages, ancient sites, historic houses, and paths and tracks for walkers and cyclists. Within the town, interesting places to visit include the Norman Church of St. Mary the Virgin, with its Cromwellian flat ceiling and a single arcade in the nave; the Priory and Garden, a fine 1820 house that stands beside the River Kennet on the site of a 14th-century Carmelite friary; the Merchant's House, built in 1656 for a silk merchant, which has a rare painted balustrade in the staircase hall and original floor-to-ceiling oak panelling in the great panelled chamber (the house is open by arrangement with the manager). At 13–15 Silverless Street are two small timbered cottages built after the Great Fire of 1653, and good examples of medieval houses with overhanging upper stories. Marlborough College, founded in 1843 as a public school intended for sons of the clergy stands near the mound where Marlborough's Norman castle once stood. Outside the town, Savernake Forest is an expanse of unbroken woodland, bridle paths and open glades. Avebury, a World Heritage Site, is a complex of prehistoric sites, including a massive bank and ditch with a large outer circle and two inner circles, a sanctuary with stones and timber circles, a conical earth mound from 2660BC and the West Kennet Long Barrow, a stone-chambered tomb.

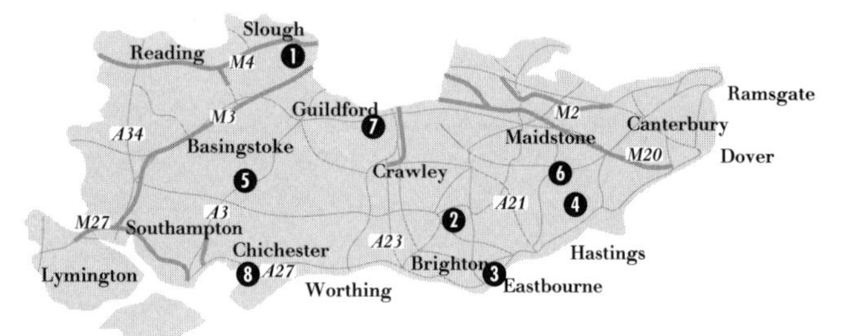
Slough
Reading
M4
1
M3
Guildford
7
A34
Basingstoke
M2
Canterbury
Ramsgate
Maidstone
M20
Dover
Crawley
6
5
A21
4
A3
2
M27
Southampton
A23
Hastings
Chichester
Brighton
3
Lymington
8
A27
Worthing
Eastbourne

The South East Tea Trail

Berkshire

❶ CROOKED HOUSE TEA ROOMS *p.* 38

East Sussex

❷ CLARA'S *p.* 39

❸ PAVILION TEA ROOMS *p.* 40

❹ THE TEA TREE *p.* 41

Hampshire

❺ GILBERT WHITE'S TEA PARLOUR *p.* 42

Kent

❻ CLARIS'S *p.* 43

Surrey

❼ HASKETTS TEA & COFFEE SHOP *p.* 44

West Sussex

❽ SHEPHERDS TEAROOMS *p.* 45

Crooked House Tea Rooms

51 HIGH STREET, WINDSOR
BERKSHIRE SL4 1LR
TEL: 01753 857534
E-MAIL: MANAGER@CROOKED-HOUSE.COM
WEB SITE: WWW.CROOKED-HOUSE.COM
OWNERS: CONCETTA & MICHAEL HARRINGTON
2000 BRITISH TOURIST AUTHORITY
NUMBER ONE ATTRACTION IN BERKSHIRE
(EXCLUDING THE CASTLE)

Crooked House Tea Rooms is in the centre of Windsor, in the high street next door to the Guildhall.

OPEN ALL YEAR EXCEPT CHRISTMAS DAY, NEW YEAR'S DAY AND EASTER SUNDAY. MONDAY–SUNDAY AND BANK HOLIDAYS, 10AM–6PM.

Built in 1687 and acquiring its tilt after restructuring in 1718, the Crooked House (historically called Market Cross House) is one of England's most unique tearooms. Originally a butcher's shop and the house owned by Silas Bradbury's family in the old market area outside the walls of Windsor Castle, the building was mysteriously pulled down in 1718 at the height of an acrimonious land dispute with the town council that ended up in the High Court of London. Within six months, the Bradburys won the dispute and rebuilt their shop and home with a mixture of original and unseasoned timber that caused the famous tilt. A secret passageway from the basement into Windsor Castle suggests a rather colourful and intriguing history. Next to the Crooked House is Britain's shortest street — Queen Charlotte Street.

The tearooms, set out on two floors, are well known for their Cornish clottedcream teas and afternoon teas with cucumber sandwiches. The menu offers a wide variety of fresh soups and light lunches, including toasted sandwiches, pasta and scrambled eggs. Favourite cakes and desserts include blueberry cheesecake, lemon lush cake, chocolate fudge cake and sticky toffee pudding with custard.

Breakfast Blend, Assam, Darjeeling, Ceylon, Lapsang Souchong, Jasmine, Japanese Sencha, Gunpowder, Rose Pouchong, Earl Grey, Lady Grey, Lemon, Decaffeinated, Iced Teas, Camomile, Camomile and Spiced Apple, Camomile and Lime Flower, Strawberry, Peppermint, Mango.

Clara's

9 HIGH STREET
EAST HOATHLY, NEAR LEWES
EAST SUSSEX BN8 6DR
TEL: 01825 840339
E-MAIL: CLARAS@NETWAY.CO.UK
WEB SITE: WWW.NETWAY.CO.UK/USERS/CLARAS
OWNER: JANE SEABROOK

East Hoathly is just off the A22 south of Uckfield. Clara's is in the centre of the village.

OPEN ALL YEAR
EXCEPT MONDAYS AND THE WEEK
BETWEEN CHRISTMAS AND NEW YEAR.
TUESDAY–SATURDAY, 10:30AM–5PM;
SUNDAY, 2PM–5PM.

The owner of this pretty tea shop, Jane Seabrook, is very interested in the history of her village, and researches the family trees and histories of local village people. East Hoathly was the home of Thomas Turner, diarist and local shopkeeper, and Jane sells copies of his writings, which chronicle his life in the late 1700s and give a rare and detailed insight into village life in those days. Clara's itself dates from the same period but has a Victorian façade; inside there are oak beams and an inglenook fireplace. In good weather there is extra seating outside.

Upstairs there is a large selection of secondhand books, with an emphasis on crafts, cookery and gardening. There is also a small permanent exhibition of knitting, sewing and related memorabilia, such as old sewing tools and knitting patterns, and the shop sells Rowan knitting yarns, pretty cards, Sussex honey, and local homemade chutneys, jams and jellies. The chutney also appears on the menu to accompany delicious rolls filled with chicken, cheese, egg mayonnaise or smoked salmon. The cake selection includes gingerbread, walnut cake and coffee sponge; the teas are locally packaged.

Traditional Blend, Earl Grey, Darjeeling. Herbal infusions are also offered.

Pavilion Tea Rooms

ROYAL PARADE, EASTBOURNE
EAST SUSSEX BN22 7AQ
TEL: 01323 410374
OWNERS: COASTLINE CATERERS, ON BEHALF OF EASTBOURNE BOROUGH COUNCIL
1997 TEA COUNCIL AWARD OF EXCELLENCE

The Pavilion Tea Rooms are situated on the seafront, half a mile east of the pier towards the Sovereign Centre.

OPEN ALL YEAR EXCEPT CHRISTMAS DAY.
SUMMER: MONDAY–SUNDAY, 10AM–6PM.
WINTER: MONDAY–SUNDAY, 10AM–5PM.

Pavilion Tea Rooms conjures up images of Victorian and Edwardian tea times at the seaside, with pots of Lapsang Souchong or Darjeeling on the terrace while enjoying a stunning vista across the bay to Beachy Head. The setting and the style re-create everyone's idea of all the essential elements of a memorable English tea set amongst beautiful gardens and croquet lawns: a light and elegant room, waiters who calmly bring you everything you could possibly want, newspapers for browsing through, the gentle sound of croquet and the music of the piano on summer afternoons and winter weekends, and a menu absolutely crammed with wonderful ideas to suit all tastes, at every time of the year, whatever the weather. You may choose to tuck into a cinnamon muffin or nibble at a slice of carrot and walnut cake; dip a long spoon into a raspberry meringue sundae that oozes ice cream, cream, raspberries and is topped with a delicious meringue; or enjoy an old-fashioned cream tea or Pavilion afternoon tea.

House Blend, Darjeeling, Earl Grey, Decaffeinated, Lapsang Souchong, Estate Assam, Ceylon Orange Pekoe, Jasmine, Camomile, Kiwi and Strawberry, Apple and Lemon.

The Tea Tree

12 HIGH STREET, WINCHELSEA
EAST SUSSEX TN36 4EA
TEL: 01797 226102
FAX: 01797 226102
E-MAIL: THETEATREE@WINCHELSEA.FSNET.CO.UK
WEB SITE: WWW.THE-TEA-TREE.CO.UK
OWNERS: JO & STEPHEN TURNER

From Rye, enter the town via Ferry Hill and take the second turning left into the high street. From Hastings, at the top of Sandrock Hill, turn right and follow the road. Turn right past the church into the high street.

OPEN ALL YEAR EXCEPT JANUARY.
APRIL–OCTOBER: WEDNESDAY–MONDAY, 10AM–6PM;
NOVEMBER–MARCH: WEDNESDAY–MONDAY, 10AM–5PM.
CLOSED TUESDAY.

A visit to the Tea Tree does not simply mean a chance to taste an excellent cup of tea. It is also an opportunity to buy your favourite of the teas served, along with gifts and tea wares. This 15th-century, Grade II-listed building was completely refurbished in 1994. With such features as the original beamed ceiling and log-burning stove, the Tea Tree possesses much of Winchelsea's own well-preserved charm.

The menu offers a good range of homemade food, ranging from hot lunches, ploughmans, and fresh sandwiches to a large selection of cakes, including the house speciality — meringues and carrot cake. Cream teas are also a particular favourite with regulars and visitors alike.

The Tea Tree is a wholesaler of coffees and speciality teas. Only loose-leaf teas are used in the tearoom, served in china pots. This tearoom has all the qualities of a traditional English tearoom, so whether you want to sip your tea by the inglenook fireplace in the light, airy 18th-century pine room or in the walled patio garden, the Tea Tree is a delightful setting. Once refreshed by tea, customers will find that Winchelsea, the smallest town in England, is steeped in history and has much to offer.

A wide selection, including Assam, Darjeeling, Ceylon, Lapsang Souchong, Earl Grey, English Afternoon and House Blend. Camomile, Peppermint, and many more fruit and herb infusions.

Gilbert White's Tea Parlour

GILBERT WHITE'S HOUSE & THE OATES MUSEUM
THE WAKES, SELBORNE
HAMPSHIRE GU34 3JH
TEL: 01420 511275
FAX: 01420 511040
E-MAIL: GILBERTWHITE@BTINTERNET.COM
OWNERS: THE TRUSTEES

Selborne is on the B3006, which links Alton to the main A3 London to Portsmouth Road. Park in the village car park behind the Selborne Arms, turn left on leaving the car park and continue along the high street. Gilbert White's house is on the left, almost opposite the plestor and church.

OPEN ALL YEAR EXCEPT
DECEMBER 25–JANUARY 31.
MONDAY–SUNDAY, 11AM–5PM.

The Rev. Gilbert White (1720 – 1793) was England's first ecologist and wrote the world-famous *Natural History of Selborne*. He lived here at the Wakes for most of his life, and visitors can wander through his house, which is furnished in the style of the day and includes his furniture, embroidered bed hangings and family portraits. Learn about the Oates family in the Oates Museum and enjoy the glorious garden — almost completely restored to its 18th-century form, with a sundial, a pond, a stone ha-ha, a fruit wall and a revolving "wine pipe" that overlooks a miniature landscape garden and a magnificent beech-clad hanger. There is also a good selection of unusual plants for sale and a good gift shop.

The dining room was added in 1794 and is today decorated and furnished in period style. Many of the dishes on the menu are based on 18th-century recipes, are all made on the premises, and use fresh produce and herbs from the garden. At lunchtime, choose from homity pie, filled with creamed potato, onion and parsley topped with melted cheese; spiced potted salmon with a watercress garnish; or turkey, herb and cranberry pasty in a light pastry. At teatime, indulge in lemon or chocolate puffs with clotted cream, plum cake, light Madeira seed cake, 18th-century scones (at the time known as corporation cakes), toasted wigs (spicy fruited buns) and lots more.

English Breakfast, Darjeeling, Ceylon, Earl Grey, Lapsang Souchong, Camomile.

Claris's

1–3 HIGH STREET, BIDDENDEN
KENT TN27 8AL
TEL: 01580 291025
WEB SITE: WWW.COLLECTABLEGIFTS.NET
OWNERS: BRIAN & JANET WINGHAM
2000 TEA COUNCIL AWARD OF EXCELLENCE
EGON RONAY RECOMMENDED

Biddenden lies at the junction of the A274 and A262, 12 miles south of Maidstone. The tearoom is in the centre of the village opposite the village green.

OPEN ALL YEAR EXCEPT
LATE JANUARY–EARLY FEBRUARY.
TUESDAY–SUNDAY, 10:30AM–5:20PM;
CLOSED MONDAY.

A row of picturesque 15th-century weavers' houses graces the gentle bend in the unspoilt main street of this quiet Kentish village, which was once the centre of the cloth trade. At the east end of the row stands Claris's tearoom and gift shop, with its windows temptingly filled with Moorcroft pottery, glass, enamels, soft toys and other gifts from the selection inside. Its arched porchway leads into the old-world charm of the shop and tearoom. The low oak beams and the two inglenook fireplaces create an atmosphere of homey cosiness, where lace tablecloths cover spacious tables, and delicious home-baked cakes and savouries are served on pretty white china.

Having settled at your table, it may take you quite a while to decide between the lemon madeira, the walnut bread served with apricot preserve, the hot bread pudding or the meringue filled with oodles of whipped double cream from a local dairy. You may decide that a Scottish smoked salmon or prawn sandwich is the ideal accompaniment to your afternoon cup of tea. Whatever you choose, this is the perfect place to relax after a wander around Biddenden Village or a ramble in the nearby Wealden countryside.

House Kenya Blend, Earl Grey, Darjeeling, Lapsang Souchong, and Assam. Fruit-flavoured teas and herbal infusions are also available.

Hasketts Tea & Coffee Shop

86B SOUTH STREET
DORKING, SURREY RH4 2EW
TEL: 01306 885833
E-MAIL: MARGARET.GARRETT@UKGATEWAY.NET
WEB SITE: WWW.GARRETSCATERING.SAGENET.CO.UK
OWNER: MARGARET GARRETT
1999 & 2000 TEA COUNCIL AWARD OF EXCELLENCE

Come into Dorking from the A24 and follow the high street until it splits at a Y junction. Continue up South Street; Hasketts is the second of two Regency bow-windowed buildings on the right, 250 metres from the Y junction.

OPEN ALL YEAR EXCEPT CHRISTMAS DAY.
MONDAY–SATURDAY, 9AM–5PM; SUNDAY, 11AM–5PM.

Hasketts has a home in a Grade II-listed building that dates back to 1693. Situated in the sandstone cave district of Dorking, it has a basement that is actually made out of a cave and a 220-foot well that is now sealed off. The interior today has a 1920s or 30s character, and enjoys the impact of all the poster art from that period that decorates the walls. The menu has a similar nostalgia, offering lots of favourite specialities from years gone by, including eggs Benedict and corned beef hash, and high tea treats such as ham carved from the bone and served with Cumberland sauce and a poached egg. There is also an excellent range of sandwiches and salads, and a vast selection of homemade cakes (never less than 20 varieties), including the delicious renowned fruit cakes. The shop also takes orders for special-occasion cakes. Hasketts is well known for its knowledge and enthusiasm for tea and for the extensive range of world speciality teas (including single-source teas) on offer. A special-occasion tray service and comprehensive take-away service are also available.

Three Assams, three Darjeelings, two Ceylons, English Breakfast, Russian Caravan, Earl Grey, Kenya, China Oolong, Gunpowder, Yunnan, Keemun, Jasmine, Rose Congou, Lapsang Souchong, Japanese, Mate, Rooibos.

Shepherds Tearooms

35 LITTLE LONDON, CHICHESTER
WEST SUSSEX PO19 1PL
TEL: 01243 774761
E-MAIL: SHEPHERDS@SHEPHERDTEA.FREESERVE.CO.UK
WEB SITE: TEAGIFTS.CO.UK
OWNERS: YVONNE & RICHARD SPENCE
1990, 1992 & 1995 TOP TEA PLACE OF THE YEAR
1989-2001 TEA COUNCIL AWARD OF EXCELLENCE
1994, 1995 & 1996 EGON RONAY RECOMMENDED

Little London is off East Street, one of the main shopping streets in Chichester.

OPEN ALL YEAR.
MONDAY–FRIDAY, 9:15AM–5PM;
SATURDAY, 9AM–5PM. CLOSED SUNDAY.

Housed in a fine Georgian listed building, Shepherds has a calm, friendly, living-room atmosphere and efficient, attentive waitresses. The cool lemon-and-lime walls with the pastel curtains combined with an oak floor, give the room a New England-style charm. The windows of the conservatory at one end flood the room with light and warmth, and make this a very popular, restful venue for tourists, local businesspeople and weary shoppers, who tuck into tasty rarebits, sandwiches and scrumptious sweet treats such as Earl Grey and sultana cake, or carrot, pecan and apricot cake. The traditional cream tea with home-baked scones and generous portions of jam and clotted cream is well worth a special visit.

Since 1987, when they acquired the tearooms, Yvonne and Richard Spence have constantly set very high standards and have researched different blends and suppliers of tea in order to offer only the best. Their special blends are so popular that they are now available via the Internet or from the small shop.

English Breakfast, Ceylon Afternoon, Darjeeling, China Black, Earl Grey, Assam, Gunpowder, Jasmine. Fruit-flavoured teas and herbal infusions are also offered.

Tea-Time Traditions from the South East

BERKSHIRE, HAMPSHIRE, KENT, SURREY, SUSSEX

The southeastern counties of England have for centuries produced supplies of apples, cherries, plums, damsons, currants and soft summer fruits. Traditional recipes from Hampshire's New Forest use wild blackberries and wild cherries in jams and jellies, and strawberries from the county were traditionally turned into jams and vinegars, as well as being served up with cream and in open tarts and cakes. Old collections of local recipes are packed with instructions for damson cheesecakes, rhubarb pies, raspberry tarts, apple cakes and plum jam. Hampshire has also for centuries been an important centre for beekeeping, and so honey cakes with spice and almonds were often served up at tea time.

Apples and cherries from Kent and Sussex were cooked in cakes and pies and harvest specialities. Cherry bumpers, like a pastry turnover, were served on Cherry Pie Sunday in August to celebrate the end of the picking season. Kentish huffkins were soft white rolls with a large indentation in the middle that were filled with cooked apples or cherries and eaten by the seasonal hop pickers who arrived in the summer from London to enjoy a working holiday in the hop fields. The hop pickers also had a special fruit cake that was taken out to the fields for lunchtime and tea-time picnics. It is a dark fruity cake made with treacle, ginger and mixed spices, and is full of sultanas, currants and candied peel. Also from Kent came oast cakes — a little like traditional shortbread biscuits, but with the addition of currants — and flead cakes were made with the fat left after the process that rendered lard for household cooking. It was crucial that the dough was rolled only once because if it was handled too much it would not rise and would remain flat and crusty like pastry, whereas if handled correctly it rose to twice its height.

In Sussex it was the custom to turn some of the local gooseberries into puddings and tarts for Gooseberry Pudding Sunday in July. Surrey is famous for Maids of Honour, the little tartlets that are said to have been invented at Hampton Court during the reign of Henry VIII. The legend says that one day the king came across some of Anne Boleyn's maids of honour eating the delicacies, and he asked to try one. He thought them so delicious and special that he insisted that from then on, they should only be made for members of the royal family. Today there are various recipes around the country, but the original version is thought to have contained sugar, brandy, curd cheese, ground almonds, nutmeg, eggs, lemon juice and cold mashed potato — a rather surprising and unusual ingredient in what was basically a typical curd cheesecake. In May and June, the cows on the farm were producing their maximum yield of milk and the hens were laying well. Some of the milk was turned into cheese, cream cheese, curds, custards and junkets, cheesecakes, and egg custard tarts that were eaten by workers in the fields and at home for tea. Kentish pudding pies were one version of these early summer tarts, and the farm workers ate them with cherry beer — a strong, cherry-flavoured ale made locally. The Sussex recipe baked a mixture of cream, eggs, sugar, mace and currants in a puff pastry tart case.

As in all areas of Britain, local fairs meant the sale of parkins, gingerbreads, toffee apples and fairings. The Ringwood fair in Hampshire took place each year at Michaelmas, and travelling salesmen hawked the traditional gingernuts. The annual church outing also involved special treats. A recipe for Scripture cake from Hampshire (but also made in many counties around Britain) gives instructions for the ingredients in quotations from the Bible: for example, "Take 4 1/2 cups of 1 Kings IV 22 'and Solomon's provision for one day was 30 measures of fine flour,' 1 1/2 cups of Judges v 25 'she brought him butter in a lordly dish,' " etc.

Things to See and Do in the South East

BERKSHIRE, HAMPSHIRE, KENT, SURREY, SUSSEX

Berkshire

Windsor is home to the Crooked House Tea Rooms. The town is full of history, and there are many interesting places to visit and things to do. Start the day with a visit to the Town and Crown Exhibition, a small heritage exhibition that charts the history of the town. Take a horse-drawn carriage ride around the town and into the Great Park of Windsor Castle, one of three official residences of the Queen and the largest inhabited castle in the world. Visitors to the castle itself can see the State Apartments, Queen Mary's Doll House, St. George's Chapel and Frogmore House in the Home Park. Parts of the park are open to the public for picnics, walking, cycling and horse riding, and gardening enthusiasts can also visit the Savill Garden, which has wonderful displays of colour all year round. Visitors can also take a tour of Eton College, founded in 1440 by Henry VI. Both Eton and Windsor are ideal for shopping — there are antique shops, and specialist dealers in teapots, jewellery, woollens, herbs and glasswares.

Hampshire

The charming 18th-century house that includes Gilbert White's Tea Parlour at Selborne, is at the heart of the town and surrounded by outstanding countryside. The house and the Oates Museum commemorate the Oates family. It was Captain Oates who uttered the famous words, "I am just going outside. I may be some time," as he left his tent to walk to his death while in the Antarctic with Captain Scott. The Field Studies Centre at the house organises courses on art and gardening throughout the year, and holds various events and special exhibitions, mostly to do with art, gardening and jazz. In the area surrounding Selbourne are Jane Austen's house at Chawton, the Mid Hants Railway (the Watercress Line) and Chawton Park Wood. A little further to the southwest, Hinton Ampner house contains fine furniture and paintings. The outstanding grounds have a 20th-century shrub garden with scented plants, and there are unexpected vistas created by the formal and informal plantings in compartments that create both intimate and expansive sections of the garden.

Kent

Biddenden High Street, home of Claris's tearoom, is flanked by half-timbered houses that were once weavers' homes. The village is famous for the two sisters who were joined at the hip and shoulders and who lived here for 34 years in the early 12th century. Today the village also has its own Biddenden Vineyards Limited a mile and a half away. Established in 1969 by the Barnes family, the 22 acres of vines now produce Muller Thurgau (a dry white wine with a fragrant nose) and Ortega wine (a distinctive white wine that accounts for 50 percent of production). Set in a traditional apple-growing region, the vineyard also produces sweet, medium and dry ciders. Visits include a vineyard walk, a winery talk and tastings, and a complimentary glass of wine. Tenterden, a few miles to the southeast, also has a vineyard at the Chapel Down Winery, located in Tenterden Vineyard Park. There are guided tours, a herb garden, a plant centre, a wine and gift shop, and the Rural Museum, which houses a collection of agricultural tools and machinery and a hive of working bees. The Kent and East Sussex steam railway, one of the U.K.'s longest and oldest railway lines, runs 11 miles from Tenterden to Bodiam. To the west of Biddenden is Cranbrook, a pretty hamlet that probably dates back to the 13th century. Places of interest include a museum, St. Dunstan's Church, Union Windmill, two chapels and an old clothier's cottage. To the west is Sissinghurst, the famous garden created by Vita Sackville-West and now maintained by the National Trust.

Surrey

Hasketts Tea & Coffee Shop is set in the historic market town of Dorking in the heart of Surrey and between the steep slopes of the North Downs and the wooded hills and open heath of the Greensand Hills. Just a stone's throw from the high street, the spire of St. Martin's Church rises high above the town. The museum in West Street houses many fascinating artefacts that tell the story of Dorking life, including farm tools, domestic equipment, local costume and children's toys. West Street is also the location for several antique shops and the interesting Italianate Congregational church, an elegant structure from the early 19th century that contains the organ from Brighton Pavilion. Intriguingly, underneath the town centre are a number of man-made caves, some of which are open to the public by arrangement with the Dorking Museum. It is rumoured that the caves have been used to store wines and spirits, as a meeting place for outlawed religious groups and as a haunt for smugglers. Close to Dorking are Polesden Lacey, a magnificent Regency house now managed by the National Trust; Box Hill, with wonderful views over Dorking; the Weald and the River Mole; and Denbies Wine Estate, which produces approximately 400,000 bottles of wine every year.

Sussex

East Hoathley in East Sussex is the setting for Clara's tea shop. The little town itself has an interesting collection of workshops in a converted petrol station where furniture makers and restorers, sign writers, saddlers and a homeopathic vet work. The county town of Lewes is few miles to the south-west, and here you can visit the castle that was laid out after the Battle of Hastings. There are excellent views of the town, the South Downs and the River Ouse from the 13th-century keep. Also in Lewes are Anne of Cleves' House and Museum, with displays of tapestries, furniture, ironwork, pottery, watercolours and a Tudor-style garden; the remains of Lewes Priory, founded in 1077 and largely destroyed by Thomas Cromwell in 1583; the Barbican House Museum, with a fine 18th-century façade and a collection of Roman and medieval artefacts; and Pelham House, built in 1579 for an Elizabethan courtier, with fine Renaissance panelling and an elegant Georgian staircase. In the countryside nearby, not far from both East Hoathley and Lewes, are all sorts of interesting houses to visit. Glynde Place is a magnificent Elizabethan manor house with a collection of Old Masters, family portraits, embroidery and silverware. Firle Place, originally a Tudor house developed from a monastery, has been the home of the Gage family for more than 500 years. To the east, Michelham Priory is surrounded by England's longest water-filled medieval moat, and has a physic garden, herbaceous borders, a watermill, a rope museum and a sculpture trail.

Shepherds Tearooms is in the heart of Chichester, a town that is steeped in 2,000 years of history. The cathedral has been the centre of community life for 900 years and is the site of the shrine of St. Richard of Chichester. Chichester District Museum explores the fascinating story of the town through geology, archaeology and social history. The medieval Guildhall was once Greyfriars Church, but was later turned into the town hall and courthouse. William Blake was brought to trial here in 1804. Chichester Harbour tours allow a view of the vast stretches of unspoilt sheltered water with all types of yachts, fishing boats, canoes and sailing dinghies. Outside the town, the Roman Palace at Fishbourne has superb mosaic flooring, under-floor heating systems and a bath suite. Petworth House has state-of-the-art Victorian kitchens, a deer park and an outstanding art collection with more than 300 paintings by such artists as Turner, Blake and Van Dyck. The Weald and Downland Open Air Museum is a museum of historic buildings and traditional rural life set in a beautiful 19th-century park. It has more than 40 period buildings, furnished interiors and complete work environments, and the 17th-century watermill produces flour that is sold in the shop.

Pavilion Tea Rooms enjoys one of Eastbourne's prime locations, right on the seafront. As well as all the traditional seaside attractions, the town has a number of museums and heritage venues. Close to the teashop is the Amazon Jungle Zoo and Jungle Pet Shop, with tropical birds, reptiles, frogs and butterflies; the Military Museum of Sussex has South East England's largest collection of military objects and memorabilia, and covers 300 years of conflict on land, sea and in the air; and the Musgrave Collection has Roman and British coins, historic documents, mini-sculptures and paintings. A little further west from the shop is the RNLI Lifeboat Museum, with tales of epic rescues and lifeboat memorabilia; the Wish Tower Puppet Museum, with a unique display of puppets and related art forms, including Punch and Judy; the Eastbourne Heritage Centre, which takes you on a journey through Eastbourne's history and its development from four hamlets; and the "How We Lived Then" Museum of Shops, with four floors of more than 100,000 exhibits, including authentic Victorian-style shops and room settings. The Winter Garden is a delightful Victorian venue used for dances and family events. There is also Beachy Head, with its white cliffs and miles of footpaths for walkers along the South Downs. The town of Battle in East Sussex is the site of the 1066 Battle of Hastings. For visitors who wish to know more about the actual battle, there is a free interactive audio tour of the battlefield and the atmospheric ruins of the abbey built by William the Conqueror in atonement for the blood he shed that day. The Battle Museum of Local History, in the Memorial Hall opposite Abbey Green, contains a print of the Bayeux Tapestry, a facsimile of the *Domesday Book* for Sussex, coins, dinosaur remains, and old toys and games. Yesterday's World, next to the Abbey, has more than 30 rooms and shop settings that take visitors back to Victorian and Edwardian days with narrations, animated figures and smells. Just a short distance from the town, the Carr Taylor and Sedlescombe Organic Vineyards offer both tours and tastings of their wines, fruit juices and farmhouse ciders.

The Tea Tree is in Winchelsea, a picturesque Georgian town with houses that have inspired artists such as Turner and Millais. The entire area surrounding the town has direct links back to the time when modern England was born with the defeat of King Harold at the Battle of Hastings. To the west is Hastings itself, with its castle built by William the Conqueror. To the east lies the ancient town of Rye, with handsome Georgian buildings; a medieval town wall; Landgate, a castle built to protect the town from the French; cobbled streets; a 12th-century church; and an Augustinian friary. The Rye Heritage Centre tells the story of the smugglers, murder, mystery and mayhem that have coloured Rye's history. The town also has interesting literary connections to writers such as Henry James, E. F. Benson, H. G. Wells, Joseph Conrad and G. K. Chesterton. Just outside the town, there are internationally important nature reserves at Rye Harbour and nearby Dungeness, and a footpath across the marshes leads to Camber Castle. North of Winchelsea, there are vineyards at Westfield at which you can sample a range of wines and fruit juices and buy hampers and unusual preserves and mustards, and at Sedlescombe, there are a woodland nature trail and a self-build low-energy house.

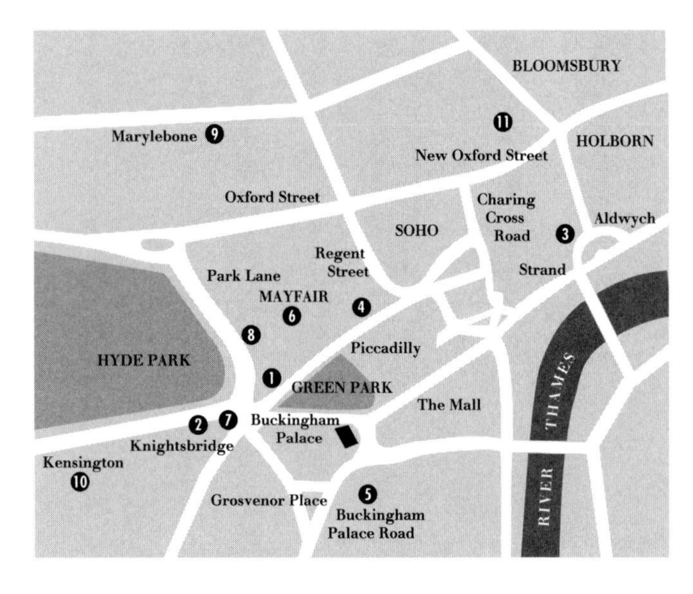
BLOOMSBURY
Marylebone 9
11
New Oxford Street
HOLBORN
Oxford Street
Charing Cross Road
SOHO
Aldwych
3
Regent Street
Park Lane
Strand
MAYFAIR
6
4
8
Piccadilly
HYDE PARK
1
GREEN PARK
The Mall
2
7
Buckingham Palace
Knightsbridge
Kensington
10
Grosvenor Place
5
Buckingham Palace Road
RIVER THAMES

The London Tea Trail

London

❶ THE LOUNGE,
FOUR SEASONS HOTEL *p.* 56

❷ GEORGIAN RESTAURANT,
HARRODS *p.* 57

❸ PALM COURT,
LE MERIDIEN WALDORF *p.* 58

❹ OAK ROOM LOUNGE,
LE MERIDIEN PICCADILLY *p.* 59

❺ CAVALRY BAR AND PALACE LOUNGE,
THE RUBENS HOTEL *p.* 60

❻ THE CONSERVATORY,
THE CHESTERFIELD *p.* 61

❼ THE CONSERVATORY,
THE LANESBOROUGH *p.* 62

❽ THE PROMENADE,
THE DORCHESTER *p.* 63

❾ THE LANDMARK HOTEL *p.* 64

❿ THE MILESTONE HOTEL *p.* 65

⓫ THE MONTAGUE ON THE GARDENS *p.* 66

The Lounge

FOUR SEASONS HOTEL
HAMILTON PLACE, PARK LANE
LONDON W1A 1AZ
TEL: 020 7499 0888
FAX: 020 7493 1895
E-MAIL: FSH.LONDON@FOURSEASONS.COM
WEB SITE: WWW.FOURSEASONS.COM
LOUNGE MANAGER: GERTRAUD JOCHL
1999 TEA COUNCIL TOP TEA PLACE OF THE YEAR
2000 TOP LONDON AFTERNOON TEA
AWARD OF EXCELLENCE

The nearest Tube station is Hyde Park Corner. Follow signs through the foot tunnels to the east side of Park Lane. Hamilton Place is set back from Park Lane, running parallel to it and at right angles to Piccadilly. The entrance to the Four Seasons Hotel is a little way up on the east side.

OPEN ALL YEAR. THE LOUNGE IS OPEN EVERY DAY FROM 8AM–11PM. AFTERNOON TEA IS SERVED FROM 3–7PM.

The soft recessed lighting, the palms and the exquisite Venetian chandeliers give the Lounge an extremely calm and relaxed atmosphere, and the air of tranquillity is enhanced by the gentle piano music played each afternoon. The walls are decorated with traditional paintings that are set in subtly lit display cabinets, and the large etched-glass and wrought-iron gates at one end of the room open to a garden that gives the impression of a tropical location.

The menu offers a Devonshire tea with traditional tea sandwiches and scones, or a seasonal tea with speciality sandwich fillings on flavoured breads. Scones are made with nectarine, dried fruits, chestnuts or similar seasonal ingredients and served with clotted cream and homemade jams. Three delicate little pastries to suit the time of year then follow, and for a refreshing finish there's a little chocolate cup filled with sorbet. A third menu option varies according to annual events and trends. Chef Eric Deblonde, who has been creating seasonal menus for tea since 1996, says, "Today's world allows us the availability of so many foods all year round. However, their optimum flavour still relies upon nature's order, and I do believe we should keep foods to their appointed seasons."

Ceylon, Assam, Darjeeling, China Black, Earl Grey, Russian Caravan, Lapsang Souchong, Gunpowder, Jasmine, Lotus, Rose Pouchong, Anniversary Blend, Queen Mary Blend.

Georgian Restaurant

HARRODS LTD
KNIGHTSBRIDGE
LONDON SW1X 7XL
TEL: 020 7225 6800
FAX: 020 7225 5903
WEB SITE: WWW.HARRODS.COM
E-MAIL: MANFRED.MAI@HARRODS.COM
MANAGER: MANFRED E. MAI

Take the Piccadilly Line to Knightsbridge Station, and follow signs for the exit to Harrods. Take the escalator at theHans Road entrance (door no. 10) to the fourth floor. Turn right at the top of the escalator and take the second doorway on your left. The entrance to the Georgian Restaurant is the first door on the right.

THE STORE IS OPEN MONDAY–SATURDAY, 10AM–7PM. AFTERNOON TEA IS SERVED EVERY DAY FROM 3:45–5:30PM. CLOSED SUNDAYS, CHRISTMAS DAY AND BOXING DAY. OPEN ALL BANK HOLIDAYS.

This elegant tea venue is part of the largest in-store restaurant in Europe. To the right as you enter is the Terrace Bar, which extends out on to the conservatory terrace; to the left is an ice cream parlour and crêperie. The area in which tea is served occupies the main part of the front of the restaurant, and the dining area stretches back and back. Everywhere you look there are palms and flowers, and the atmosphere is one of stylish and gracious living. The tables are covered with crisp white linen, and when you wish to order your meal a helpful, smiling member of the staff arrives at your side and when your tea arrives it is in a silver pot. The plush chairs are rose-pink, a gentle light filters into the room through the Art Nouveau glass ceiling, and even when the pianist is not seated at the instrument, it goes on playing anyway. The menu offers a selection of elegant sandwiches (smoked salmon, ham, cheese and tomato, watercress and egg, and cucumber), scones with clotted cream and preserves, and a variety of neat tea pastries. With its rooftop views and sense of space and calm, this is a marvellous place to recover from the inevitable shopping that you are bound to do in the store.

Harrods Afternoon Blend, Earl Grey, Lapsang Souchong, Darjeeling, Assam, Iced Tea.

Palm Court

LE MERIDIEN WALDORF
ALDWYCH, LONDON WC2B 4DD
TEL: 020 7759 4091
FAX: 020 7240 9277
PALM COURT MANAGER: MARK GLASS

Nearest Tube stations are Holborn, Covent Garden, Temple or Charing Cross.

OPEN ALL YEAR.
TEA IS SERVED MONDAY–FRIDAY, 3–5:30PM.
TEA DANCES: SATURDAY, 2–4:30PM;
SUNDAY, 4–6:30PM.

The Waldorf Hotel opened its doors in 1908 and very quickly became a favourite place for an elegant and refined afternoon tea. In 1910 the tango arrived from Buenos Aires and prompted the beginning of that rather eccentric mix of Argentine dancing and English tea drinking — the tea dance. By 1913, the Waldorf's gold-and-white ballroom was one of London's most popular venues for tango tea dances.

Today, tea is served in the magnificent Palm Court, where exotic plants, a marble terrace, gentle Edwardian colours and twinkling lights create a unique setting for a stylish tea or tea dance. The menu suggests a three-course tea with sandwiches (including prawns Marie Rose on citrus bread, cream cheese and chives with cucumber on raisin and pecan bread, turkey with mustard-grain mayonnaise on rye bread), fruit and plain scones, and neat little slices of tiramisu, chocolate mille feuilles or passion fruit cheesecake. Tea dances on Saturday and Sunday afternoons are sparkling occasions for both dance and tea enthusiasts. Indulge in slow elegant waltzes, energetic jives and cha cha chas, or the sultry steps of a tango.

Waldorf Blend, Assam, Darjeeling, Ceylon, Earl Grey, Jasmine, Kenya, Lapsang Souchong, Mint Iced Tea. Herbal infusions are also available.

Oak Room Lounge

LE MERIDIEN PICCADILLY
21 PICCADILLY
LONDON W1J 0BH
TEL: 0870 400 8400
FAX: 020 7437 3574 OR 020 7851 3030
WEB SITE: WWW.LEMERIDIEN-PICCADILLY.COM
MANAGER: AJAZ SHEIKH

Le Meridien Piccadilly is at the Piccadilly Circus end of Piccadilly, just along the road from the Royal Academy and Burlington Arcade. The nearest tube stations are Piccadilly Circus and Green Park.

OPEN ALL YEAR. DAILY, 9AM–9PM.
AFTERNOON TEA IS SERVED FROM 3–6PM.

After three years of offering afternoon tea in the second-floor Terrace Restaurant, Le Meridien has decided to move its tea event back to the Oak Room Lounge on the ground floor. The lounge is a wonderfully elegant, calm Edwardian room with pale oak panelling set with gilded musical motifs, Venetian chandeliers with twinkling candle bulbs, a sophisticated décor that uses rich burgundy colours, and an atmosphere of comfort and refinement. This room is an oasis, a true haven away from the noise and bustle of London's shopping centre.

The afternoon tea menu offers an assortment of sandwiches, including prawn cocktail, smoked salmon, turkey with tomato chutney, cucumber and egg mayonnaise. Next come warm scones with clotted cream, jellies and jams, and a selection of French pastries. For special occasions, choose the Oak Room champagne tea, which spoils you with a platter of smoked fish served with caviar and blinis, and a glass of champagne.

Assam, Darjeeling, Ceylon, Earl Grey, Lapsang Souchong, Keemun, China Oolong, Gunpowder, Jasmine, various herbals.

Cavalry Bar and Palace Lounge

THE RUBENS HOTEL
39 BUCKINGHAM PALACE ROAD
LONDON SW1W 0PS
TEL: 020 7834 6600
FAX: 020 7828 5401
GENERAL MANAGER: PAUL HEMMINGS

The nearest Tube station is Victoria on the Victoria, District and Circle lines. Come out of Victoria Station and turn right into Buckingham Palace Road. The Rubens is between Victoria Street and Palace Street, opposite the Royal Mews.

AFTERNOON TEA IS SERVED IN THE PALACE LOUNGE EVERY DAY FROM 2:30–5PM.

The Rubens Hotel's Cavalry Bar and Palace Lounge, in keeping with its location opposite the Royal Mews (which stands at the southwest corner of the grounds of Buckingham Palace) has just been refurbished with a royal theme. The hotel is so close to Buckingham Palace that you only have to walk a very short distance before you are standing gazing into the famous royal forecourt. The hotel has a splendid view of arrivals and departures to and from the Mews itself. After a walk or jog in Green Park or a stroll up the Mall or to the Houses of Parliament in Westminster Square, what could be better than to relax in such luxurious surroundings and take tea?

When you take afternoon tea at the Rubens Hotel you will enjoy a selection of delicate finger sandwiches (filled with smoked salmon, cream cheese and cucumber, egg mayonnaise and ham), freshly baked scones with clotted cream or toasted teacakes, and little cakes that include chocolate eclairs, fresh fruit tartlets and fruit cakes. The all-day menu offers English and continental-style breakfasts, snacks and light meals, main dishes and desserts to suit all palates.

Assam, Darjeeling, Earl Grey, Indian Blend, House Blend, Iced Tea. Fruit and herbal infusions are also offered.

The Conservatory

THE CHESTERFIELD
35 CHARLES STREET
MAYFAIR, LONDON W1J 5EB
TEL: 020 7491 2622
FAX: 020 7491 4793
WEB SITE: WWW.REDCARNATIONHOTELS.COM
DEPUTY GENERAL MANAGER: DUNCAN PITFIELD

The nearest Tube station is Green Park on the Victoria, Jubilee, and Piccadilly lines. Come out of the tube station into Piccadilly; walk a short distance towards Piccadilly Circus, then turn left into Berkeley Street. Charles Street is the third street on the left. The hotel is on the corner of Charles Street and Queen Street, which is the second turning on the left.

AFTERNOON TEA IS SERVED IN THE CONSERVATORY, 3–5PM EVERY DAY.

The Chesterfield is more like a private club than a hotel, combining Georgian elegance and gracious living with modern standards of comfort and convenience. A crystal chandelier lights the reception area where paintings and classic leather sofas and chairs create a traditional charm. The rooms are furnished with antiques and decorated generously with fresh flowers, and the service is attentive and courteous. The Conservatory has a cool, tranquil atmosphere, which is perfect for a light lunch, afternoon tea or supper before or after a West End show. The light, al fresco-style room is decked with fresh flowers and plants; the tables are elegantly laid with beautiful green cloths covered with lace; the teapots, milk jugs and cake stands are silver and the food is temptingly arranged to make tea time attractive as well as delicious.

The traditional afternoon tea consists of assorted finger sandwiches, freshly baked scones with clotted cream and preserves, homemade fruit cakes and French pastries, or you can simply enjoy the scones, jam and clotted cream that make up the Devonshire cream tea.

Darjeeling, English Breakfast, Orange Pekoe, Earl Grey, Lapsang Souchong, Lemon, Decaffeinated, Ophir Blue. Camomile, Peppermint, and Rosehip and Hibiscus herbal infusions are also offered.

The Conservatory

THE LANESBOROUGH
HYDE PARK CORNER
LONDON SW1X 7TA
TEL: 020 7259 5599
FAX: 020 7259 5606
MANAGER: DEREK ANDREWS

The nearest Tube station is Hyde Park Corner on the Piccadilly Line. The Lanesborough is situated on the corner of Knightsbridge and Hyde Park Corner.

AFTERNOON TEA IS SERVED 3:30–6PM EVERY DAY.

The Lanesborough, a building that dates back to 1828, was once a fine country house that commanded magnificent views over Hyde Park. It has been meticulously restored to its original grandeur and now captures the gracious style and warm hospitality of an early 19th-century residence. The glass-domed conservatory is inspired by a chinoiserie theme and styled with the frivolity of Brighton Pavilion. The ambience is enhanced by trickling fountains, palms and piano music played throughout afternoon tea. Tables are laid with elegant bone china and silver tea services, and the tea is brewed using water that has been boiled in exquisite silver samovars that stand out on view for guests to enjoy.

Afternoon tea offers a selection of finger sandwiches, homemade scones, crumpets with homemade fruit preserves and Devonshire clotted cream, English tea breads and pastries. The Belgravia tea adds fresh strawberries and cream, and a glass of Taittinger Champagne or an afternoon Champagne cocktail to the full afternoon-tea menu. Alternatively, you may select individual servings of any of the tea-time treats, or choose from a further mouthwatering menu of sandwiches and savouries, the patissier's dessert of the day, and homemade ice creams and sorbets.

Afternoon Blend, Lapsang Souchong, Earl Grey Blue Flower, Rose Congou, Darjeeling, Lychee, Ceylon, seasonal speciality estate teas.

The Promenade

THE DORCHESTER
PARK LANE, LONDON W1A 2HJ
TEL: 020 7629 8888
FAX: 020 7495 7351
WEB SITE: WWW.DORCHESTERHOTEL.COM
MANAGER: MR F. PALMINTERI
2000 TOP LONDON AFTERNOON TEA AWARD
1998 TEA COUNCIL AWARD OF EXCELLENCE
EGON RONAY RECOMMENDED

The Dorchester is halfway up Park Lane.
The nearest Tube station is Marble Arch.

OPEN ALL YEAR. MONDAY–SUNDAY, 8AM–1AM.
AFTERNOON TEA IS SERVED 2:30–6PM.

Tea at the Dorchester is quite spectacular. No one can fail to enjoy the elegant yet leisurely surroundings, where marble pillars, exquisite carpets, stately plants and magnificent flowers in fine vases and planters, and amazingly comfortable sofas and armchairs create around you a sense of total calm and refinement. Despite such grand style, the extremely friendly staff make sure you are relaxed and comfortable and have everything you need. The opulence of the occasion recalls the style of the very first afternoon teas, which took place at the beginning of the 19th century in palaces and stately homes around England.

Tea at the Promenade is brought one course at a time — first the neat finger sandwiches, then the scones with Devonshire clotted cream and jam, and finally, the pastries freshly made by the restaurant's patissier. Second and third servings are always offered, but it is doubtful whether many will be able to accept further indulgences. For special occasions, choose a glass of Dorchester champagne to accompany the delicious food.

Dorchester House Blend, Earl Grey, Darjeeling, Assam, China Keemun, Lapsang Souchong, China Caravan, China Oolong, Jasmine, English Breakfast, Russian Caravan. Fruit-flavoured teas and herbal infusions are also offered.

The Landmark Hotel

222 MARYLEBONE ROAD
LONDON NW1 6JQ
TEL: 020 7631 8000
FAX: 020 7631 8080
E-MAIL: RESERVATIONS@THELANDMARK.CO.UK
WEB SITE: WWW.LANDMARK.CO.UK
MANAGER: NIELS WEIS

The nearest Tube stations are Marylebone and Baker Street. Paddington Station is about 10 minutes' walk away.

OPEN ALL YEAR.
TEA IS SERVED IN THE
WINTER GARDEN FROM 3-6PM

The Landmark Hotel was originally opened in 1899 as the Great Central Hotel, the last of the great Victorian railway hotels. It was the dream of Sir Edward Watkins, who planned a rail network linking his Great Central Railway to Europe via a Channel Tunnel that terminated at Marylebone Station. It was never built, but the hotel reflects the wealth and power of the time, and the ambition of the architects to create an opulent and luxurious hotel. It was designed around a central courtyard that allowed horse-drawn carriages to deliver guests in privacy and comfort to the heart of the building. This central area was transformed in the 1920s into a dance floor and is now the Winter Garden. The soaring glass-roofed, eight-storey atrium covers the calm elegance of the tea area, where rattan-style furniture, tall palm trees and conservatory plants create a light and spacious turn-of-the-century colonial atmosphere.

Afternoon tea consists of a selection of finger sandwiches and Viennese bridge rolls, freshly baked scones with clotted cream and preserves, and assorted pastries. The Marylebone tea adds to that assorted tea breads, muffins and miniature gateaux.

Landmark Blend, Darjeeling, Assam, Ceylon, English Breakfast, Lapsang Souchong, Earl Grey, Earl Grey Blue Flower, Russian Caravan, Gunpowder, Jasmine, Japanese Sencha, a wide selection of fruit-flavoured teas and herbal infusions.

The Milestone Hotel

1–2 KENSINGTON COURT
LONDON W8 5DL
TEL: 020 7917 1000
FAX: 020 7917 1010
OWNER: RED CARNATION HOTEL COLLECTION
MANAGER: CAROLINE KING

The Milestone is on the corner of Kensington Court and Kensington Road, opposite Kensington Gardens. The nearest tube station is Kensington High Street. As you come out of the station, turn right and walk along Kensington High Street, which then becomes Kensington Road. The hotel is on the corner of the fourth street to the right.

THE HOTEL IS OPEN ALL YEAR, 24 HOURS A DAY. TEA IS SERVED IN THE LOUNGE FROM 3-6PM.

The Milestone takes its name from the old cast-iron milestone that stands within its boundaries. The original building that once stood here, Kensington House, was built in 1689, and after 140 years as a private house it served as a private lunatic asylum. It was replaced by a second house, but in the 1880s two new houses were built, and today these form the hotel. In 1986 a mysterious fire that took three hours to bring under control badly damaged the hotel, but it has now been beautifully restored to five-star standards.

The lounge where tea is served has the atmosphere of a family drawing room, with its rose-pink and gold décor, comfortable sofas and armchairs, wood panelling around the walls, thick gold carpet and an open hearth where a fire blazes in cold weather. The leaded light windows on one side of the room have a direct view over Kensington Gardens, which slope gently up towards Kensington Palace. A second wall is lined with bookshelves, and a third has display cabinets that hold antique porcelains.

Guests can choose a cream tea or a traditional afternoon tea of finger sandwiches, freshly baked scones with clotted cream and preserves, and a selection of French pastries.

English Breakfast, Earl Grey, Darjeeling, Assam, Lapsang Souchong, Decaf English Breakfast, Jasmine, Green Peach Tea, Camomile, Peppermint, Strawberry and Rose.

The Montague on the Gardens

15 MONTAGUE STREET
BLOOMSBURY, LONDON WC1B 5BJ
TEL: 020 7637 1001
FAX: 020 7637 2516
MANAGER: ANDREW PIKE

The nearest Tube station is Russell Square. From the Tube station, go into the square by the gate closest to the Tube station and head diagonally across the square. Turn into Montague Street; the hotel is a little way down on the left-hand side. From the main entrance of the British Museum, turn left along Great Russell Street and take the first left into Montague Street.

AFTERNOON TEA IS SERVED IN THE CONSERVATORY OR ON THE TERRACE EVERY DAY FROM 3–6 PM.

The Montague Hotel is set in a Grade II-listed building that was originally built in 1675 as part of the Bloomsbury Estate begun by the fifth Duke of Bedford and continued by the sixth Duke on the site of Bedford House. Part of the terrace of buildings developed then now houses the Georgian-fronted hotel. The name is taken from Ralph, the Duke of Montague, whose portrait still hangs in the foyer today. The hotel has an intimate atmosphere, and a genteel afternoon tea is served in the comfortable conservatory, with direct views onto the gardens, or on the terrace beneath large sunshades, also overlooking the peaceful gardens.

The pretty, traditional china and the silver three-tier cake stand set the scene for a classic afternoon tea of finger sandwiches, scones and pastries of the day, or a cream tea with scones and Devonshire clotted cream, jam and a pot of tea. The menu provides a brief history of tea as "invented" by the Duchess of Bedford and a description of the teas on offer.

Assam, Ceylon, Darjeeling, Earl Grey, Jasmine, Keemun, Lapsang Souchong, Green Teas from China and Japan. Herbal infusions are also offered.

Tea-Time Traditions from London

The best known London sweetmeat is the Chelsea bun. The Old Chelsea Bun House stood in Pimlico Road and the owner, Richard Hand (known by all as Captain Bun), sometimes sold as many as a quarter of a million buns in one day. The shop, which sadly was destroyed in 1839, stood opposite the entrance to the Stromboli House and Pleasure Gardens, and the famous buns — and Mr. Hand's eccentric manner of running his business attired in a long dressing gown and fez — attracted crowds of eager customers.

Some of London's 18th-century pleasure gardens were well known for their own particular specialities. Bread and butter was always the staple fare served with tea, and White Conduit Garden became very well known for its loaves. As well as being on offer at the pleasure garden, they were sold around the streets so that slices of the popular bread could be served for tea at home. Similarly, Bagnigge Wells became famous for its buns when tea shops became a feature of London life in the 1880s and 90s. Lyons quickly gained a reputation for its cakes and pastries and, in particular, eclairs and cream buns, while Fullers, of course, was famous for its coffee and walnut cake.

Little cheesecakes have for centuries been a popular sweet treat, and London's favourites were flavoured with almonds. Around the country pastry cases were baked with a variety of different fillings that varied from egg custards with a hint of nutmeg, to brandy- or lemon-flavoured curd cheese mixtures. London's almond cheesecakes were mentioned by Samuel Pepys in his diary in 1669, and in the 18th century, a Mr. Trusler advertised them for sale at Marylebone Gardens.

Potted shrimps were also available in the pleasure gardens and were popular with buttered toast as a high tea dish at home. If the muffin man had been along your street ringing his bell, there were toasted muffins as well as (or instead of) toast.

Boodle cake, made to a recipe from Boodles, a club founded in St. James's Street, Westminster, in 1763, is a rich dark fruit cake that is absolutely packed with raisins and brown sugar. One of London's Lord Mayors was honoured with a special trifle at his banquet, the recipe for which later appeared in Cassell's *Dictionary of Cookery*. Served to all the guests at Mansion House, it was an elaborate confection of ratafias, strawberry jam, heavy cream, macaroons, brandy or sherry, egg custard, fruits and nuts.

Things to See and Do in London

This section concentrates on places to visit in the immediate vicinity of each of the hotels or tea lounges, and also includes some of the entertaining and informative guided walks organised by London Walks throughout the year. For more information about any of the walks mentioned, and others, please telephone 020 7624 3978.

The Chesterfield Hotel is set in Mayfair, the elegant Georgian residential part of London bordered to the north by Oxford Street, to the east by Regent Street, to the south by Piccadilly, and to the west by Park Lane and Hyde Park. Berkeley Square at its centre has some wonderful 18th-century houses set around an elegant garden. Shepherd Market, a village within a village, is a fascinating jumble of narrow lanes and streets full of restaurants, pubs and bars. The district is named after Edward Shepherd, who laid out the market and built Crewe House in Curzon Street in the early 18th century. Mount Street Gardens provide a peaceful resting place, and Grosvenor Square is the location of the U.S. Embassy and the Canadian High Commission. London Walks organises a tour around "Old Mayfair" that they advertise as "a champagne cocktail of a London walk." This area was home to Admiral Nelson and his mistress, Emma Hamilton, Clive of India, Disraeli, Handel, Florence Nightingale, Peter Sellers, Jimi Hendrix and Earl Mountbatten.

The Landmark Hotel stands on Marylebone Road just along from Regent's Park. The open area was laid out as a public park by John Nash in 1812, and today there is a boating lake with many varieties of water birds, a bandstand that is regularly used for the public performance of music, and in summer Queen Mary's Gardens are full of colour and powerful perfumes. London Zoo is situated on the north side of the park and has more than 600 species of animals. South of Regent's Park, Marylebone is full of wonderful Georgian houses, many of which are now used as clinics and private hospitals. Just along Marylebone Road from the Landmark, Madame Tussaud's waxwork museum has galleries filled with famous historical and contemporary people from the worlds of politics, entertainment and sport. Next door, the London Planetarium shows models of the sky at night.

London Walks organises two walks in this district. The Beatles "In My Life" walk takes you to the film locations of *A Hard Day's Night* and *Help*, the registry office where two of the Beatles got married, and the apartment immortalised by Ringo, John and Yoko. You will also see the house where Paul lived with his girlfriend, actress Jane Asher, and where Paul and John wrote "I Want to Hold Your Hand." The tour finishes with a visit to the famous Abbey Road studios. "The Sherlock Holmes Walk" visits the Victorian house at 221B Baker Street, home of the famous detective where Watson and he puzzled over many a crime.

From the Bond Street Tube station on Oxford Street, you can take a walking tour with London Walks to discover "Old Marylebone." It's the greenest walk in London, and takes you into an area where all the streets are very different from one another. You will catch glimpses of private dwellings, world-famous paintings and suits of armour.

The Lanesborough Hotel, the Dorchester Hotel and the Four Seasons Hotel are all extremely close to Hyde Park. Once the land of the ancient manor of Hyde, its 340 acres have been a royal park since the days of Henry VIII. Henry and Queen Elizabeth used it as a royal hunting ground, but James I opened it to the public, and it became popular for foot and horse racing, walking and relaxing. In 1851, the Great Exhibition was held here in the Crystal Palace, a great glass structure that was built specially for the event and was later moved, piece by piece, to Sydenham. Today the park is used for concerts, parades, political demonstrations and horse riding. An artificial lake, the Serpentine, has been used for boating and bathing since 1847, and at the Marble Arch corner, Speakers' Corner is available for anyone who wishes to speak publicly about absolutely anything. A law of 1872 made it legal for anyone to address a gathering on any subject, and this part of the park attracts all types of speakers and hecklers — especially on a Sunday. Marble Arch, designed by John Nash, was built as a main gateway to Buckingham Palace but was found to be too small for the horse-drawn carriages and so was moved to its present location near the site of the old Tyburn gallows where criminals were hanged. Next to Hyde Park is

Kensington Gardens, once the grounds of Kensington Palace and now a public park. There is a sunken garden, a memorial garden to Princess Diana, a statue of Peter Pan, modern statues, fountains and flower borders. Parts of Kensington Palace, previously home to Princess Margaret and Princess Diana, are open to the public every day and contain a costume gallery with an exhibition of court dress, and ornate state rooms.

London Walks takes groups on a tour called "Old Kensington" that includes a visit to Kensington Palace and the gardens, and that guides walkers through "cobbled little soigné lanes and mews, girt with pretty cottages and charming old shops."

Le Meridien Piccadilly stands in an area that became fashionable in the 16th century when Henry VIII built St. James's Palace. South of Piccadilly, the narrow streets are full of elegant shops, and in Piccadilly itself, there are major bookshops, china shops, gift shops and an important Japanese shop that sells books, tablewares and all sorts of foods from Japan. Fortnum and Mason, founded in 1707 by one of Queen Anne's footmen, is today one of the classiest department stores in London and sells an extensive range of British foods in its food halls. The Royal Academy, founded by Sir Joshua Reynolds in 1768, has popular permanent and temporary exhibitions throughout the year. Nearby Burlington Arcade has traditional shops selling cashmere, jewellery and British leather goods, and just around the corner, Regent Street has yet more fashionable shops. In the centre of Piccadilly Circus, the famous statue of Eros is one of London's landmarks.

London Walks organises a "Spies and Spy Catchers" walk that starts at Piccadilly Circus Tube station and takes you round "the secret places of a murky netherworld" of cloak-and-dagger London. You will visit the covert places of MI5 and MI6 and close in on a Soviet agent, pinpoint the "dead letter box" and unmask the fifth man.

The Meridien Waldorf in the Aldwych is surrounded by fascinating bits of old London. Round the corner is Covent Garden, once upon a time London's main fruit and vegetable market, but now humming with shoppers, theatregoers and opera and dance lovers. Places of interest include the Theatre Museum; the piazza, which was once the heart of the market and is today filled with shops, restaurants and bars; the

London Transport Museum; St. Paul's Church, with its façade by Inigo Jones; the newly refurbished Royal Opera House; and Neal Street and Neal's Yard, with its speciality food shops. North of the Meridien Waldorf is London's legal district with the neo-Gothic Law Courts and the 15th-century buildings of Lincoln's Inn. You can visit the Church of St. Clement Dane, which stands on the site of a seventh-century mission and synagogue built by the Danes in 886 and named after a Roman bishop. Severe bombing in 1941 reduced it to ruins, but it was rebuilt in 1955. On the south side of Fleet Street, Temple includes the four Inns of Court, the Middle Temple and the Inner Temple — the names derive from the Knights Templar who had their base here and who travelled with pilgrims to the Holy Land in order to protect them. It is a fascinating area to wander around, full of unexpected corners, archways and alleys. Prince Henry's Room, part of a Fleet Street tavern, has the coat of arms of the Prince of Wales, son of James I, and also contains an exhibition about the diarist Samuel Pepys. In Chancery Lane, the London Silver Vaults are an excellent source of silver tea wares.

There are several excellent London Walks around this area — "Somewhere Else" London reveals parts of Dickens' London and includes a dramatic river crossing; "Lost Palaces and Hidden Byways" encounters ghosts and discovers riverside palaces and the King's Barge Room and ends up in the Floral Hall of Covent Garden; "Classic Murders and Crimes" takes in murder at the Savoy, death at the Café Royale, the silk stocking murders and the Kray brothers; "Secret London" takes walkers around Dr. Johnson's part of the city and reveals traces of Roman London and a Norman crypt; "Legal and Illegal London" visits the Inns of Court, a warren of cloisters and courtyards, passageways and gardens; "In the Footsteps of Sherlock Holmes" explores the Strand's gaslit alleys and Covent Garden and ends in a re-creation of Holmes' study; "Charles Dickens' London" takes you round a lost city, a London "of nooks and crannies and alleyways and gas lamps and 18th- and 19th-century houses." This one is led by a guide dressed in Victorian costume.

The Montague on the Gardens Hotel in Bloomsbury is close to the British Museum, an imposing building opened in 1759 and housing collections of prehistoric, Bronze Age, early medieval, Romano-British, Oriental, Egyptian and Greek antiquities. The new Great Court is a huge internal courtyard with the old British Library Reading Room at its heart and cafes, a restaurant, a bookshop and a gift shop all under the cover of a stunning glass roof. This is also an area closely associated with learning, literature and art, and was the centre of the Bloomsbury group of writers and artists from 1900 to the 1930s. The main campus of the University of London is here, as are many of the academic bookshops. The streets and squares in the area are lined with elegant Georgian houses, several with blue plaques marking some of them as residences of famous people. Russell Square was once part of the estate of the Duke of Bedford, and his statue stands on the south side of the gardens. Bloomsbury Square is the oldest in the quarter, having been laid out in 1661. Famous residents include Virginia Woolf, Lytton Strachey and Duncan Grant. North of Bloomsbury is the Post Office Tower, which has a panoramic view over the capital and a revolving restauraunt at the top from which diners have splendid views while they eat.

Walks around the area include "Old Bloomsbury," which points out some of the handsome Georgian squares and the warren of little streets around the British Museum, and tells group members all sorts of fascinating stories and anecdotes about some of the famous people who once lived and worked here. The "British Museum Walk" guides walkers around the museum, pointing out such things as the Rosetta stone, the Elgin marbles, the 2,000-year-old Lindow bog man and the Sutton Hoo treasure.

The Rubens is within two minutes' walk of Buckingham Palace and St. James's Park. Queen Victoria was the first British monarch to live at the palace, and it is still the main official London residence of the royal family. Some state rooms are open to the public in August and September each year. The Changing of the Guard takes place daily from April to July, and on alternate days from August to March. Round the corner from the palace's main entrance, and opposite The Rubens, is the Queen's Gallery in what was once a conservatory. This contains one of the finest collections in the world of paintings by masters such as Vermeer and Leonardo. The Royal Mews along the road is only open for a few hours each week; visitors can see the stables and coach houses that were designed by John

Nash in 1825. The most important exhibit is the gold state coach built for George III in 1761. Further up the Mall from the palace stands Clarence House, designed in 1825 by Nash for William Duke of Clarence and, until her death, the London home of the Queen Mother. St. James's Park is bordered on one side by the Mall, which connects the palace with Trafalgar Square, and on the other by Birdcage Walk, where Charles II used to keep his collection of caged birds. The park was once marshland but was turned into a hunting ground by Henry VIII. Green Park, also once part of Henry's hunting grounds, became a public park in 1666.

London Walks organises a "Diana Princess of Wales" walk from Green Park Tube station around the places that were important to the Princess — Dodi Fayed's penthouse, her ancestral home, Spencer House in St. James's Place, Buckingham Palace, the Royal Chapel and the Mall. "The London of Oscar Wilde" walk takes groups around the London of the 1890s with gaslit streets, hansom cabs, theatre personalities and drama. "The Westminster Nobody Knows" walk explores "narrow streets, secret courtyards and superb, old-fashioned shops hidden away behind all the tinsel of the West End" and reveals Henry VIII's cow shed, a fine Georgian shopping arcade, the Queen Mother's home and London's most exclusive gentlemen's club.

The Georgian Restaurant in Harrods department store in Knightsbridge is set in what was once a small village outside the city of London that was surrounded by mudbanks and fields. Harrods was established as a small grocery shop in 1849 by Henry Charles Harrod, and from very humble beginnings it became a world-famous store that claims to be able to supply just about anything shoppers could want. Knightsbridge is generally an excellent area for all types of shopping.

London Walks takes groups on an "Old Knightsbridge Village Pub Walk" around cobbled pathways, hidden churchyards and other quiet places that "could be a million miles from Harrods and the hustle-and-bustle of the Brompton Road."

A short bus ride from Knightsbridge will take you to Kensington, where the Milestone Hotel is an excellent base from which to enjoy Kensington Gardens, with its beautiful, recently refurbished Albert Memorial designed by Sir George Gilbert Scott and completed in 1876, 15 years after the death of Albert, Queen Victoria's consort. Alternatively, shop in Kensington High Street and Kensington Church Street, and walk down to the Cromwell Road, where some of London's best museums stand close to each other. The Victoria and Albert Museum has amazing collections of textiles, furniture, design, ceramics and glass, sculpture, metalwork, jewellery, costume, Indian art and Far Eastern art. The Natural History Museum explains life on earth and has a dinosaur exhibition, an ecology gallery, a bird gallery, a mammals exhibition and earth galleries. The Science Museum has impressive exhibitions on space, navigation and surveying, flight, medical history and computing. The Royal Albert Hall is a vast circular concert hall used for performances of all types of music, sporting events and business conferences.

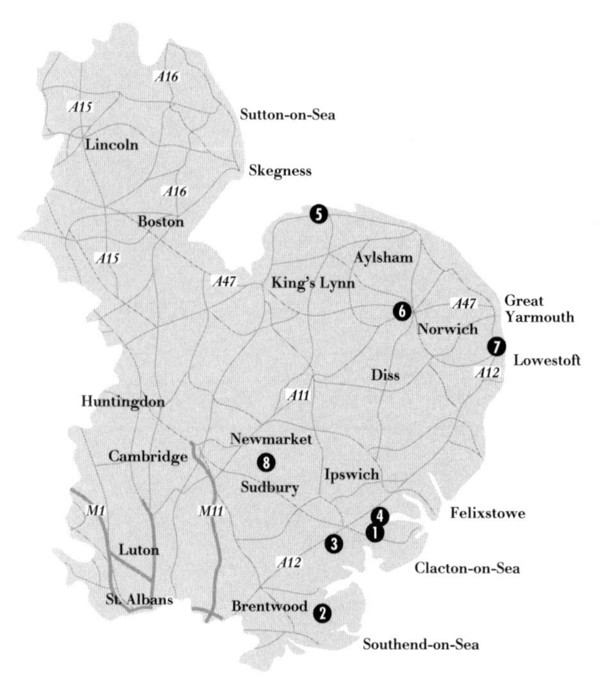
A16
A15
Sutton-on-Sea
Lincoln
Skegness
A16
Boston
5
A15
Aylsham
A47
King's Lynn
6
A47
Great
Yarmouth
Norwich
7
Lowestoft
A12
Diss
A11
Huntingdon
Newmarket
Cambridge
8
Ipswich
Sudbury
M1
M11
4
Felixstowe
1
3
Luton
A12
Clacton-on-Sea
St. Albans
Brentwood
2
Southend-on-Sea

The East Tea Trail

Essex

1. POPPYS TEA ROOM *p.* 78
2. SQUIRES *p.* 79
3. TEA ON THE GREEN *p.* 80
4. TRINITY HOUSE TEAROOM & GARDEN *p.* 81

Norfolk

5. MARGARET'S TEA ROOMS *p.* 82
6. NORWICH TEA & COFFEE SHOP *p.* 83

Suffolk

7. FLYING FIFTEENS *p.* 84
8. THE SWAN *p.* 85

Poppys Tea Room

17 TRINITY STREET
COLCHESTER, ESSEX CO1 1JN
TEL: 01206 765805
OWNERS: GILL CALENDAR & JAN COOPER
EGON RONAY RECOMMENDED

Take the A12 from the M25 and follow to Colchester. Poppys is in the town centre close to the Clock Museum.

OPEN ALL YEAR.
MONDAY–THURSDAY, 9:30AM–5PM;
FRIDAY AND SATURDAY, 9:30AM–5:30PM;
CLOSED SUNDAY.

Poppys gets a lot of visits from foreign tourists, and one group wrote in the guest book, "We didn't expect such big meals in such a small restaurant — we will be back!" It is small, but its large reputation as being the best in Colchester has spread beyond the immediate locality because of its charming Victorian style and delicious food. The building is full of old beams and Victorian bric-a-brac, with relaxing classical music playing in the background and the staff wearing period uniforms with mobcaps.

As well as a very wide range of all-day dishes — quiches, hot jacket potatoes, pastas and pies — there is an excellent choice of hot and cold sandwiches (honey roast ham with cheese, prawn mayonnaise, mackerel and orange, pork sausage, BLT, the ultimate cucumber sandwich and CBLT). For the health-conscious, the menu includes large helpings of seasonal mixed salads and homemade soups. Tea time brings six set menus with sandwiches, scones, croissants, crumpets, teacakes, and a whole host of cakes and puddings known as Poppys Pudding Club.

Darjeeling, Earl Grey, English Breakfast, Yorkshire, Lapsang Souchong, Lady Grey, Assam. Fruit-flavoured teas and herbal infusions are also available.

Squires

11 HIGH STREET
RAYLEIGH, ESSEX SS6 7EW
TEL: 01268 741791
WEB SITE: WWW.SQUIRESCOFFEESHOP.COM & CO.UK
OWNERS: HELEN & CARL WATSON
THE SOUTHEND & DISTRICT BEST
NEW SMALL BUSINESS AWARD 1988

Rayleigh is situated on the A129 within easy access of the A127. Squires is located at the upper end of the high street close to Trinity Church.

OPEN ALL YEAR.
MONDAY–SATURDAY, 9AM–5PM; CLOSED SUNDAY.

The 300-year-old building that houses Squires is one of only a few original buildings in this busy high street. Old wooden beams run across the ceiling, and a red brick fireplace gives the tearoom a traditional atmosphere. Bentwood chairs, dark wooden tables and a professional standard of service carry this through. Both Helen and Carl gave up a career at sea to open Squires, and Helen has a strong link with tea since her father once worked for a major tea importing firm. They have created a really friendly, welcoming atmosphere where locals pop in regularly for lunch or tea.

Squires has achieved a reputation for excellent food, professionally served and made to order. This includes many homemade dishes such as quiches, soups and traditional crumbles. Squires now offers 17 pure arabica coffees and 25 loose-leaf teas. Customers are often encouraged to sample teas in the restaurant using specialist glass teapots before purchasing in the retail area, where they also sell themed gifts as well as specialist hampers.

Ceylon, Assam, First Flush Darjeeling, Second Flush Darjeeling, English Breakfast, Kenya, Keemun, Black Dragon Oolong, Jasmine Monkey King, Earl Grey, Lapsang Souchong, Advent of Winter, Tea of Life Green Tea. Herbal and fruit infusions are also offered.

Tea on the Green

3 EVES CORNER, DANBURY
ESSEX CM3 4QF
TEL: 01245 226616
E-MAIL: MICK@TEAONTHEGREEN.FSNET.CO.UK
OWNER: MICK HELLIER
1999 TEA COUNCIL AWARD OF EXCELLENCE

Leave the M25 at Junction 28 and take the A12 towards Chelmsford. Bypass Chelmsford and then take the A414 off the A12 to Maldon. Danbury is approximately five miles along this road. When you reach the village green, turn left into Little Baddow Road and the tearooms are immediately opposite the village duck pond.

OPEN ALL YEAR EXCEPT CHRISTMAS AND NEW YEAR.
MONDAY–FRIDAY, 8:30AM–4:30PM;
SATURDAY, 10AM–5PM; SUNDAY, 11AM–5PM;
BANK HOLIDAYS, TIMES VARY, PLEASE TELEPHONE AHEAD.

The large pink building that houses this delightful tea-room overlooks the village green and duck pond set in National Trust land. Inside, the décor is soft pastel colours, floral tablecloths and fine white bone china, and has a cricket and golf theme that always provokes comments and conversation from guests. There are also numerous teapots of all shapes and sizes displayed around the room, and a collection of books on tea and coffee for customers to browse through. The atmosphere is relaxing and fun.

The informative menu offers a good selection of breakfast and light lunchtime dishes, and an excellent range of tea-time toasts, breads and scones. As well as traditional hot buttered crumpets, English muffins and cinnamon toast, you can also choose waffles with maple syrup, cinnamon muffins or toasted bagels. The house special Tea on the Green afternoon tea includes a choice of tasty finger sandwiches, a sultana scone with cream and strawberry jam, and a slice of homemade cake. For children there are small portions at reduced prices and an imaginative list of treats, with Mouse Trap (cheese sandwich plus drink and cake), Flipper (tuna sandwich), and Monkey Business (banana sandwich) adding to the fun.

English Breakfast, Afternoon Blend, Earl Grey, Lady Grey, Jasmine, Assam, Darjeeling, Ceylon, Lapsang Souchong, Decaffeinated. Herbal and fruit infusions are also offered.

Trinity House Tearoom & Garden

47 HIGH STREET, MANNINGTREE
ESSEX CO11 1AH
TEL: 01206 391410
FAX: 01206 391216
MANAGERS: RAY & HEATHER ABLETT

Take the A137 from Ipswich, or the A131 from Colchester into the centre of Manningtree. Trinity House is situated in the main street.

OPEN ALL YEAR, INCLUDING EASTER.
MONDAY–SATURDAY, 9AM–4:30PM.

Trinity House Tearoom overlooks the River Stour and is a very attractive spot to sit and watch boats, birds and wild fowl. The tearoom is run to help support and provide work for the residents of Acorn Village — a community within Manningtree for people with learning disabilities. A great deal of care and thought goes into the organisation of the tea shop and its menu. Trinity House holds the local council's Hygiene Award and Heartbeat Award for healthy living, and the healthy options include all sorts of lunchtime savoury dishes, filled rolls and sandwiches. There's a tempting array of homemade cakes (including indulgent treats such as lemon meringue pie with cream, Danish pastries, and fruit pies with custard, ice cream or cream) and fat-free tea breads and sponge cakes.

The tearoom is on the scenic Coastal Route from Harwich, in a prime position in Manningtree where Matthew Hopkins, witchfinder general, is said to have operated in the 17th century. The popular Essex Way is also nearby, and Manningtree is a favourite stop for cyclists and walkers. The beautiful tea garden is entered each year in the local Floral Manningtree Competition, in conjunction with "Anglia in Bloom."

House Blend, Yorkshire Blend, Assam, Earl Grey, Lady Grey, Darjeeling, Lapsang Souchong, English Breakfast, Decaffeinated, fruit-flavoured, various herbals.

Margaret's Tea Rooms

CHESTNUT FARMHOUSE, THE STREET
BACONSTHORPE, NEAR HOLT
NORFOLK NR25 6AB
TEL: 01263 577614
OWNERS: MARGARET & ROGER BACON
1997, 1998, 2000, 2001 TEA COUNCIL
AWARD OF EXCELLENCE

Four hundred yards from the Holt-Norwich (B1149) roundabout (off the Holt bypass) is the road to Baconsthorpe. Stay on this road for three miles and you will come straight to Margaret's Tea Rooms (300 yards from the village post office). There is a car park for up to 15 cars.

CLOSED DECEMBER, JANUARY AND FEBRUARY. OPEN MOTHERING SUNDAY–OCTOBER 3: TUESDAY–SUNDAY, 10:30AM–5PM; CLOSED MONDAYS EXCEPT BANK HOLIDAYS.

Margaret and Roger Bacon's mid-17th-century farmhouse is a warm and welcoming home with two tearooms — the Harebell and Strawberry parlours. Lace tablecloths and themed china enhance the traditional settings, and in cooler months, a wood-burning stove in the Harebell and an oak surround open fire in the Strawberry, add to the warm ambience. During the summer months, refreshments are also served in the farmhouse garden, where poppies, foxgloves and roses create a colourful backdrop.

Margaret's home cooking makes every visit special. She gets up at 5am every day to make all the breads, cakes, biscuits, scones, soups, jams and pickles herself in the farmhouse kitchen. Daily choices may include delicious pies and quiches, open sandwiches, various salads and a selection of cheeses served with Margaret's unusual pickles. Favourite cakes (which vary from day to day) include carrot cake, banana and brazil nut, hazelnut meringue, hot marmalade bread pudding with cream, traditional Norfolk scones and different varieties of shortbread. The cream teas are a must — plain scones with homemade jam and fresh double cream from the local dairy. All the flour used in the baking comes from the local watermill.

House Blend, English Breakfast, Irish Breakfast, Kenya Breakfast, Assam, Ceylon, Darjeeling, Dimbula, Nilgiri, Earl Grey, Earl Grey Decaffeinated, Orange Pekoe, Gunpowder, Jasmine, various Keemuns, various Lapsang Souchongs, Formosa Oolong, Rose Congou, Russian Caravan, Rwanda, Yunnan, Camomile and fruit infusions.

Norwich Tea & Coffee Shop

33 ORFORD PLACE, NORWICH NR1 3QA
TEL: 01603 760790
FAX: 01603 722122
OWNER: ALAN DEAN
2001 TEA COUNCIL AWARD OF EXCELLENCE

The Tea & Coffee Shop is right in the middle of Norwich in a row of shops that includes Marks & Spencer, Debenhams and Pizza Hut, and then the tea shop.

OPEN ALL YEAR. MONDAY–SATURDAY, 9:30AM–4:30PM; CLOSED SUNDAY AND BANK HOLIDAYS. THE RETAIL SHOP IS OPEN MONDAY–SATURDAY, 9AM–5:30PM.

Alan Dean first became involved in the tea and coffee trade in 1974, when he and his brother purchased a very old Norwich company by the name of Lamberts & Co — tea and coffee wholesalers, coffee roasters and tea merchants. In 1982, Alan started the wholesale side of Norfolk Tea & Coffee Company, added the city centre retail shop in 1995 and the first-floor air-conditioned tearoom in 1999. The list of teas which the company now sells is truly amazing and offers customers the chance to taste some really unusual and special flavours. To ensure that the teas are brewed to the very best possible standard, the tearoom has two separate boilers — one using hard tap water for the strong Assams and Breakfast Blends and the other with filtered water for all the other teas. The leaves are brewed inside the teapots in disposable t-sacs that are removed before the pot is served to the table — thus ensuring that your tea cannot stew and become bitter. All the teas served in the tearoom are on sale in the ground-floor shop. The menu offers sandwiches and light lunches, and a selection of homemade biscuits and cakes. This is a must for anyone interested in really fine teas.

Various Assams (second flush, third flush, CTC organic), various Darjeelings (first flush, second flush, third flush, autumnals), various Ceylons, Kenya, Rwanda, various Keemuns, Rose Congou, Jasmine, various Lapsang Souchongs, Yunnan, Formosa Oolong, Earl Grey, Russian Caravan, various Breakfast Blends, Gunpowder, Green Hyson, Chun Mee, Mango, Peach, Lemon, Turkish Apple Tea, various fruit and herbal infusions.

Flying Fifteens

19A THE ESPLANADE, LOWESTOFT
SUFFOLK NR33 0QG
TEL: 01502 581188
FAX: 01502 586991
OWNERS: PETER & DIANA KNIGHT
1999 TEA COUNCIL AWARD OF EXCELLENCE

The tea shop is located on the seafront promenade of the South Beach between the South Pier and the Claremont Pier, near the Hatfield Hotel.

CLOSED EARLY OCTOBER–EASTER; OPEN WEEKENDS ONLY FROM EASTER TO SPRING BANK HOLIDAY. FROM SPRING BANK HOLIDAY TO EARLY OCTOBER: TUESDAY–SUNDAY, 10:30AM–5PM. CLOSED MONDAYS EXCEPT BANK HOLIDAYS.

Since opening in 1996, Flying Fifteens has gained a reputation for good food and service. The unusual name for this delightful tearoom comes from the Flying Fifteen sailing boats designed by Uffa Fox. In 1958 he brought Prince Philip's Flying Fifteen "Cowslip" to Lowestoft for the June egatta.

A great deal of thought has gone into the design of the tearoom, and the light décor of pale yellow and pale turquoise reflects the colours of sea and sand. Customers can also sit in the attractive seafront garden, which has won several gold awards in the "Lowestoft in Bloom" competition.

There is a simple menu of homemade soup, omelettes, toasted and fresh sandwiches and baguettes that are well presented on china designed by Jeff Banks. The smoked salmon is produced in Lowestoft especially for Flying Fifteens, and on Saturday, fresh dressed Cromer crabs and crab sandwiches are usually available. All the cakes are homemade, and the special strawberry scones and strawberry meringues are particularly popular, as is the boozy fruit cake. Lowestoft porcelain, which is produced nearby by their sister company, is on display and workshop visits are recommended.

More than 25 different teas, including Assam, Darjeeling, English Breakfast, Earl Grey. Various fruit and herbal infusions are also available.

The Swan

HIGH STREET, LAVENHAM
SUDBURY, SUFFOLK CO10 9QA
TEL: 01787 247477
FAX: 01787 248286
GENERAL MANAGER: FRANCIS GUILDEA

Lavenham is on the A1141 between Bury St. Edmonds and Hadleigh. The Swan is located in the centre of the medieval village of Lavenham.

OPEN ALL YEAR.
TEA IS SERVED IN THE LOUNGE FROM 3–5:30PM.

In the 15th century, four timbered houses in the centre of this incredibly unspoilt and picturesque town were united to form the Swan Hotel, and today it is still a hotel of great character and charm, and a perfectly wonderful place to stop for a traditional English tea. The cosy, comfortable lounge has quaint snug corners that are ideal for a quiet, refined cup of tea, open fireplaces where roaring log fires crackle their welcome in winter months, generous arrangements of fresh and dried flowers all over the room, and a lovely view of the walled, cloistered garden, with its lawn surrounded by pretty borders. In summer, customers spill out into this beautiful space for their three course tea served on silver tiered cake stands, or cream teas with home-baked scones, homemade jams and Cornish clotted cream.

You will feel as if you have settled into a genteel country house where afternoon refreshment is an essential part of each day's enjoyment.

House Blend, Earl Grey, Assam, Darjeeling, Lapsang Souchong.

Tea-Time Traditions from the Eastern Counties

ESSEX, NORFOLK AND SUFFOLK

England's Eastern Counties have a rich history of speciality foods resulting from a thriving fishing and shellfish industry, the plentiful production of soft fruits, apples and damsons grown for the London markets, the once-famous saffron fields in Essex, and the traditional farming of wheat, barley and oats.

Although Cornwall later became recognised for its importation of the spice, saffron fields were established in Essex during the 14th century. For some reason, the industry there did not survive, and the only evidence today is in the name of the town of Saffron Waldon and in recipes for saffron cakes, breads and wigs that have survived down through the centuries. It took between 60,000 and 192,000 stamens from the saffron crocuses to make one pound of saffron, and the harvesting work must have been backbreaking.

This part of England has long been famous for its bees and their honey. Traditionally, the bees lived in straw hives called skeps, and their honey was used in all sorts of honey breads, cakes and buns. The town of Walsingham has its own honey cake recipe for a rich sweet sponge filled with candied peel, cherries and raisins and covered with a honey, almond and butter topping.

Essex used to produce many different types of loaves — Dannicks made from stone-ground wheatmeal; oval paddles or pads; and Essex huffers, made by flattening a two-pound piece of well-fermented dough into a round and then dividing it into eight triangular pieces. Small round flat loaves were confusingly called biscuits in Essex, and Epping buns were made with ground rice, spices and clarified lard, as well as the standard flour, sugar, eggs and milk. Cymbals were little round spiced buns made for Ash Wednesday, and the Essex name for hot cross buns was hock-a-buns. As in other parts of Britain, when the Easter buns were made each year, every housewife or cook would set one of the batch aside and dry it so that it could not go mouldy. It was then hung up in the kitchen in order to ward off bad luck, and if anyone fell ill during the following 12 months, a piece of the charmed bun was crumbled in water and given to the patient to drink to help them recover quickly.

Norfolk and Suffolk both have old recipes for treacle tarts that do not contain breadcrumbs but are creamy and set like a jelly, and are a little less sweet than other treacle tarts. Norfolk gingers and Norfolk fair buttons were typical fairings, made with a little ginger and sometimes a little lemon juice. Suffolk and Norfolk, rusks were eaten with butter and cheese or jam. They were like a rather dry scone, plain and pale in Norfolk and slightly smaller and richer in Suffolk. Norfolk shortcake was the local version of lardy cake made with pastry rather than bread dough, and Stiffkey cakes were again a little like scones but drier and crisper.

Suffolk fourses were made for the harvesters' mid-afternoon break out in the fields. Recipes vary around the county, but most were doughy, currant-filled round cakes divided into four sections by knife markings and then sprinkled with sugar before being baked. November 23 is St. Clement's Day and in Essex, little Clementy cakes made for the festive day were rather like the Cattern cakes made for St. Catherine's Day (November 25) in lace-making and spinning areas. They were usually made by rolling out a rectangle of sweetened, almond-flavoured dough and sprinkling over it a handful of currants. The pastry was then rolled up like a Swiss roll, cut into slices and baked until pale golden.

In all these eastern Counties fruit was plentiful, and so apple pies, tarts and puddings were standard fare. Fen Counry apple cake was like a pie but made with semolina and lemon juice. In Colchester, the gooseberry harvest was celebrated on Gooseberry Pie Day, and other fruits such as blackberries, raspberries, redcurrants, damsons and cherries were baked and bottled and turned into jams and jellies.

High tea was a feast of savoury dishes — raised game pies made with locally caught pheasant, partridges, hare and venison; oysters from the nearby oyster beds; smoked herrings and other fish caught by the local fishermen; and bloater paste made from Yarmouth's famous bloaters. Victorian tea tables in Norfolk were never quite complete without locally made bloater paste on toast.

Things to See and Do in the Eastern Counties

ESSEX, SUFFOLK, NORFOLK

Essex

Colchester, home to Poppys Tea Room, is Britain's oldest recorded town, dating back to Roman times. In the centre of the old part of the town is Castle Park, where visitors can stroll through the gardens, walk through the oldest wall in Britain, learn about the town's history in the Castle Museum and imagine the fate that befell those who were held in the castle prisons. Elsewhere in the town, the Hollytrees Museum has an exhibition of life in Colchester over the past 300 years; the Natural History Museum gives a "hands-on" perspective on the local natural environment since the Ice Age, and Bourne Mill is a picturesque 16th-century fishing lodge converted into a mill (now owned by the National Trust) with much of the machinery still intact. For countryside lovers, High Woods Country Park is just a couple of miles outside the town centre and offers 300 acres of grassland, woodland, wetland, farmland and a visitors centre.

To the northeast of Chichester, Manningtree is the location of Trinity House Tearoom and Garden. The smallest town in England, in Tudor times it was a thriving port and many of today's imposing Georgian façades conceal Elizabethan and Tudor houses. The local museum has exhibitions of items and photographs relating to the heritage of Manningtree and the neighbouring town of Mistley. Both towns stand on the river Stour and the estuary is one of the most important wildlife areas of Europe. Swans guard the river where barges once loaded and unloaded their cargoes, and smugglers landed illicit goods. At Mistley, the former County Nuclear War Bunker is open to the public and has displays, cinemas and sound effects relating to the Cold War. Also in Mistley is the Mistley Place Park Animal Rescue Centre, where children can play among the rescued animals and birds that roam free in 25 acres of countryside overlooking the Stour Valley. West of Colchester, railway enthusiasts will love the East Anglian Railway Museum at Chappel Station, Chappel. The collection spans 150 years of railway history and includes explanations of the workings of signals and steam engines. A few miles to the southwest, near Coggeshall, stands Paycocke's, a handsome half-timbered merchant's house built around 1500 and now owned by the National Trust.

Tea on the Green is in Danbury, southwest of Coggeshall. Danbury and Lingwood Commons, the countryside that surrounds the tearoom, belong to the National Trust and are at the highest point of the gravel ridge that runs between Chelmsford and Maldon. The Commons once belonged to the medieval manors of St. Clere and Herons, and incorporated an area of common grazing land. There is evidence of Napoleonic defences and old reservoirs, and visitors can follow a circular nature trail. Just south of the town is Danbury Country Park. Created in 1088, it has a formal garden (separated from the park by two ha-has that stop deer and domestic farm animals from straying into the gardens); lakes with water lilies, ducks and the occasional kingfisher; woodland with rare native trees and ancient hedgerows and a meadow picnic area. Just north of Danbury, Blakes Wood at Little Baddow is a "Site of Special Scientific Interest" with its ancient woodland of hornbeam and chestnut trees and its famous bluebells. At Woodham Walter to the north there is a large expanse of common, the ruins of Woodham Walter Hall and a nature trail. At Maldon, on the estuary of the River Blackwater, there's a heritage museum; the old 15th-century Moot Hall; the Millennium Garden, a representation of a 10th-century garden created in 1991 to mark the millennium of the Battle of Maldon; and the Edwardian-style gardens of Promenade Park by the river, which include a marine lake, an adventure playground, sporting facilities and a programme of events throughout the year.

Just inland from the eastern reaches of the Thames estuary and on the northern borders of Southend-on-Sea, Rayleigh's high street is where Squires tearoom stands. The National Trust owns Rayleigh Mount and its windmill, the former site of a Domesday castle built by Sweyn of Essex. Visitors can visit it and the Dutch Cottage, which is lived in but is open to the public on certain days each year. As well as its famous seafront and seaside attractions, Southend also has the Southchurch Hall Museum, housed in a 13th- and 14th-century timber-framed manor house that stands in a moated landscaped garden and has exhibitions that include period room settings from the Middle Ages to the 19th century. Leigh-on-Sea, to the west of Southend, is home to Belfairs Park and Nature Reserve, which includes woodland walks, a nature reserve and remnants of the ancient oak, birch and hornbeam woodland that once covered much of this area.

Norfolk

Margaret's Tea Rooms is in Baconsthorpe, which is set in gently undulating countryside. There is a castle and just to the west is Holt, a small Georgian town set on the edge of the Glaven Valley. On the outskirts of the town lies Holt Country Park, with more than 100 acres of woodland, picnic areas, nature trails and an adventure playground for children. The village of Letheringsett, a mile west of Holt, has an early 19th-century watermill that still stone-grinds corn in the traditional way. From Holt, the North Norfolk Steam Railway, the Poppy Line, runs to Sheringham on the coast. The area around Sheringham is ideal for walking and cycling, and Sheringham Park, two miles southwest of Sheringham, is a stunning National Trust property, particularly beautiful in May and early June when the rhododendrons are in full bloom. To the south of Baconsthorpe is Mannington Hall, a medieval moated manor house with lake, shrubs, trees and roses, and neighbouring 18th-century Wolterton Hall is set in beautiful historic parkland.

Norwich, a busy city within easy reach of the Norfolk Broads, is where you will find the Norwich Tea and Coffee Shop. Dominated by its 13th-century cathedral, it is a delightful jumble of medieval streets and alleys with small speciality shops and half-timbered houses, and there are a number of interesting museums and historic buildings. The medieval Merchant's Hall in King Street has an outstanding timber-framed great hall, crown post roof, living hall with an imposing screens passage, cellars and vaulted undercroft. St. Julian's Church, tucked away in St. Julian's Alley off King Street, is also a fascinating piece of history and a place of extreme calm and quiet. Julian of Norwich, the first woman to write a book in English, lived here and wrote *The Revelations of Divine Love.* Although the hermitage was pulled down during the Reformation, it was rebuilt after wartime bombing. Up the hill at the 12th-century castle, Norwich Castle Museum houses the Twinings Teapot Gallery, with its collection of more than 3,000 teapots. Other museums in town include the Bridewell Museum, which tells the story of how the town found fame through shoes and mustard, textiles and beer; Strangers' Hall, one of the oldest and most fascinating buildings in Norwich where mayors and sheriffs have left traces of their occupation; and the Royal Norfolk Regimental Museum, which houses a collection of three centuries of military equipment, souvenirs and memorabilia. Three miles north of Norwich, at Horsham St. Faith, the City of Norwich Aviation Museum features a Vulcan bomber. Nine miles to the east, Fairhaven Woodland and Water Garden has more than three miles of woodland walks with wonderful views across the South Walsham Inner Broad, daffodils and azaleas in spring, massed wild flowers, butterflies, birds and dragonflies in summer, and the superb colours of trees and shrubs in autumn. The Broads offer opportunities for relaxing river trips, skippering your own boat or enjoying short trips on a picnic boat or cruiser.

Suffolk

Flying Fifteens tearoom in Lowestoft is situated in a town that has a wide variety of museums and other attractions. There's a Transport Museum, a Maritime Museum, the Royal Navy Patrol Service Museum and the War Memorial Museum. The Heritage Workshop Centre documents the town's history, its people and crafts, and Peto Craft has a re-creation of Lowestoft's porcelain industry, which ended 200 years ago, and small workshops so that visitors can see pieces being made and decorated. At Somerleyton, just northwest of the town, stands Somerleyton Hall, a splendid early Victorian stately home with impressive architectural features, state rooms and 12 acres of gardens that include original ornamentation, a fine collection of trees and shrubs, a miniature railway and a maze constructed in 1846 from yew hedges. Beccles, a few miles south west of Lowestoft, is home to the Beccles and District Museum at Leman House, with displays of the social life and traditional crafts and industries of the area. The William Clowes Print Museum documents the development of printing from 1800 with machinery, woodcuts and books. Also in Beccles is Winter Flora, a unique workshop and shop associated with flowers, herbs and plants for garden lovers. Wonderful thatched houses that date from medieval days surround the Swan at Lavenham. The Guildhall and Little Hall are fine examples of the timbered and whitewashed buildings that flank the narrow streets of a town that flourished as a result of a thriving wool trade. The late 15th-century Guildhall overlooks and dominates the market place and contains exhibitions on the cloth industry, the medieval woollen trade, local history, farming and railways. Its delightful walled garden contains dye plants and a 19th-century lock-up and mortuary. The Little Hall, which was built in the 14th century, modernised in the 16th, extended in the 17th and restored in the 1920s and 30s, now contains interesting furniture and pictures. Lavenham Church is a magnificent 15th-century perpendicular church with richly carved misericords and screens and some very fine glass. The Priory is a timber-framed house dating from the 14th century with paintings and a herb garden.

M60
A1
Mansfield
M1
A5
Shrewsbury
M54
M6
Wolverhampton
M1
Leicester
Birmingham
Coventry
M43
Northampton
M1
Worcester
M5
Hereford
Cheltenham
M40
Gloucester
Oxford
Stroud
A46
A34

The Middle England Tea Trail

Gloucestershire

❶ THE BAY TREE *p.* 96

❷ THE BLACK CAT *p.* 97

❸ TETBURY GALLERY TEA ROOM *p.* 98

❹ TWO TOADS *p.* 99

Nottinghamshire

❺ OLDE SCHOOL TEAROOM *p.* 100

❻ OLLERTON MILL TEA SHOP *p.* 101

❼ THE LOCK HOUSE TEA ROOMS *p.* 102

Oxfordshire

❽ ANNIE'S TEA ROOMS *p.* 103

Shropshire

❾ ANN BOLEYN TEA ROOM *p.* 104

❿ BIRD ON THE ROCK TEA ROOM *p.* 105

⓫ DE GREYS *p.* 106

⓬ THE MARSHMALLOW *p.* 107

The Bay Tree

1 VICTORIA STREET
BOURTON-ON-THE-WATER, CHELTENHAM
GLOUCESTERSHIRE GL54 2BT
TEL: 01451 821818
OWNER: CHRISTINE O'NEILL

Follow the A429 from Stow-on-the-Wold and turn left into Bourton. Victoria Street runs off the main high street and the Bay Tree is approximately 100 yards from the famous Cotswold Perfumery. Access is by any of the bridges over the river.

OPEN ALL YEAR. SUMMER OPENING TIMES VARY. MONDAY-THURSDAY, 10AM-LATE EVENING; FRIDAY AND SATURDAY, 9AM–LATE EVENING; SUNDAY, 10AM–8PM.

This pretty tea shop is housed in one of Bourton's typical, picturesque honey-coloured stone buildings and once inside you will find a traditional tearoom atmosphere with dark wood furniture, flower prints on the walls, fresh flowers on each table and a menu offering traditional meals throughout the day. The emphasis is on individual friendly service and a menu that offers healthy options. The Bay Tree has won Heartbeat awards for the range of low-fat meals (low-fat cheese salad, broccoli and cheese bake, mushroom stroganoff) and vegetarian dishes (vegetable curry, tomato pasta, vegetable chili) that Christine O'Neill offers. At teatime, cream teas are served with fruit scones and Cornish clotted cream, and the Bay Tree special cream tea includes sandwiches, scones and a slice of cake. When you've finished lunch or afternoon tea, why not wander into the Bay Tree's shop next door and browse amongst the wide selection of collectable teapots, speciality teas and coffees that offer something to suit everyone's taste, and other tea paraphernalia.

Traditional English Blend, Cotswold Blend, Earl Grey, Darjeeling, Assam, Ceylon, Yunnan, Lapsang Souchong, Jasmine, Lemon, Iced Teas. Herbal and fruit infusions are also offered.

The Black Cat

HIGH STREET
LECHLADE ON THAMES
GLOUCESTERSHIRE GL7 3AD
TEL/FAX: 01367 252273
E-MAIL: BLACKCATCAFE@HOTMAIL.COM
OWNERS: ALAN & VALERIE WATKINS

Follow signs to the centre of Lechlade. From Market Square, continue along the high street past the post office, the Red Lion Inn and Thames Street, which runs off to the left. The Black Cat is a little further along on the left-hand side, opposite the Crown Inn.

OPEN ALL YEAR.
MONDAY-FRIDAY, 9:30AM-5PM;
SATURDAY, 9:30AM-5:30PM; SUNDAY, 10AM-5:30PM.

The Black Cat is a very successful combination of a specialist tea and coffee retail operation and a fully fledged tearoom that gives customers the chance to sample any of the shop's teas, tisanes and coffees before choosing which one to buy to take home. As an independent family business, the Watkins feel that it offers an old-fashioned standard of service that is sadly missing from so many catering outlets today. The menu contains an excellent range of traditional savouries (ploughmans with various meats and cheeses, rarebits, sandwiches, and daily specials such as deep-fried brie and Normandy pork). There are special choices for children, and for tea there are homemade scones, tea cakes and a variety of cakes from the trolley.

The shop also sells a wide range of tea- and coffee-making equipment and accessories, and offers advice as to which leaf teas and coffee beans will suit different customers' requirements. They also give advice on how to brew them. The Black Cat now also takes bookings for evening meals on Thursdays, Fridays and Saturdays, and has an excellent restaurant menu.

English Breakfast, two Darjeelings, Assam, two Ceylons, Earl Grey, Keemun, Lapsang Souchong, Jasmine, Gunpowder, Russian Caravan, Formosa Finest Oolong, Rose Congou, Japanese Genmaicha, various fruit-flavoured teas, various fruit and herbal infusions.

Tetbury Gallery Tea Room

18 MARKET PLACE, TETBURY
GLOUCESTERSHIRE GL8 8DD
TEL: 01666 503412
E-MAIL: JANEOFTETBURY@AOL.COM
WEB SITE: WWW.TETBURYGALLERYTEAROOM.CO.UK
OWNER: JANE MAILE

Tetbury is 10 miles from Junction 17 on the M4 and 10 miles from Cirencester. The Gallery Tea Room is situated in the centre of town, just along the road, on the opposite side, to the pillared Market House.

OPEN SEVEN DAYS A WEEK ALL YEAR.
TIMES VARY ACCORDING TO SEASON.

Tetbury's documented history dates from the seventh century and many of its town centre buildings date from the 17th and 18th centuries.

The Tea Room is situated in the cosy drawing room of one of these 18th-century houses, and the linen tablecloths, white china and walls hung with fine art help create its timeless atmosphere. The food is exceptional, with all the cakes and scones made by Jane on the premises. There are many traditional favourite cakes on offer and a very wide range of scones. The dozen or so different varieties include a plain cheese scone that is very popular, especially served with a bowl of homemade soup. Another lunchtime favourite is the cheese and walnut wholemeal scone served with camembert and grapes. The chocolate scone, or the apricot and almond version with jam and clotted cream, make a perfect accompaniment to a cup of tea. It is clear why the American author Bruce Richardson listed this as one of "the great tea rooms of Britain." Jane has been described as having "turned the humble scone into an art form," and her fans will be delighted that a book of her tea room recipes has now been published.

Earl Grey, Lady Grey, Darjeeling, Assam, Lapsang Souchong, Ceylon, Jasmine, Rose Pouchong, Decaffeinated, various fruit-flavoured teas and herbal infusions.

Two Toads

19 CHURCH STREET, TETBURY
GLOUCESTER GL8 8JG
TEL: 01666 503696
OWNERS: KEN & PETA QUATERMASS

Two Toads is located on the Bath Road that runs from Bath to Cirencester. As you come into the village, the shop is halfway between St. Mary's Church and the Town Hall.

OPEN ALL YEAR EXCEPT CHRISTMAS.
MONDAY–SATURDAY, 9AM–5PM;
SUNDAY, 10AM–5PM.

Ken and Peta both gave up their jobs — Ken as an aerospace executive and Peta as a catering manager — to open Two Toads and say they have absolutely no regrets. The building in which they have created this bright, sunny yellow tearoom was built in 1675, and the middle section was once a barn. The decor is light and fresh, with pale ash bentwood furniture, flowers on the tables, country and garden prints on the walls (some for sale by local artists), waitresses' aprons in green and black stripes over black uniforms, and the calm, elegant, easy music of the 1920s and 30s. In the beautiful courtyard garden at the back, a very popular spot for up to 30 guests in summer, there is a cherry tree, a rose arch and borders and tubs filled with plants and flowers.

The menu lists soups and jacket potatoes, pasties and quiches, filled baguettes and fresh-cut sandwiches served with mixed salad leaves. Several of the products used — the cheeses, ham and fruit juices — come from local award-winning suppliers. For tea time, order Cornish clotted cream to eat with scones and jam, or try the scrumpy cider cake or some of the homemade produce.

House Morning Blend, Assam, Ceylon, Darjeeling, Earl Grey, Lapsang Souchong, China Oolong, Yunnan, Gunpowder, Jasmine, Kenya.

Olde School Tearoom

CARBURTON, NEAR WORKSOP
NOTTINGHAMSHIRE S80 3BP
TEL: 01909 483517
OWNER: GWEN ELLIOTT
1992 TEA COUNCIL AWARD OF EXCELLENCE

Carburton is on the B6034 that runs from Worksop to Ollerton. The Olde School Tearoom is at the crossroads with the road that runs from Clumber Park to Norton Village.

OPEN ALL YEAR EXCEPT JANUARY.
TUESDAY–FRIDAY, 10AM–4:30PM;
SATURDAY AND SUNDAY, 10AM–5PM;
CLOSED MONDAY.

Many of the regular customers in this converted 1930s school are local people who love the peace and quiet of a country tearoom. But it is also an ideal place for tourists after a drive or ramble in Sherwood Forest or Clumber Park. Gwen Elliott has preserved the spirit of the school building and has an old school desk in the entrance, her menu written up on the blackboard and easel, and the original children's hand basins in the washrooms. The old school shelves, once used for reference books and stacks of homework, now display woodwork, greeting cards and handmade prints by local artists. The partition, which in the past divided the main classroom into two, is now used to make a separate room for private parties, and the old school bell is still available to attract the attention of large groups if they are being too jolly and making too much noise.

Good service and value are important to Gwen, and her menu offers a very reasonably priced selection of homemade savouries, cakes and freshly cut sandwiches. The most popular cake is something her mother used to make when Gwen was a child — a fruit slice with a pastry base, a layer of jam and a topping of sponge full of dried fruits.

House Blend, Assam, Darjeeling, Earl Grey, Ceylon.

Ollerton Mill Tea Shop

OLLERTON MILL, MARKET PLACE
OLLERTON, NEWARK, NOTTINGHAMSHIRE NG22 9AA
TEL: 01623 824094/822469
OWNERS: KATE & ELLEN METTAM
1994, 1995, 1999 & 2001 TEA COUNCIL
AWARD OF EXCELLENCE

Ollerton lies at the junction of the A614 and B616, between Worksop and Nottingham. The watermill and tea shop are in the centre of the village, almost opposite the church.

OPEN MARCH–MID-NOVEMBER.
TUESDAY–SUNDAY, 10:30AM–5PM.
OPEN EVERY BANK HOLIDAY AND ANY
OTHER TIME BY ARRANGEMENT.

Ollerton is situated on the edge of Sherwood Forest in a corner of rural England that has remained unchanged for 300 years, and the Mill, built in 1713, stands on the same spot as the medieval mill mentioned in the *Domesday Book*. Since 1921 it has been in the Mettam family, who have been millers for many generations and whose family tree has been traced back to 1635. In 1993, it was lovingly restored by them, and now sisters-in-law Kate and Ellen Mettam run the tea shop, which is housed in the old millwright's workshop. The entrance has a wonderful view of the waterwheel and mill race, and the tea shop itself looks directly over the River Maun. This is a delightful spot, and visitors have the chance to learn a little about what life was like for a working miller in the 18th century while at the same time enjoying a really special afternoon tea. The cakes, quiches and mouthwatering puddings are baked on the premises with flour that is sold in the mill. The Ollerton Mill cream tea is just perfect — three dainty fruit or plain scones served with lashings of jam and cream.

House Blend, Earl Grey, Assam, Darjeeling, Lady Grey. Fruit and herbal infusions are also offered.

The Lock House Tea Rooms

TRENT LOCK
LOCK LANE, LONG EATON
NOTTINGHAMSHIRE NG10 2FY
TEL: 07974 544939
FAX: 0115 972 2288
E-MAIL: LOCKHOUSE@LINEONE.NET
OWNERS: MARK & TERRY ASHBY

Lock House Tea Room is situated three miles from the M1. Leave the motorway at Junction 24 and take the A50 towards Derby. Follow signs towards Long Eaton. Turn right in Sawley for Trent Lock.

OPEN ALL YEAR, INCLUDING BANK HOLIDAYS. CLOSED MONDAYS AND TUESDAYS.

Lock House Tea Rooms is run by the talented Ashby family: Keith, who specialises in sculpture, ceramics and paintings; Margaret, who is an antiques collector; Mark, an award-winning chef; and Terry, a traditional folk painter and graphic designer. The tearoom is located inside the old Lock House, which was built in 1794 by the Erewash Canal Carrying Company at the point where the River Trent meets the River Soar, the Erewash, and the Trent and Mersey canals. Inside the décor is an historic centre containing artefacts and canal memorabilia of a bygone age. Adjoining the tearoom is the old toll house where tolls were taken for use of the waterway. Today it contains a fine range of antiques, gifts and souvenirs.

To complement the fascinating historical setting, the menu creates a nostalgic atmosphere by offering old-fashioned treats such as dripping toast, a high tea with ham roasted on the bone and served with salad, bread and butter, a prawn high tea with Atlantic prawns and seafood dips, a traditional cream tea with fruit scones and Cornish clotted cream, Welsh cakes, and granny apple cake with clotted cream. The Ashbys also boast "the biggest Knickerbocker Glory this side of the Trent."

House Blend and more than 50 different teas including classic Indian and China teas and various botanical and fruit teas.

Annie's Tea Rooms

79 HIGH STREET
WALLINGFORD, OXFORDSHIRE OX10 0BX
TEL: 01491 836308
OWNER: JEAN ANN ROWLANDS

Wallingford is situated at the junction of the A329 Reading to Oxford road and the A4130 Henley to Wantage road. Annie's is in the High Street, just along from the crossroads of St. Martin's Street and Castle Street.

OPEN ALL YEAR. MONDAY, TUESDAY, THURSDAY–SATURDAY, 10AM–5PM; CLOSED SUNDAY, WEDNESDAY AND BANK HOLIDAYS.

Wallingford's history goes back to the granting of its charter in 1155, and it has links with a number of interesting personalities from the past, including Oliver Cromwell. The ruins of the largest castle in England stand round the corner from Annie's, and stones from here were included in the building of Windsor Castle.

Right in the centre of town, in a Grade II-listed building that is more than 300 years old, Jean Ann Rowlands gives a warm welcome to visitors from all over the world who come to taste her cakes, scones, pies and especially the homemade tea cakes, which are served with homemade jams.

The pink and burgundy room is a relaxing setting in which to enjoy your tea. The walls are decorated with old paintings and views of Wallingford, and paintings by local customers are displayed for sale. On fine days, a small walled garden at the back allows for alfresco teas after you have explored the ancient highways of the town.

Indian, Earl Grey, Ceylon, Darjeeling, Traditional English Blend, Assam, Lapsang Souchong. Fruit-flavoured teas and herbal infusions are also offered.

Ann Boleyn Tea Room

SMALLWOOD LODGE, UPPER BAR
NEWPORT, SHROPSHIRE TF10 7AP
TEL: 01952 813232
FAX: 01952 813606
E-MAIL: ZOLAROY@BTINTERNET.COM
OWNERS: ROY STEPHENSON & OWEN LAVELLE

Leave the M54 at Junction 3 and take the A41 to Whitchurch. Follow signs to Newport. The Tudor building that houses the Ann Boleyn Tea Room is situated in the main high street.

OPEN ALL YEAR. MONDAY-SATURDAY, 9AM–5PM; CLOSED SUNDAY. OPEN MOST BANK HOLIDAYS EXCEPT CHRISTMAS AND NEW YEAR.

This is more than simply a wonderful place to go for tea — it is also a shop and showroom in which to organise your interior design, buy fabrics and decorative objects, browse in the upstairs bookshop, and enjoy the 1600s interior of what is one of only two buildings left standing after the Great Fire of Newport. It is also the only building in Newport High Street with its own front garden, where Owen has created a Tudor knot garden with box hedges, lavender bushes and white standard roses.

In summer, this is a perfect setting for tea. As you enter the sweet-smelling black-and-white building, the first rooms you come to are showrooms for the interior design business, and these lead through to the oak-panelled tearoom with its Tudor beams, beautiful ochre walls above the panelling and chenille drapes in ochre and gold. The menu offers a selection of sandwiches and baguettes, breakfast dishes such as Welsh rarebit and eggs benedict, lunchtime favourites of steak and ale pie, cottage pie and in summer, amazing salads. There are also all the traditional tea-time favourites: scones, tea cakes, small "fancies," banoffee pie, eclairs and — the most popular, which disappear rapidly — white chocolate torte and seasonal fruit tartlets. A warm welcome awaits all.

House Blend, Assam, Darjeeling, Earl Grey, Camomile, Rosehip, Ginseng, Vanilla, Lemon Honey and Ginger, Ginger Honey and Orange, Blackcurrant Bracer, Peppermint, Elderflower and Lemon.

Bird on the Rock Tearoom

ABCOTT, CLUNGUNFORD
SHROPSHIRE SY7 0PX
TEL/FAX: 01588 660631
OWNERS: DOUGLAS AND ANNABEL HAWKES
2001 TEA COUNCIL AWARD OF EXCELLENCE

The tearoom is eight miles from Ludlow and is situated on the B4367 between the Craven Arms and Hoptonheath.

OPEN ALL YEAR.
CLOSED MONDAY, TUESDAY EXCEPT BANK HOLIDAYS.
SUMMER: WEDNESDAY–SUNDAY, 10AM–6PM.
WINTER: WEDNESDAY–SUNDAY, 10AM–5PM.

Cottage garden flowers and climbers create a memorable sight as you approach this pretty 17th-century house, and inside the traditional Welsh longhouse, with its oak beams and quarry tiles, Annabel and Douglas Hawkes have created a marvellous early 20th-century atmosphere with 1920s, 30s and 40s music and memorabilia, collected during their careers in the film industry. As costume designers for several period films and TV dramas (including *Poirot, Pride and Prejudice* and *House of Elliot*), the couple have a real flair for re-creating the past. Both the interior and garden of this excellent, charming tearoom delight everyone who visits.

The Just William Schoolboys Tea allows you to choose preserves to go with your toasted muffin, followed by a scone of your choice from a list of nine — all, of course, washed down by "lashings of ginger beer" (or tea). The Claude Greengrass Poacher's Tea of hot buttered crumpets and a slice of Mrs. Beaton's half pound cake has a true old-fashioned appeal. In summer, the Hercule Poirot Sleuth Tea serves Poirot's favourite lemon tea with bread and jam and wonderful cakes.

Assam, Darjeeling, Nilgiri, Dimbula, Nuwara Eliya, Keemun, Yunnan, Russian Caravan, Rose Pouchong, Lapsang Souchong, Gunpowder, Chunmee, Formosa Oolong, Earl Grey, Lady Grey, Lemon, Old English Fruits, Spice Imperial, various own blends including a good strong Shropshire blend of Assam, Kenya, Nuwara Eliya and Lapsang Souchong, various herbals.

De Greys

5-6 BROAD STREET
LUDLOW, SHROPSHIRE SY8 1NG
TEL: 01584 872764
FAX: 01584 879764
WEB SITE: WWW.DEGREYS.CO.UK
OWNER: MRS. S. UNDERHILL
"COMMENDED" BY THE HEART OF ENGLAND TOURIST BOARD IN TEA SHOP OF THE YEAR COMPETITION

Ludlow is just off the A49, halfway between Shrewsbury and Hereford. The tearoom is located in the heart of the town, close to the Buttercross.

OPEN ALL YEAR.
MONDAY–THURSDAY, 9AM–5PM;
FRIDAY AND SATURDAY, 9AM–5:30PM;
SUNDAY, 11AM–5PM; OPEN BANK HOLIDAYS.

De Greys dates back to 1570, and the building has retained many of its original features and lovely oak beams. The tearoom has been tastefully refurbished with luxury fabrics, rich colours and hanging tapestries, and a real old-world charm is created by the copper wares on display and the china plates arranged on the Welsh dresser. Waitresses wear old-fashioned black-and-white outfits and serve customers in a friendly and efficient manner.

Ludlow's Food and Drink Festival each September attracts a lot of interest amongst visitors from all over the country, and De Greys aims to add to the town's reputation with their very high standards and the quality of the food they serve. At lunchtime, customers can enjoy rarebits, quiches and omelettes, or choose from a variety of sandwiches served on home-baked bread and with delicious fillings such as smoked salmon and cream cheese, tandoori chicken with mint yoghurt dressing and chicken with lemon mayonnaise. Tea time brings homemade cakes and scones, cream cakes and pastries, Danish pastries, meringues, toasted tea cakes and a selection of buns and fancy cakes.

Tea Room Blend, Earl Grey, Darjeeling, Assam, Ceylon, Keemun, Lapsang Souchong, Iced Teas, various fruit teas and herbal infusions.

The Marshmallow

HIGH STREET, MORETON-IN-MARSH
GLOUCESTERSHIRE GL56 0AT
TEL: 01608 651536
OWNER: VALERIE WEST
1996, 1998 & 2001 TEA COUNCIL
AWARD OF EXCELLENCE

Moreton-in-Marsh is on the A429 between Stratford-upon-Avon and Stow-on-the-Wold. The tea shop is at the north end of the town, in the main shopping street, not far from the station.

OPEN ALL YEAR.
MONDAY, 10AM–5PM; TUESDAY, 10AM–4PM;
WEDNESDAY–SATURDAY, 10AM–9:30PM;
SUNDAY, 10:30AM–9:30PM.

Having never been involved in catering before acquiring this lovely Grade II-listed building, Valerie West now runs a thriving restaurant and tearoom right in the heart of the busy town that was once very important in the wool trade. Within 10 days of moving in, Valerie had rebuilt and opened her 96-seat dining room, and is busy all year with tourists, regular customers and passing visitors, particularly on Tuesdays when the traders' market comes to town.

The front of the building is covered with Virginia creeper and in the flagstoned courtyard at the back, there are more tables and hanging flower baskets that create a very restful place to sit and have tea.

The waitresses are dressed in gentle shades of peach and pale green; furnishings are pine, set against original stone walls; and there is a view through to the homey kitchen where copper pots and pans decorate the walls and the chefs create wonderful cakes and savouries. The cake trolley is laden with truly delicious creations — chocolate mousses, roulades, mille feuille gateaux, pecan Danish pastries and so much more to tempt you.

House Blend, Earl Grey, Assam, Lapsang Souchong, Darjeeling, Traditional. Fruit-flavoured teas and herbal infusions are also offered.

Tea-Time Traditions from Middle England

GLOUCESTERSHIRE, NOTTINGHAMSHIRE, OXFORDSHIRE, SHROPSHIRE

When man-made canals forged a link between London and the industrial midlands in the 18th century, exotic foods started arriving in those areas to add colour and interest to the diet of the wealthy. So while poorer families continued to eat local produce, the rich fed off apricots, figs, dates, almonds, quince and cocoa shipped in on the barges. Meanwhile, the regional diet benefited from copious supplies of milk that gave cheeses, curds, butter and cream, domestic animals such as pigs and sheep, and plenty of wild creatures that were hunted, shot or fished. Market gardens supplied apples, gooseberries, rhubarb, blackberries and strawberries, and meal tables were rich with pies, puddings, cakes and all sorts of savoury specialities.

It was said that if you ate an apple before St. Swithin's Day on July 15, it would cause a bad stomachache, and that if a teaspoonful of rain collected on Ascension Day was added to the bread dough, it would prevent the bread from being heavy. As in other areas, ordinary dough was enriched for special occasions with raisins, orange peel, spices, and extra sugar and fat. Seede cake was rather like a lardy cake, but had caraway seeds added. Coventry God cakes, given to godchildren by their godparents at New Year and Easter, and very similar to Eccles cakes and Chorley cakes, were made by filling pastry triangles with currants, sugar, butter, spices and rum. The triangular shape was said to represent the Holy Trinity. Oranges were significant to nearby Warwickshire, as Kineton market was famous until the 1940s for the sale of cheap oranges. The local strawberry and portynggale shortcake was named after oranges imported from Portugal — also referred to by Shakespeare as portynggales.

In Shropshire, apples and other fruits were readily available, so the county has many surviving recipes for apple cakes, apple shortcakes, apple cobs (apples filled with honey and spices and completely encased in short crust pastry) and fidget pie (a savoury dish made with potatoes, onions, bacon, sugar, apples and spices) — perhaps served for high tea. Shropshire's soul cakes were made for All Souls' Day on November 2, when children went "a-souling." They would go from house to house chanting, "A soul-cake, a soul-cake, please, good missus, a soul-cake. One for Peter, two for Paul and three for Him who saved us all." The biscuit-like cakes were made with butter, sugar, eggs, flour, spices and currants and sometimes had strands of saffron added. Other Shropshire tea-time treats were caraway soda bread, Welsh border tart (a meringue-topped lemon pie) and cakes for particular times of the year, such as a spicy lambing cake that kept workers going through the long cold nights when the first spring lambs were born, and shearing cake, devoured after the shearing was finished. This was a rich spicy cake with brown sugar, caraway seeds, lemon rind, honey and ginger.

In Oxfordshire, some favourite cakes were wiggs (yeasted dough flavoured with caraway seeds), curd cheesecakes that contained sultanas and currants; Burford dough cake with currants, old English cider cakes, gingerbreads, oatmeal biscuits, apple cakes and Banbury apple pie with ginger, currants, candied peel and cinnamon in a short-crust pastry. And, of course, Banbury cakes — puff-pastry ovals similar to Coventry God cakes and Eccles cakes, and filled with dried fruits, spices, rum, sugar and butter. They are thought to date back to pagan days and to have had close links with May Day celebrations.

Nottinghamshire lace makers, like their colleagues around the country, always celebrated St. Catherine's Day with Cattern cakes — dough with butter or lard and sugar, currants and caraway seeds added. At other times of the year, folk in Nottinghamshire enjoyed ginger cakes, ground rice cakes, gooseberry pies from the Mansfield area and tea cakes. One recipe from Scarthingmoor for fruited buns (which doubled as hot cross buns at Easter) dates back to the 1740s. An old recipe for Nottinghamshire harvest cake instructed, "Rub a tidy dollop of lard into a pound of flour with a pinch of salt and a teaspoon of baking powder. Put in currants according to what you have. Mix up stiff with a nice drop of parsnip wine and water. Fry in hot fat when they come up lovely and brown. Don't hang about, but sit down and eat them. Hot's hot!"

High teas from these counties included Shropshire faggots (also called savoury duck or poor man's goose), pork pies, young Oxford sausages made with the meat from young pork, Shropshire chicken pie with apples, fried cakes (a mixture of flour, sugar, lard and milk, fried in bacon fat), Warwick pig's pudding (rather like black pudding) and Brummy bacon cakes from Birmingham.

Things to See and Do in Middle England

GLOUCESTERSHIRE, NOTTINGHAMSHIRE, OXFORDSHIRE, SHROPSHIRE

Gloucestershire

At Bourton-on-the-Water, the Bay Tree tearoom is set in what has been described as "everyone's idea of the perfect Cotswold village." The houses are built of local quarried stone and the oldest dates back to the 17th century. It has several attractions. The Cotswold Perfumery has an exhibition, a specially constructed theatre, an ingredients room, a perfume quiz, and a beautifully laid-out Perfume Garden with masses of fragrant flowers and herbs. Bourton Model Railway has some of the finest indoor railway layouts in the country, with more than 40 British and continental trains running automatically through imaginative scenery. The Cotswold Motoring Museum and Toy Collection features fine old cars, motoring memorabilia, motorbikes and bicycles, and a large collection of old enamel advertising signs. At Birdland Park and Gardens, you can watch the penguins, flamingos, pelicans and cranes in various water habitats, and see tropical birds such as parrots and toucans in more than 50 aviaries. At the Model Village, you can stroll through a replica of the village that was is made of local stone in one-ninth scale and has the River Windrush flowing under Bourton's famous bridges. There is even a model of the model.

The Black Cat is in the heart of Lechlade-on-Thames, a historic market town surrounded by green meadows. The tall slender spire of the Parish Church of St. Lawrence has been a landmark since the 15th century, and Ha'penny Bridge used to mark the end of the navigable part of the Thames. Next door to the Black Cat is the Old Bell Pottery, and just along the road, Market Place is flanked by several fine listed buildings, including the New Inn Hotel and the old vicarage. Sherborne House, a short walk away, still has one of five gazebos that were raised heated summerhouses where 18th-century ladies could sit and watch passersby. A specialist dollhouse and miniatures shop now occupies an old stable-barn behind 17th-century Bridge House; and Downington, an area to the west of the town, has several 17th-century gentlemen's houses, some of which were improved in Georgian times by a local architect. The surrounding area is full of opportunities for wonderful walks alongside the riverside and through beautiful Gloucestershire and Oxfordshire countryside. Moreton-in-Marsh is another of the Cotswold's beautiful villages, and it is here, in the high street, that the Marshmallow tearoom stands. Also in the high street is the Curfew Tower, which dates from the 16th century and was once used as the local lock-up. On the corner is the White Hart Royal Hotel, where Charles I is said to have stayed during the Civil War, and the Manor House Hotel, also on the high street, is reported to have been haunted for the past 200 years. A further stroll around the town will take visitors to St. David's Church and the Victoria Gardens, which commemorate Queen Victoria's diamond jubilee. At the Cotswold Falconry Centre at Batsford Park, eagles, hawks, owls and falcons are flown throughout the day, and visitors have a chance to appreciate their speed and grace and their close relationship with the falconer. To the north, near Chipping Camden, Hidcote Manor Garden is one of England's most delightful gardens. It is in effect a series of gardens within a garden, each section separated from the next by a wall or hedge or herbaceous border. To the west, at Broadway, Snowshill Manor is a museum of samurai armour, musical instruments, clocks, toys, bicycles and weaving and spinning tools and it has a beautiful organic garden. Broadway Tower and Park is a unique folly that was once the home of William Morris. At Mill Dene Garden, there is a 2.5-acre watermill garden with steep terraces, a pool, a stream and a grotto, a rose walk and a "fantasy" fruit garden.

In Tetbury, the two Guild members — Tetbury Gallery Tea Room and Two Toads — are set in the centre of one of the Cotswold's prettiest and oldest towns. In prehistoric days it was the site of a hill fort, and the first written record of it is in 618 when there was a Saxon monastery there. In the Middle Ages it became prosperous as the centre of the Cotswold wool trade but declined in the 19th century to be left as a peaceful undisturbed town. The parish church of St. Mary the Virgin was recently described by an English

Heritage inspector as "the best Georgian Gothic church I have ever seen" and has the fourth highest spire in England. The market house, built in 1655, is a fine example of a Cotswold pillared market house, and Chipping Steps was for centuries the site of "Mop Fairs" at which domestic staff made themselves available for employment. It is said that at the bottom of Gumstool Hill, one of Tetbury's most ancient streets, there was once a pool where scolding wives were tied to a ducking stool or "gumstool" and ducked under the water as punishment. Today, the town has more than 20 antique shops dealing in furniture, decorative objects, silver and porcelain. Also close by is Malmesbury Abbey, once part of a Benedictine monastery founded in the middle of the seventh century and now open to the public. Its five acres of garden contain flower borders, an herb garden, a stew pond and wildlife. To the west, Chavenage House is an Elizabethan dwelling with tapestry rooms, furniture and relics of the Cromwellian period. Westonbirt Arboretum has 600 acres of landscaped gardens and woodland, with 17 miles of paths to explore and 18,000 specimens of trees and shrubs.

Nottinghamshire

The Olde School Tearoom in Carburton is surrounded by wonderful countryside. Clumber Park, the jewel of the Dukeries and part of ancient Sherwood Forest, offers 400 acres of land with areas for walking, birdwatching, cycling and generally exploring woods, heathland, marsh, scrub, streams, lakes, tracks and pathways. If visitors leave Clumber Park by Carburton Gate, they will see the Church of St. Giles on the right. The tiny Norman church was originally older, and the arches seen on the outside once led into the south aisle. A few miles north is Worksop, where you can visit Mr. Straw's House, the Edwardian terraced house at 7 Blyth Grove that Mr. Straw bought with proceeds from his grocery business and sales of tea. The interior of the house has remained unaltered since the 1930s and contains contemporary wallpaper, Victorian furniture and household objects. Also in Worksop is "The Pilgrim Fathers Story and Exhibition," for it was in the quiet north Nottinghamshire villages that the Pilgrim movement was started. A few miles south of Nottingham, at Trent Lock, the Lock House Tea Rooms sit beside the Erewash Canal in an area where a network of waterways and canals once served local industry. The coal trade from pits adjoining the Cromford and Nottingham canals relied heavily on the Erewash Canal. Trent Lock stood at the very hub of the canal network and was often referred to as "Waters Meet" by the local boatmen. This is an extremely attractive area for boating, fishing and walking, and Lock House can provide details of the best walks from Trent Lock. A short distance to the east, Ruddington has three interesting places to visit. The Ruddington Framework Knitters Museum shows the life and labour of a Victorian knitting community; Powers Pottery is a working pottery where you can view brushwork decoration and traditional hand-throwing; and Nottingham Transport Heritage Centre has a seven-mile train ride, a vintage and classic bus collection; and a country park.

North of Nottingham, Ollerton Mill Tea Shop is itself an exciting venue for both historical interest and for tea. The mill has an exhibition which tells the story of the mill, and a video shows the mill grinding corn and producing flour. For those who want to spend more time exploring the area, Ollerton is also close to Vicar Water Country Park and to Sherwood Forest Visitors Centre, Farm Park, Sherwood Pines Forest Park and the Art and Craft Centre.

To the southeast of Ollerton is Rufford Abbey and Country Park, which has a monastic history exhibition, wonderful gardens and lakeside walks, a ceramic centre and a craft gallery.

Oxfordshire

Annie's Tea Rooms is set in the centre of Wallingford, a town that dates back to Saxon times. King Alfred founded the town in the 10th century and remains of the town moat and earthworks are still visible. William the Conqueror came to the town after his victory at Hastings and ordered a royal castle to be built. King John, Edward the Black Prince and the young Henry VI all spent time here. Today, visitors can wander through the Castle Gardens, which offer wonderful views over the town from the top of the castle moat, and then follow the Town Trail that takes walkers past some of the places of historic interest. The Town Hall (1670) contains a collection of town plate, fine paintings and wall boards; Flint House, which is the home of the Wallingford Museum, tells the story of the town; the Corn Exchange now houses a theatre and cinema; and the Market Place and surrounding narrow streets enclose an antiques centre and a picturesque river pathway where river craft can moor. On the outskirts of the town is the Chorley and Wallingford Railway with its steam engines; the railway's Preservation Society runs the old "bunk" line between Chorley and Wallingford at weekends throughout the year.

Shropshire

The nearest large village close to Bird on the Rock Tearoom in Clungunford is Craven Arms, famous for Stokesay Castle, a unique example of a 13th-century fortified manor house. In the second half of the 19th century, the railway came to the town, and tens of thousands of sheep were brought in each year for the annual sales. On the southern edge of Craven Arms, the Secret Hills Discovery Centre tells the story of the Shropshire hill landscape.

A little further to the south east lies Ludlow, home to De Greys and often described as "the perfect historic town." There are more than 500 listed buildings and an almost intact medieval street pattern. The town is still dominated by its market square just outside the castle, a Norman stronghold that was once the home of royalty and one of the most interesting castles in the Welsh marshes. Ludlow Museum on Castle Street tells the story of the town from the construction of the castle 900 years ago, through medieval prosperity and political intrigue, to the town's fashionable days in the 18th century when glove making was the major industry. Other interesting old buildings to see include The Feathers, a timber-framed Elizabethan town house that is now a hotel; the 1743 Buttercross, Castle Lodge, another fine Elizabethan town house; and the 13th-century Broadgate, the only remaining gateway through the town walls. Each year, in late June and July, Ludlow hosts a festival, the centrepiece of which is the performance of a Shakespeare play in the open air inside the Castle. Ann Boleyn Tea Room, in Newport, is on the Shropshire/Staffordshire border in the heart of a rural farming area. It was planned as a new town in the 12th century during the reign of Henry I. The usual ravages of time and a great fire in 1665 destroyed most of the medieval buildings, but there are many very fine Georgian and Regency façades. The Parish Church of St. Nicholas, the patron saint of fishermen, was founded in the 12th century and restored in the 19th to its present condition. The town has an indoor market that is open on Fridays and Saturdays. Outside Newport to the south, Boscobel House is a 17th-century hunting lodge that sheltered Charles II after the Battle of Worcester in 1651. It contains panelled rooms and secret hiding places, and on the grounds stands the great Royal Oak where Charles hid from Cromwell's men. Near Telford, Hoo Farm Animal Kingdom allows visitors to bottle-feed lambs, feed deer, collect eggs, dip candles and ride mini-quad bikes. To the north at Market Drayton, Hodnet Hall has 60 acres of landscaped gardens, woodland walks, ornamental pools and lakes with flowering shrubs.

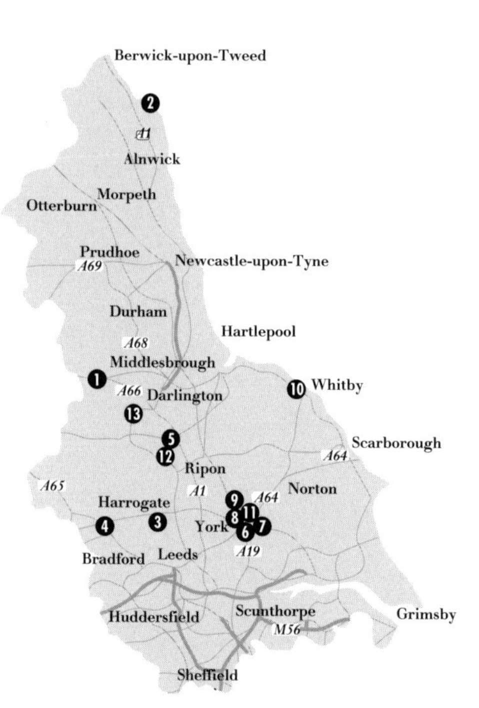
Berwick-upon-Tweed
2
A1
Alnwick
Morpeth
Otterburn
Prudhoe
A69
Newcastle-upon-Tyne
Durham
Hartlepool
A68
Middlesbrough
1
A66
Darlington
10
Whitby
13
5
Scarborough
A64
12
Ripon
A65
A1
9
A64
Norton
Harrogate
3
8
11
4
York
7
6
A19
Bradford
Leeds
Huddersfield
Scunthorpe
M56
Grimsby
Sheffield

The North East Tea Trail

County Durham

1. THE MARKET PLACE TEASHOP *p.* 120

Northumberland

2. THE COPPER KETTLE TEA ROOMS *p.* 121

Yorkshire

3. BETTYS CAFÉ TEA ROOMS, HARROGATE *p.* 122
4. BETTYS CAFÉ TEA ROOMS, ILKLEY *p.* 123
5. BETTYS CAFÉ TEA ROOMS, NORTHALLERTON *p.* 124
6. BETTYS CAFÉ TEA ROOMS, YORK *p.* 125
7. BULLIVANT OF YORK *p.* 126
8. CLARK'S OF EASINGWOLD *p.* 127
9. CLARK'S TEAROOMS *p.* 128
10. ELIZABETH BOTHAM & SONS *p.* 129
11. LITTLE BETTYS *p.* 130
12. THE MAD HATTER TEA SHOP *p.* 131
13. THE PRIEST'S HOUSE *p.* 132

The Market Place Teashop

29 MARKET PLACE, BARNARD CASTLE
COUNTY DURHAM DL12 8NE
TEL: 01833 690110
OWNER: ROBERT HILTON
EGON RONAY RECOMMENDED
GOOD FOOD GUIDE

The tea shop is in the centre of the cobbled market place.

OPEN ALL YEAR EXCEPT TWO WEEKS
AT CHRISTMAS. MONDAY–SATURDAY, 10AM–5PM;
MARCH–NOVEMBER: SUNDAY, 2:30PM–5:30PM;
DECEMBER–FEBRUARY: CLOSED SUNDAY.

In the very heart of this attractive old market town, you will find the Market Place Teashop in an early 17th-century building that long ago was a house before it became a pub, and later a gentleman's outfitters selling typical country garments to local farm workers. The front of the tea shop was probably the original master's house and servants quarters, and the stables were behind and alongside in Waterloo Yard. Today, the upstairs artisan shop and picture gallery has a good selection of gifts, prints and original paintings.

The tea shop itself, which is celebrating its 30th anniversary this year, is a charming room full of character, with flagstones on the floor and an open stone fireplace. Tea is served in silver teapots by friendly waitresses in smart burgundy-striped uniforms, and they will bring you whatever you choose from a tempting list of home-baked cakes that changes daily. Try the meringues filled with cream and strawberries, the strawberry tarts or the Yorkshire curd cheesecake. The high quality of all the food and the attractive, welcoming atmosphere make this an excellent place for lunch or afternoon tea.

Typhoo, Earl Grey, Ceylon, Traditional English, Assam, Darjeeling, Lapsang Souchong, China. Fruit-flavoured teas and herbal infusions are also offered.

The Copper Kettle Tea Rooms

21 FRONT STREET, BAMBURGH
NORTHUMBERLAND NE69 7BW
TEL: 01668 214315
OWNERS: PAT & HEATHER GREEN

From the A1, take either the B1341 or the B1342 to Bamburgh. The Copper Kettle is in the heart of the village.

OPEN FROM MID-FEBRUARY TO END OF NOVEMBER:
TUESDAYS–SUNDAYS, 10:30AM–LATE AFTERNOON;
CLOSED MONDAYS EXCEPT IN SEASON;
OPEN ALL BANK HOLIDAYS.

After a visit to Bamburgh Castle or a walk in the sea air, don't miss the opportunity of afternoon tea in the old-fashioned charm of the Copper Kettle's 18th-century tearoom or cottage patio. Outside, a bright display of colourful flowers at the front door and windows welcomes you, while inside your eye will be caught by the collection of gleaming copper kettles, old teapots and interesting knick-knacks. In summer, the patio garden is a riot of colour and provides a sun trap where refreshments are served under the shade of large umbrellas.

Everything on the menu is homemade and the selection is extremely tempting — from the Copper Kettle Ploughman's Platter to the toasted and traditional open sandwiches, or salads made with such treats as locally caught crab, prawns and cottage cheese, chicken mayonnaise and home-cooked ham, to name just a few. These all come with freshly tossed salads or garnishes. And don't forget the best-kept secret — Pat's pickles. The cakes and desserts are equally mouthwatering — mini-Pavlovas, cream horns, pastries, carrot cake, chocolate cake, blueberry muffins, lemon loaf and Heather's South African apple cake — and, of course, traditional cream teas and tea cakes.

Assam, Ceylon, China, Darjeeling, Earl Grey, Traditional English, Lapsang Souchong, Rose Pouchong, Decaffeinated, Organic. Fruit-flavoured teas and herbal infusions are also offered.

Bettys Café Tea Rooms

1 PARLIAMENT STREET
HARROGATE, NORTH YORKSHIRE HG1 2QU
TEL: 01423 502746
FAX: 01423 877307
WEB SITE: WWW.BETTYSANDTAYLORS.CO.UK
MANAGER: ANDREW BRIDGFORD
1994 TEA COUNCIL TOP TEA PLACE OF THE YEAR
1990, 91, 92, 93 & 96 TEA COUNCIL
AWARD OF EXCELLENCE
EGON RONAY RECOMMENDED

Bettys is located on the main route through the centre of Harrogate from Leeds to Ripon, opposite the War Memorial and overlooking Montpellier Gardens.

OPEN ALL YEAR.
MONDAY–SUNDAY, 9AM–9PM.

The Harrogate branch of Bettys was the first tearoom opened by Frederick Belmont in 1919. The young confectioner arrived from Switzerland and settled in North Yorkshire where he found the clear air very much to his liking. His natural talent for creating exceptionally good cakes and his Swiss flair for hospitality were the perfect combination to build a thriving business, and very soon he opened more shops in other Yorkshire towns. Today, the company is still owned by direct descendents of Frederick's family, now half Swiss, half Yorkshire, but still no one knows the identity of Betty.

Frederick Belmont's guiding principle was, "If we want things just right, we have to make them ourselves," and today, Bettys Bakery still makes all the cakes, pastries, chocolates, breads, rolls, fruit loaves, scones and muffins, and the dishes on the menu are freshly prepared on the premises.

Teas and coffees are specially imported and blended by Bettys' sister company, Taylors of Harrogate. A café pianist plays every evening from 6pm to 9pm.

Tea Room Blend, Special Estate Darjeeling, Special Estate Tippy Assam, Earl Grey, Lapsang Souchong, Yunnan Flowery Orange Pekoe, China Gui Hua, Mountains of the Moon, Zulu, Iced Tea in summer, various fruit-flavoured teas, various herbal infusions.

Bettys Café Tea Rooms

32–34 THE GROVE, ILKLEY
WEST YORKSHIRE LS29 9EE
TEL: 01943 608029
FAX: 01943 816723
WEB SITE: WWW.BETTYSANDTAYLORS.CO.UK
MANAGER: JULIE JUDD
1993 TEA COUNCIL TOP TEA PLACE OF THE YEAR
1990, '91, '92 & '96 TEA COUNCIL
AWARD OF EXCELLENCE
EGON RONAY RECOMMENDED

Bettys is in Ilkley town centre, backing on to the main Pay and Display car park and not far from the station and tourist information centre.

OPEN ALL YEAR.
MONDAY–SUNDAY, 9AM–5:30PM.

This is one of the five hugely successful Bettys Café Tea Rooms in Yorkshire, and the special feature of this branch is the wonderful, colourful collection of more than 200 teapots arranged on a high shelf that runs all round the tea-room. Recently refurbished, Bettys in Ilkley boasts a striking wrought-iron canopy and an extensive tea and coffee counter, stacked with antique tea caddies. The tearoom has some specially commissioned stained-glass windows that depict some of the wild flowers found on the Yorkshire moors and *La Chasse*, the largest marquetry picture ever made in the Spindler studio, which shows a medieval hunting scene.

This is a haven for ramblers who reach the town tired and in need of refreshment after walking for miles across the rugged, wind-swept moorland. They and other visitors can relax and enjoy the fabulous selection of pastries, breads and cakes that arrive fresh from Bettys Bakery every day. To add to the attraction, a pianist plays every Thursday, Friday, Saturday and Sunday from 10am-noon.

Tea Room Blend, Special Estate Darjeeling, Special Estate Tippy Assam, Earl Grey, Lapsang Souchong, Yunnan Flowery Orange Pekoe, China Gui Hua, Mountains of the Moon, Zulu, Iced Tea in summer, various flavoured teas, various herbal infusions.

Bettys Café Tea Rooms

188 HIGH STREET
NORTHALLERTON, NORTH YORKSHIRE DL7 8LF
TEL: 01609 775154
FAX: 01609 777552
WEB SITE: WWW.BETTYSANDTAYLORS.CO.UK
MANAGER: LINDSAY JUDD
1987 TEA COUNCIL TOP TEA PLACE OF THE YEAR
1990 TEA COUNCIL AWARD OF EXCELLENCE
EGON RONAY RECOMMENDED

Bettys is situated in the town centre, in the main shopping street.

OPEN ALL YEAR. MONDAY–SATURDAY,
9AM–5.30PM; SUNDAY, 10AM–5.30PM.

This is the most northerly of the five branches of Bettys and it is a real treasure, tucked away in the Saxon market town of Northallerton. It is said that Roman soldiers once marched along the Great North Road that passes very close by, and the town is mentioned in the *Domesday Book*, so there is lots of history here. It was in this delightful setting that Bettys opened the most recent addition to their chain of fantastic Yorkshire tea shops. The company is still owned by the family of the founder, Frederick Belmont, and the teas and coffees are specially blended for the shops by the sister company Taylors of Harrogate.

The sunny golden room here in Northallerton is small and intimate and decorated with Art Deco mirrors and antique teapots. As you step inside the red brick Georgian building, your attention will be caught by the selection of wonderful cakes and pastries that fill the counter. How does one ever decide what to eat? There are just so many delicious things to try. More than one visit is recommended in order to work your way through at least some of the selection.

Tea Room Blend, Special Estate Darjeeling, Special Estate Tippy Assam, Earl Grey, Lapsang Souchong, Yunnan Flowery Orange Pekoe, China Gui Hua, Mountains of the Moon, Zulu, Iced Tea in summer, various fruit-flavoured teas, various herbal infusions.

Bettys Café Tea Rooms

6–8 ST HELEN'S SQUARE
YORK, NORTH YORKSHIRE YO1 8QP
TEL: 01904 659142
FAX: 01904 627050
WEB SITE: WWW.BETTYSANDTAYLORS.CO.UK
MANAGER: PAULA KAYE
1997 TEA COUNCIL AWARD OF EXCELLENCE
EGON RONAY RECOMMENDED

Bettys is located in the city centre, just round the corner from York Minster.

OPEN ALL YEAR. MONDAY–SUNDAY, 9AM–9PM.

This "continental style" tearoom is set in the heart of York, and from the huge picture windows that dominate the ground-floor tearoom you can look out over the cobbled streets of this historical city. The elegant surroundings were inspired by the interior of the luxury liner the *Queen Mary*. Frederick Belmont, Bettys' founder, travelled on the maiden voyage of this ocean liner in 1936, during which time he dreamt up the plans for a new flagship café in York. The liner's interior decorators were commissioned to design the new tearoom, recreating the magnificent panelling, pillars and mirrors that had adorned the *Queen Mary*. Many of the original 1930s features have recently been refurbished, and the Belmont Room on the first floor has reopened after many years for group bookings and private parties.

The cakes and pastries are still made daily by hand at Bettys Craft Bakery, just as they were back in the 1930s. Today, an added attraction is the café pianist who plays every evening from 6pm to 9pm.

Tea Room Blend, Special Estate Darjeeling, Special Estate Tippy Assam, Earl Grey, Lapsang Souchong, Yunnan Flowery Orange Pekoe, China Gui Hua, Mountains of the Moon, Zulu, various fruit-flavoured teas, various herbal infusions.

Bullivant of York

15 BLAKE STREET
YORK YO1 8QJ
TEL: 01904 671311
OWNER: CHRISTINE BULLIVANT

From York Minster, walk along Duncombe Place to the crossroads. Turn left into Blake Street and the tea shop is about 150 yards along.

OPEN SEVEN DAYS A WEEK.
PLEASE TELEPHONE FOR DETAILS.

Christine Bullivant's main concern is that her customers should feel pampered and relaxed in her charming, intimate tearoom, and she is almost always on duty to welcome you. Her smiling and efficient staff will do their very best to make your visit a memorable one. The pretty pink decor, the pink Lloyd Loom chairs and the tables dressed in the Victorian breakfast table style make it a very special place to stop at any time of the day. A peaceful courtyard at the rear provides more seating in good weather, and here you can sit surrounded by tubs full of flowers and climbing plants. Table reservations can be made.

Bullivant's menu offers an incredible range of sandwiches, club sandwiches, luncheons of wonderful cheeses, pies, pâtés, savoury pancakes and roast meats, and at tea time all the traditional favourites are on offer — cinnamon toast, cream teas with delicious homemade scones, with Cornish clotted cream and homemade preserves, toasted tea cakes, hot buttered crumpets and a really special rich dark fruit cake served with Wensleydale cheese.

The shop also has an enormous range of superb collectors' teapots; if you are interested, Christine's helpful staff will bring items of interest to your table so that you can choose in comfort what to buy to take home with you.

Select Blend, Traditional English, Earl Grey, Ceylon, Lapsang Souchong, Rose Pouchong, China, Lemon. Fruit-flavoured teas and herbal infusions are also available.

Clark's of Easingwold

195 LONG STREET
EASINGWOLD, YORK YO61 3JB
TEL: 01347 821285
E-MAIL: CLARKS@FAMILYBAKERS.FREESERVE.CO.UK
WEB SITE: WWW.CLARKSBAKERS.SAGEWEB.CO.UK
OWNERS: JUDY & GERALD CLARK

Easingwold is situated equidistant between York and Thirsk and is bypassed by the A19.

OPEN ALL YEAR. WINTER: MONDAY–SATURDAY, 8:30AM–4PM; SUMMER: MONDAY–SATURDAY, 8:30AM–5PM.

Gerald Clark's mother, who served tea and homemade scones from the kitchen window to the tarmac men who came down from Middlesborough to repair the roads, established Clark's in 1925. She developed this promising business into a bakery and built a wooden hut in the garden to serve as a café. This was used for many years until it was eventually demolished and replaced by the present café, which was set up within the bakery shop in 1995.

Both Judy and Gerald are narrow-boat enthusiasts and so have decorated the café with all sorts of canal wares to create an attractive interior. Plates, pictures, posters and tea towels are on display and there is an old milk churn decorated in the style of the narrow boat *Buckby Ware*. In good weather, there are chairs and tables in the pretty garden at the rear of the café. The menu offers sandwiches, pies, pastries, ploughmans, soups, salads and omelettes, and there is a wide variety of fresh cream cakes and confectionery available. Tea time brings tea cakes, scones with jam and cream, cakes and pastries, and a set tea with a selection of savouries and sandwiches, scones and cakes. Everything is made on the premises.

Yorkshire Blend, Earl Grey.

Clark's Tearooms

MARKET PLACE
EASINGWOLD, YORKSHIRE YO61 3AG
TEL: 01347 821285
E-MAIL: CLARKS@FAMILYBAKERS.FREESERVE.CO.UK
WEB SITE: WWW.CLARKSBAKERS.SAGEWEB.CO.UK
OWNERS: JUDY & GERALD CLARK

Easingwold, now bypassed by the A19, is 13 miles north of York and 10 miles south of Thirsk. Clark's Tearooms is situated in the market square

OPEN ALL YEAR. MONDAY–THURSDAY, 10AM-5PM; FRIDAY, 9AM-5PM; SATURDAY, 9:30AM-5PM; CLOSED SUNDAYS.

All breads, pastries and cakes served and sold at Clark's Tearooms are made at the shop's bakery, which was set up 76 years ago and now houses Judy and Gerald's other tearoom and main bakery shop about three-quarters of a mile away on the edge of town. This branch of the business in the central market place is in a perfect location for shoppers and tourists, whether for lunch or a refreshing pot of tea and one of the wonderful homemade cakes. It is divided into three rooms with traditional dark furniture set off by colourful curtains and tablecloths.

The menu includes sandwiches, home-baked savouries, breads and cakes, and local specialities such as Wensleydale cheese with Yorkshire fruit cake, Yorkshire curd tarts and delicious fruit pies with cream. If you would like to buy some of these to take home, the Clarks have a bakery on the other side of the street that sells their breads, pastries and cakes. The selection of breads includes granary, wholemeal and seed loaves. Amongst the pastries there are lardy cakes, Sally Lunns, Cornish pasties, pork pies and all sorts of traditional favourites. As well as all the homemade products, there are fine quality goods from Switzerland, France and Italy.

House Blend, Darjeeling, Earl Grey, various fruit-flavoured teas, various herbals.

Elizabeth Botham & Sons

35/39 SKINNER STREET
WHITBY, NORTH YORKSHIRE YO21 3AH
TEL: 01947 602823
FAX: 01947 820269
WEB SITE: WWW.BOTHAM.CO.UK
E-MAIL: MJ@BOTHAM.CO.UK
MANAGING DIRECTOR: MIKE JARMAN

Botham's is at the top of Skinner Street on the West Cliff. There is a car park nearby.

OPEN ALL YEAR. SEPTEMBER–MAY: TUESDAY–SATURDAY, 9AM–4:30PM; JUNE, JULY, AUGUST: MONDAY–SATURDAY, 9AM–4:30PM; CLOSED SUNDAYS. TELEPHONE TO CHECK OPENING TIMES.

In 1865, Elizabeth Botham established a bakery in Whitby and today, Sarah, her great-granddaughter, is carrying on the tradition with her husband, Mike Jarman, and her two brothers, Jo and Nick. Not only does the company continue to make the same biscuits, breads, cakes and pastries that the Victorian shop was famous for, they have expanded the business and now have a restaurant and café (originally set up in the 1860s), and a celebration cake and hamper service, as well as a retail shop and mail order/web site options for those who can't get to Yorkshire to taste or buy.

To get to the restaurant on the first floor, you have to walk past the truly mouthwatering array of cakes and confectionery. If you manage to drag yourself away from the display and climb the stairs, you will find yourself in a welcoming comfortable room where waiting staff in reassuring black and white are attentive and helpfully friendly. The menu includes plenty of traditional English dishes for indulgent breakfasts, satisfying lunches and excellent teas, any of which may be enjoyed with a pot of fine loose-leaf tea.

Botham's Special Blend Resolution Tea (this is the only Botham's tea packed in tea bags), Ceylon Orange Pekoe, Darjeeling, English Breakfast, Earl Grey, Gunpowder, Jasmine, Lapsang Souchong.

Little Bettys

46 STONEGATE, YORK
NORTH YORKSHIRE YO1 8AS
TEL: 01904 622865
FAX: 01904 640348
WEB SITE: WWW.BETTYSANDTAYLORS.CO.UK
MANAGER: HAZEL BONE
1991, 1992 & 1993 TEA COUNCIL
AWARD OF EXCELLENCE
EGON RONAY RECOMMENDED

Little Bettys is very close to York Minster in Petergate.

OPEN ALL YEAR.
MONDAY–SUNDAY, 9AM–5:30PM.

There's a second Bettys Café Tea Rooms in York — the adorably named "Little Bettys" situated in a Grade II-listed building in medieval Stonegate, just a stone's throw from York Minster.

Little Bettys, just as the name implies, is the smallest of the Bettys Café Tea Rooms. In the café, situated up a flight of winding stairs, the roaring fires, wooden beams and beautiful interior are almost as much a source of refreshment as the tea itself. As with all the Bettys Café Tea Rooms, there's an outstanding selection of teas and coffees, chocolates, breads, cakes and Yorkshire specialities such as fat rascals, spiced Yorkshire teacakes and Yorkshire curd tarts.

The downstairs shop is the perfect place to buy freshly made cappuccinos, espressos and cups of fine teas, along with sandwiches and cakes to take away for a picnic by the River Ouse.

Once you have tried and become addicted to the excellent foods and teas, you can have a regular supply sent by post by telephoning Harrogate 01423 886055.

Tea Room Blend, Special Estate Tippy Assam, Earl Grey, Lapsang Souchong, Mountains of the Moon, Kwazulu, Ceylon Blue Sapphire, Good Luck Green Tea, English Breakfast, China Rose Petal, Peppermint Tisane.

The Mad Hatter Tea Shop

MARKET PLACE, MASHAM
NEAR RIPON, NORTH YORKSHIRE HG4 4EA
TEL: 01765 689129
OWNERS: ANDREW ATKINSON & STIRLING JEBB

Masham is 20 miles north of Harrogate on the A61 between Glasshouses and Jervaulx, and eight miles west off the A1 along the B6267. The tea shop is in the heart of the town in the market square.

OPEN ALL YEAR. MONDAY–WEDNESDAY, FRIDAY AND SATURDAY, 10AM–5PM; SUNDAY, 11AM–5PM; CLOSED THURSDAY (ALL YEAR); NOVEMBER–MARCH: CLOSED MONDAY.

The Mad Hatter Tea Shop is a Grade II-listed building dating from the 1830s and overlooks the huge four square Market Place in Masham. The two tearooms are decorated in a traditional style, still with many original features. The Mad Hatter is an appointed Spode stockist and has one of the largest selections of Spode china and giftware in the area. Even the tea is served in Spode's finest bone china.

The menu includes plenty of healthy options. The philosophy at the Mad Hatter is to use only the freshest of ingredients to produce a wide range of meals. The most popular dishes include filled French-style baguettes (baked fresh each morning on the premises), open sandwiches, crispy salad bowls (all with a wide range of fillings/toppings) and Welsh rarebit with bacon.

The range of cakes proves to be an ever-popular reason for customers returning to the Mad Hatter Tea Shop. The choice varies, but the favourites include baked lemon cheesecake, coconut and lime cake, and coffee cake. The homemade scones with a hint of nutmeg always go down well.

On Friday and Saturday evenings, the Mad Hatter re-opens its doors as Lewis's Restaurant with a full à la carte menu. The restaurant has also established itself as a firm favourite in the area.

Assam, Ceylon, Darjeeling, China, Earl Grey, English Breakfast, Formosa Lapsang Souchong, Yorkshire. Fruit-flavoured teas and herbal teas are also available.

The Priest's House

BARDEN, NEAR SKIPTON
NORTH YORKSHIRE BD23 6AS
TEL: 01756 720616
WEB SITE: WWW.THEPRIESTSHOUSE.CO.UK
OWNERS: ROBERT HODGSON & JO PARKINSON

From Leeds, take the A65 to Addingham. Follow directions to Bolton Abbey. Take the B6160 to Burnsall. Barden is between Bolton Abbey and Burnsall, approximately three miles from Bolton Abbey. You will see the ruins of Barden Tower on the right. The gateway is signposted.

OPEN MID-MARCH–END OCTOBER:
10:30AM–5PM; CLOSED THURSDAY AND FRIDAY.
PLEASE RING TO CONFIRM IN WINTER.

The restaurant lies in the heart of the beautiful Yorkshire Dales and is located in a 15th-century building next to the ruins of Barden Tower. Since establishing the business here in 1991, Robert and Jo have built up a regular year-round trade with visitors and locals. The restaurant is open for morning coffee between 10:30 am and noon, and for lunch between noon and 2:30 pm. Customers dine in the Oak Room, so called because of its oak beamed ceiling and magnificent oak dressers, which house a fine collection of antique Willow pattern meat platters. Many people comment on the wonderfully relaxed atmosphere of the Oak Room, with its historic features and gentle period background music.

Light refreshments are served throughout the day on the tea terrace overlooking the ruins. Sultana and lemon scones with jam are a particular favourite with summer customers, whilst toasted crumpets and hearty soups go down well with chilled hikers in the winter months. The water from the restaurant's moorland spring makes fantastic tea, and some customers even bring bottles to fill so that they can take some away to enjoy at home.

Traditional Blend, Assam, Ceylon, Darjeeling, Earl Grey and Lapsang Souchong. Various herbal infusions are also available.

Tea-Time Traditions from the North East

COUNTY DURHAM, NORTHUMBERLAND, YORKSHIRE

As in Scotland, locally grown oats traditionally made up a major part of the daily diet in these north-easterly counties. Yorkshire haverbread and Northumbrian oat bread were baked on a griddle over the open fire and then left on a rack or hung up to dry. Bread was also made from barley or rye flour, potato flour or from pea or bean meal. Flat oatcakes, also known in the 17th century as tharve cakes, riddle cakes and clapbread, and similar to those made elsewhere in Britain, were mixed in a kneading trough called a knade-kit and then, like the bread, baked on the bakestone or griddle. Once cooked, they were stored in a container known as an ark and then eaten with butter, cheese, bacon or treacle. Although oat recipes have survived in many places and oats continued to be used in many local dishes, from the early 19th century oatmeal was gradually replaced by wheat flour. Yorkshire harvest buns use wholemeal wheat flour, Scarborough and Keighley muffins both use a wheat-flour dough, and York fingers are made with a wheat-flour pastry folded over grated Wensleydale cheese and spread with horseradish and more cheese.

Oatmeal was also a staple ingredient of parkins and gingerbreads, and with the strong Danish and Norse influences in the region, pepper cakes and ginger cakes are very similar to Scandinavian recipes. Pately Bridge pepper cake is made with ground cloves, treacle and ginger, and brandy snaps, closely associated with the Hull Fair that was first held in 1279, have a brittle texture and a hot gingery flavour. Most parkins were cooked on the bakestone, but Yorkshire parkin is generally baked as a dark rich oaty slab cake in a shallow tin. As it is stored it tends to get more sticky and delicious.

The north-eastern ports brought supplies of spices, dried fruits, lemons and oranges into the area, providing extra ingredients for enriching cakes and biscuits for festive occasions. Drop fritters (or frutterses) were made by frying spoonfuls of a yeasted batter made with grated apple, currants, candied peel, brandy and nutmeg. Fat rascals are round, golden tea-time biscuits made by rolling out a fairly dry, firm dough flavoured with currants and dredged with sugar. Nuns biskett was made with orangeflower water, ground almonds, sugar, eggs and lemon rind. Singin' hinnies are soft rounds of dough made tastier and more interesting by the addition of currants, ground rice and cream, and then baked on the griddle until golden — delicious with butter and jam. Ripon Christmas bread is a yeasted bread dough enriched with lard, raisins, candied peel, currants and allspice. Old Peculier ale makes the fruit cake that bears its name, a much more interesting tea-time feast than ordinary fruit cakes.

In May, a copious milk supply gave one of the main ingredients for Yorkshire curd cheesecakes and curd tarts, popular at Whitsuntide and during sheep shearing. Crops of local apples meant that apple tarts, shortbreads and cakes were also popular. Wilfra apple cake, made with the local Wensleydale cheese, and almond-flavoured Wilfra tarts were traditionally made for St. Wilfred's Day on the first or second Saturday of August. St. Wilfred is the patron saint of Ripon ,and his feast falls on the same day as the August Bank Holiday. Festivities used to include a procession through the streets of the town to re-enact the saint's return to his home town after a long absence abroad.

High tea treats in the North East included kippers from Craster, whitebait and other fish caught off the North East coast, fish pies, rabbit pies, potted beef, tatie pies and black puddings. Halifax high tea beef was made by boiling salted brisket with bacon pieces, carrots, onions, herbs and spices such as allspice, mace and cloves. After four hours of gentle braising, the meat was put into an earthenware dish and pressed overnight, ready for slicing at tea the next day. Yorkshire rarebit adds stout to the cheese mixture and tops the bubbling cheese with a slice of bacon and a poached egg.

Things to See and Do in the North East

COUNTY DURHAM, NORTHUMBERLAND, YORKSHIRE

County Durham

Barnard Castle, where you can have tea at the Market Place Teashop, is a small market town set beside the ruins of the 12th-century castle, now owned by English Heritage. It stands high above the River Tees on a rugged outcrop of stone, and there is a free audio tour that tells the story of the castle and its place in the history of this part of County Durham. In the town, County Bridge was built in the 16th century and at one time spanned the boundaries of two counties, so illicit weddings were conducted in the middle of the bridge where neither of the two bishops from the two areas could object. Sixteenth-century Blagraves House is said to have entertained Oliver Cromwell, and the Market Cross has over the centuries been used as a "lock-up" and a town hall. A quarter of a mile outside the town, the Bowes Museum is a French-style chateau in an English setting and houses a collection of furniture, paintings and ceramics from the second Napoleonic period. For those who wish to venture further than the town itself, the Teesdale countryside offers miles of quiet open roads, walks on waymarked footpaths that include the Pennine Way and the Teesdale Way, pony-trekking through heather and woodland, cycling on small country lanes and forest tracks, and canoeing, sailing and fishing on five reservoirs in Balderdale and Lunedale.

Northumberland

Bamburgh, home to the Copper Kettle Tea Rooms, is the ancient capital of Northumbria. In the 1890s its dramatic castle became a passion of the first Baron Armstrong, an engineer, shipbuilder and industrialist, and it is a treasure trove of fascinating rooms and exhibitions. The public tour takes you through the King's Hall, the Cross Hall, reception rooms, the backhouse, the Victorian scullery, the armoury and the dungeon. The former laundry building houses the

Armstrong industrial heritage museum. A few miles south of Bamburgh is the Seahouses Marine Life Centre, where visitors can follow a fisherman's life on shore and at sea, and compare today's fishing industry with that of the past. There are also tanks showing various forms of marine life. From Seahouses harbour, boats will take you to the Farne Islands, a sanctuary that provides homes for many types of sea birds and a colony for grey seals.

Yorkshire

It was in Whitby, location of Elizabeth Botham & Sons teashop, that James Cook served his seaman's apprenticeship. He lodged in a handsome 17th-century house in Grape Lane, close to the harbour, and visitors to the house can climb up to the attic where Cook and other apprentices slept and studied by candlelight. Whitby Museum, founded in 1823, is located in Pannett Park and is full of unique treasures and historical items. From the town, climb the 199 steps up to Whitby Abbey, and you can explore the gaunt ruins of the clifftop church that has over the years inspired painters, writers and engravers. For those who enjoy spooky experiences, you can take a Ghost Walk through the streets of the town to discover strange and supernatural tales of murder, mystery and suspense.

Crathorne Hall Hotel is on the northern borders of North Yorkshire and is not far from Osmotherley, where the Mount Grace Priory is the best-preserved Carthusian monastery in the Hambleton Hills. The extensive remains, restored monk's cell, medieval herb garden, monk's fishpond, 17th-century manor house and wonderful large gardens make it worth the journey a few miles south. Further east, Great Ayton has a sculpture of James Cook at the age of 16 and the 12th-century church where Cook worshipped as a boy. The Cook family grave is in the churchyard, and the peaceful candlelit interior of the church is a favourite place for visitors. At the Captain Cook Schoolroom Museum there is a reconstruction of an 18th-century schoolroom and interactive displays of James Cook's life and of his later achievements. A granite memorial also marks the site of the Cook family cottage, which was dismantled and shipped to Australia in 1934.

The Mad Hatter Tea Shop is in Masham, close to the breathtakingly beautiful Yorkshire Dales and a centre for arts, crafts and local producers of glass and pottery. Black Sheep and Theakston both have breweries and visitor centres in the town, and offer the opportunity of seeing how the speciality ales are made and a chance to taste them. A weekly market takes place every Saturday and Wednesday, and there are sheep fairs, a steam engine and fair organ rally, and a Victorian market followed by a torchlight procession every December. Nearby at Leighton Reservoir, Island Heritage has rare breeds of sheep on a farm that produces clothing and accessories from the undyed sheep's wool. In Ripon, a few miles to the south-east of Masham, the cathedral is also well worth a visit. Built in the seventh century, it is among the finest in Britain and has one of the oldest crypts. The Yorkshire Law and Order Museum in the former Ripon Union Workhouse has 19th-century vagrants' wards with displays of how paupers were treated in those days. Three miles to the west of Ripon lies Fountains Abbey and Studley Royal Water Garden. Here you can explore the almost complete remains of the Cistercian abbey and 10 historic buildings, including an Elizabethan mansion and the medieval deer park with 500 deer.

The Priest's House in Barden enjoys the beautiful countryside of the Southern Dales, with their remote fells and gritstone moors, bare limestone rock and lush pastures, steep cliffs and gorges. Bolton Priory is a few miles down the road ,and visitors can explore the historic Yorkshire estate of the Duke and Duchess of Devonshire, with its medieval buildings set beside the River Wharfe. Nearby Skipton, "the Gateway to the Dales," has a rich variety of interesting specialist shops in the ancient courts, or "folds" that lead off the high street, including Craven Court, the covered Victorian-style shopping arcade. Skipton Castle, once the home of the Clifford Lords, has dominated the town for more than 900 years. Fully roofed and with a dungeon and watchtower, chapel and conduit court, it is one of the best-preserved and most complete medieval castles in England. The Craven Museum, housed in the Town Hall in the centre of the town, is crammed full of exhibits about the Craven Dales from prehistoric and Roman days to Victorian homes and the lead mining industry. The Leeds-Liverpool canal runs right through the town, providing an ideal walking route.

Bettys Café Tea Rooms in Harrogate is set in what is often described as "England's Floral Town" because of its acres of immaculate gardens that blaze with colour throughout the year. The Valley Gardens feature dramatically colourful displays alongside the streamside pathways, and at the top of the gardens are lush pinewoods leading to Harlow Botanical Gardens, home of the Northern Horticultural Society. Other highlights include the Museum of Gardening, a gift shop and a plant centre. There is still plenty of evidence around the town of Harrogate's spa heritage, the most important being the Royal Pump Museum inside an 1842 building that originally housed the Old Sulphur Well, the main watering hole for visitors. The sulphur water can still be sampled. Harrogate is also the antiques centre of the north and there are a number of quality antique shops around the town centre.

Ilkley, home to another of Bettys Café Tea Rooms, is an attractive town set in the valleys of the River Wharfe and surrounded by wonderful countryside. Ilkley Moor is the backdrop to the south and to the north, woodland covers the sloping landscape and in spring this is well worth a visit to see the bluebells. In the town itself, the Manor House Art Gallery and Museum in Castle Yard dates from the 15th, 16th and 17th centuries and has mullioned windows, carved beams and open fireplaces. The ground-floor exhibitions trace the history of Ilkley while the upper floors house the art gallery. Behind the Manor House is the site of the Roman fort of Olicana, built in about 79 AD. Between the fort and the River Wharfe, Riverside Gardens provide grassy banks for relaxing, pathways for strolling and an adventure playground for children. The Old Bridge dates back to 1675 and stands on the site of several previous bridges that were washed away by floods.

Bettys Café Tea Rooms in Northallerton is at the centre of a lively market town that has several interesting historic buildings. The Old Grammar School, now occupied by a firm of solicitors, was built in 1776 on the site of an original school building that dated from the 14th century. Porch House is the oldest private house in Northallerton, and traditions tell how Charles I was a guest there in 1640, but was held prisoner in 1647 and tried to escape. Marks on an upstairs beam are thought to record the counting of the ransom paid for the king's release. The Golden Lion, built in 1700 on the high street, was one of several important coaching inns on the Great North Road, and famous coaches such as the Royal Mail and the High Flyer called here for refreshment, rest and to change the horses. The old Georgian Theatre was opened in 1800, and it is here that Edmund Keen began his acting career in 1806. The building has subsequently been a Methodist chapel, the town's abattoir, a gymnasium and a club. A plaque on the wall records its varied history.

York is home to three of the Guild's teashops — Bettys Café Tea Rooms, Bullivant of York and Little Bettys. It is a charming, fascinating town packed with interesting things to see and do. York Castle Museum has reconstructions of Victorian and Edwardian streets, the prison cell of notorious highwayman, Dick Turpin, a Victorian bank and police station, and an Edwardian shop. The Treasurer's House is an elegant town house restored by Yorkshire industrialist Frank Green. The National Railway Museum tells the story of the train, and has royal trains, toy trains and steam engines. Other attractions include the Micklegate Bar Museum in the old gate and walls of the city, the York Dungeon with more than 2,000 years of history, Clifford's Tower (the central keep of the medieval castle), the Impressions Gallery in a Georgian town house, the York City Art Gallery, with 600 years of European paintings and York Museum, set in 10 acres of botanical gardens. Outside York, Castle Howard and Beningborough Hall are both beautiful historic houses with wonderful grounds and gardens.

There are two Clark's tearooms in Easingwold, a small town south of Thirsk. Thirsk is the old cobbled Yorkshire town famous for its connections with James Herriot and the TV series *All Creatures Great and Small.* "The World of James Herriot," in Skeldale House, is a tribute to Alf Wight, author of the James Herriot novels, and exhibitions explore veterinary science and combine history, nostalgia, humour and education. The room settings and memorabilia from the TV series take visitors back to the 1940s and 50s. Also in Thirsk, St. Mary's Church has medieval woodwork in the chapel, door, roof and font, and medieval glass in the chapel. James and Helen Herriot (Alf and Joan Wight) were married here in 1941. In the old maltings, "Trees to Treske" is an award-winning exhibition of traditional furniture making.

Northeast from Easingwold, Shandy Hall is an early 15th-century house where Laurence Stern wrote his two novels, and the 12th-century Newburgh Priory, still the home of the Earls of Fauconberg and the Wombwell family, contains family pictures and furniture and the tomb of Oliver Cromwell.

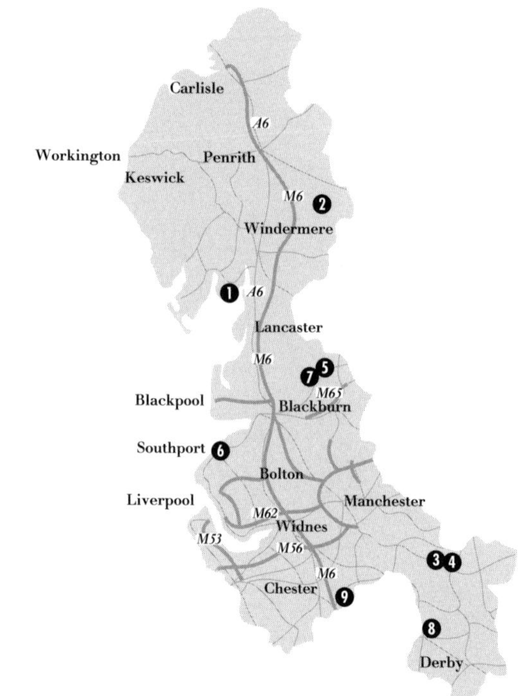
Carlisle
A6
Workington
Penrith
Keswick
M6
2
Windermere
1
A6
Lancaster
M6
7
5
M65
Blackpool
Blackburn
Southport
6
Bolton
Liverpool
Manchester
M62
Widnes
M53
M56
3
4
M6
Chester
9
8
Derby

The North West

Cumbria

❶ THE HAZELMERE CAFÉ & BAKERY *p.* 144

❷ NEW VILLAGE TEA ROOMS *p.* 145

Derbyshire

❸ THE COTTAGE TEA ROOM *p.* 146

❹ NORTHERN TEA MERCHANTS *p.* 147

Lancashire

❺ CAFÉ CAPRICE *p.* 148

❻ NOSTALGIA TEAROOMS *p.* 149

❼ THE TOBY JUG TEA SHOP *p.* 150

Staffordshire

❽ GREYSTONES 17TH CENTURY TEA ROOM *p.* 151

❾ ROYAL DOULTON VISITOR CENTRE *p.* 152

The Hazelmere Café & Bakery

1 YEWBARROW TERRACE
GRANGE OVER SANDS, CUMBRIA LA11 6ED
TEL: 01539 532972
FAX: 01539 534101
OWNERS: DOROTHY & IAN STUBLEY
1998 TEA COUNCIL AWARD OF EXCELLENCE

When coming into Grange over Sands on the B5277, you will pass Grange Station on the left. Shortly after this, there is a mini-roundabout. Take the first exit and the café is about 25 yards along, on the right.

OPEN ALL YEAR.
WINTER, 10AM–4:30PM; SUMMER, 10AM–5PM.

Grange over Sands is one of those towns that just would not be complete without a high-class tea shop and the Hazelmere, set in a parade of Victorian shops fronted by a beautiful, ornate glass-and-cast-iron veranda, provides the perfect venue for tea and also manages to recapture the spirit of traditional tea time. Dorothy and Ian Stubley specialise in homemade quality food using only the best local ingredients, including free-range eggs and fresh cream. They make everything on the premises and like to include a mixture of local specialities as well as their own original recipes.

You can be absolutely sure that you will not be disappointed by the selection of real treats — Cumberland rum nicky, Yorkshire curd tart, date and walnut fudge tart, a variety of homemade scones with damson jam and Lakeland cream, and sandwiches filled with cheddar cheese and home-made piccalilli, or oak-roasted salmon with horseradish or turkey breast and applesauce. Light meals are also available. All the teas served are single-estate, and the menu gives helpful tasting notes and source descriptions.

Five China, two Japanese, three Indian, seven Ceylon, two African, Argentinian, various "guest" teas, various herbals.

New Village Tea Rooms

ORTON, PENRITH
CUMBRIA CA10 3RH
TEL: 01539 624886
OWNER: CHRISTINE EVANS

Leave the M6 at junction 38 and take the Appleby road. In Orton, take the Shap road in front of the George Hotel. The tearooms are straight ahead, opposite the stores and post office, where the road turns left and leaves the village.

OPEN ALL YEAR. JULY–AUGUST, 10AM–6PM; APRIL, MAY, JUNE, SEPTEMBER, OCTOBER, 10AM–5PM; NOVEMBER, MARCH, 10:30AM–4:30PM.

The New Village Tea Rooms are housed in an 18th-century building that has had a varied history and was most recently a cottage. The downstairs tearoom was once the cottage living room, and the kitchen is open to the friendly area where customers now sit to enjoy their tea. This means that they can chat to the staff while their food is being prepared and feel really at home.

On hot summer days, the tearooms remain cool and comfortable, but sun lovers can bask outside in the pretty cottage garden. In winter, an open coal fire keeps visitors warm and cosy and creates a haven for walkers. Californian "Coast to Coast" walkers who visited when walking west to east in 1992 and again when walking east to west in 1994, said that the sticky toffee pudding was the best in the country and took the recipe home, vowing to keep it a secret forever.

All the food is prepared on the premises using traditional methods and locally produced quality ingredients. The menu offers a wide range of homemade cakes, tempting desserts, sandwiches and hot lunch dishes in a totally smoke-free environment.

Earl Grey, Ceylon, Darjeeling, Assam, Lapsang Souchong, PG Tips. Fruit-flavoured teas and herbal infusions are also offered.

The Cottage Tea Room

3 FENNEL STREET, ASHFORD-IN-THE-WATER
NEAR BAKEWELL, DERBYSHIRE DE45 1QF
TEL: 01629 812488
E-MAIL: WILLWAT@BUSHINTERNET.COM
OWNERS: BILL & BETTY WATKINS
1998 TEA COUNCIL AWARD OF EXCELLENCE
EGON RONAY RECOMMENDED

Ashford-in-the-Water lies on the A6, two miles north of Bakewell and eight miles south of Buxton Spa. The tearoom is just above the ford by the ancient sheepwash bridge.

OPEN ALL THE YEAR EXCEPT ONE WEEK IN MID-SEPTEMBER, CHRISTMAS DAY, BOXING DAY AND NEW YEAR'S DAY. MONDAY, WEDNESDAY, THURSDAY, SATURDAY AND SUNDAY TEAS ARE SERVED 2:30–5PM; CLOSED TUESDAY AND FRIDAY AFTERNOONS.

You take a step back in time when you find the charming Cottage Tea Room in this unspoilt village on the old Drovers Road from Inverness to London. A place of refreshment since the early part of the last century, long before the Peak District became Britain's first National Park, the tearoom has been run by Betty and Bill Watkins for the past 21 years. In that time, the Watkins have earned the commendation of all the leading food and travel guides.

The unchanging high quality is a feature of the Cottage, and customers are served freshly brewed leaf tea and delicious home-baked breads, cakes and scones, as were their grandparents in earlier decades. Open throughout the year, a friendly welcome awaits you on sun-drenched summer days and on snowy winter ones, when tea by an open fire is especially tempting.

The accent is on genuine home cooking. There is a wonderful array of traditional English cakes and hand-kneaded breads, and a variety of feather-light scones is baked daily. The warm cheesy herb scones are a great favourite on winter days. Six set meals are served, and you can choose anything from a simple pot of tea and a slice of cake to the full afternoon tea.

House Blend, six China, five Ceylon, three Indian, Kenya, Formosa Oolong, Russian Caravan, Earl Grey, English Breakfast, various herbals.

Northern Tea Merchants

CROWN HOUSE
193 CHATSWORTH ROAD, BRAMPTON
CHESTERFIELD, DERBYSHIRE S40 2BA
TEL: 01246 233243
FAX: 01246 555991
WEB SITE: WWW.NORTHERN-TEA.COM
OWNER: DAVID POGSON

Northern Tea Merchants is situated one mile from the centre of Chesterfield on the A619 (the road to Chatsworth House).

OPEN ALL YEAR
EXCEPT BANK HOLIDAYS AND FOR
A WEEK FROM CHRISTMAS TO NEW YEAR
AND SUNDAYS. MONDAY–FRIDAY, 9AM–5PM;
SATURDAY, 9AM–4:30PM;
CLOSED SUNDAY.

The windows of Northern Tea Merchant's double-fronted store, not far from the famous crooked spire, are full of eye-catching tea and coffee equipment — scales, caddies, grinders, tea chests, tea wares and attractive packages. The family business, dating back to 1936, specialises in tea blending and packing and the manufacture of tea bags (as well as coffee roasting, grinding and packaging) and handles enough for 100 million cups a year. Proprietor David Pogson is recognised as an authority on tea and acts as a judge in the Tea Council's tea-tasting competitions. His shop is an absolute treasure trove of speciality teas, coffees and equipment, and the shelves are stacked high with an incredible choice of packages. This is a place of serious tea drinking where you can sample some of the unusual varieties at the tea bar before selecting your purchases from a range of 24 blends and single-source teas. Visitors can also choose from a mouthwatering selection of scones, cakes and pastries to accompany their tea.

Golden De Luxe Classic, Silver De Luxe, Rwanda, Guangxi Guihua, Darjeeling, Assam, Ceylon, Ceylon Orange Pekoe, Keemun, Lapsang Souchong, Earl Grey, English Breakfast, Kenya, Russian Caravan, Formosa Oolong, Gunpowder, Jasmine. Fruit-flavoured teas and herbal infusions are also available.

Café Caprice

6–8 MOOR LANE
CLITHEROE, LANCASHIRE BB7 1BE
TEL: 01200 422034
OWNER: PETER & JOYCE JENKINSON

Leave the A59 at the Clitheroe turnoff.
On entering the town centre, Café Caprice is on the left.

OPEN ALL YEAR. MONDAY, TUESDAY,
THURSDAY, FRIDAY, SATURDAY, 9:30AM–4:30PM;
CLOSED WEDNESDAY AND SUNDAY.

Café Caprice has a brand new image and menu. The neutral shades have gone and instead the colour scheme is vibrant and lively, with bright colours — strong blues and yellows on the walls and tablecloths in salmon and green, yellow and blue.

The pictures on the wall and the bright blue and yellow outfits worn by the waiting staff add more splashes of similar colours to create a cheerful, friendly and happy atmosphere. But the modern look doesn't mean that the old-fashioned friendliness and service have gone. They are still very much in evidence, as are Joyce Jenkinson's talents in the kitchen and interest in food and traditional cookery. There is now a book room in the shop where you can browse through and buy from a collection of more than 2,000 books on cookery, food and drink.

The menu features an excellent range of tea-time traditionals and cakes, including Cumbrian lemon loaf, carrot cake, chocolate cake, orange Victoria sandwich, and lime and coconut slice. The shop also specialises in parkins and gingerbreads and the menu suggests a pairing of a particular tea with the parkin of the month.

House Blend, Ceylon, Assam,
Darjeeling, Earl Grey, Formosa Oolong, Lemon.

Nostalgia Tearooms

215–217 LORD STREET, SOUTHPORT
LANCASHIRE PR8 1PF
TEL: 01704 501294
E-MAIL: COUZENS@TOTALISE.CO.UK
MANAGER: ANN COUZENS
2000 TEA COUNCIL AWARD OF EXCELLENCE
1991 FINALIST IN BUSINESS WOMEN MERSEYSIDE

Nostalgia is opposite the tourist information centre, on the first floor of the black and white building, above the Early Learning Centre.

OPEN ALL YEAR EXCEPT
MID-JANUARY TO MID-FEBRUARY.
WEDNESDAY–FRIDAY, 9:30AM–4:30PM;
SATURDAY, 9:30AM–5PM; SUNDAY, 10AM–5PM.
CLOSED MONDAY, EXCEPT BANK HOLIDAYS.
CLOSED TUESDAY, EXCEPT IN AUGUST.

Ann Couzens had already enjoyed considerable success with her first tearoom in Birkdale before opening this Southport branch in one of the town's typical Victorian arcades. Ann used to be a catering teacher at the local college. She also designed the furniture and the interior decoration herself so that the large airy room would look absolutely right. Styled on a conservatory, with bamboo chairs and a colour scheme in pale peach and green, this is an elegant and restful place to take tea, where waitresses in pretty Victorian black-and-white costumes look after you in the old-fashioned way.

The generous menu, which is supplemented by a daily blackboard, includes modern as well as traditional cakes — the Pavlova and cream teas are extremely tempting, along with the very popular tea snack. There are ice cream sundaes too, with exotic names such as Mississippi Steamboat and Singapore Surprise. But even if you settle for just a cup of tea and a flapjack, you are bound to enjoy the reassuring Englishness of the experience.

Yorkshire, English Breakfast, Earl Grey, Darjeeling, Assam, Ceylon, various fruit and herbal infusions.

The Toby Jug Tea Shop

20 KING STREET, WHALLEY
CLITHEROE, LANCASHIRE BB7 9SL
TEL: 01254 823298
FAX: 01254 823298
OWNERS: PETER, MARIE & JANE IRELAND

The Toby Jug is in the main street of Whalley Village, by the bridge over the River Calder.

OPEN ALL YEAR.
TUESDAY–FRIDAY, 10:30AM–4:30PM;
SATURDAY, 10:30AM–5PM;
CLOSED SUNDAYS AND MONDAYS.
IN NOVEMBER AND DECEMBER,
THE TEA SHOP CLOSES AT 4PM.

The Toby Jug Tea Shop, originally King Street Farm and now a Grade II-listed building, in days gone by would have provided a welcome resting place for weary pilgrims on their way to the mother church in Whalley, which dates back to 1206 and today houses the beautiful 15th-century choir stalls taken from the Cistercian abbey nearby. In the churchyard are three Celtic preaching crosses. The village, in the heart of the Ribble Valley, nestles beneath Pendle Hill, where the Quaker founder, George Fox, preached in 1652 and which is closely associated with the infamous Pendle witches and their subsequent trial and hanging in Lancaster in 1612.

The Toby Jug, the Irelands' family home, offers traditional Lancashire hospitality and creates a cosy atmosphere with its oak beams and panelling plundered from the abbey. The lunchtime menu (11:30am–2:30pm) offers an extensive selection of freshly prepared savoury specialities, including a variety of healthy wholemeal sandwiches, jacket potatoes with delicious fillings and highly recommended homemade soups. For afternoon tea there are scones and an extensive range of tempting cakes, gateaux, and fresh fruit pies, all made on the premises in the Irelands' family kitchen.

Yorkshire, Yorkshire Gold, Earl Grey, Assam, Darjeeling, South African Kwazulu, Ceylon, Lapsang Souchong, Lemon China, Orange and Lemon Peel, Moroccan Mint, various exotic flower teas, Peppermint Tisane.

Greystones 17th Century Tea Room

STOCKWELL STREET
LEEK, STAFFS, ST13 6DH
TEL/FAX: 01538 398522
OWNERS: ROGER & JANET WARRILLOW
2000 TOP TEA PLACE OF THE YEAR
1999 & 2001 AWARD OF EXCELLENCE

Greystones is situated on the A523, the main road through Leek from Macclesfield to Ashbourne. The tearoom is next door to Leek library, which is housed in the copper-domed Nicholson Institute — a landmark for miles around.

OPEN ALL YEAR. WEDNESDAY, FRIDAY, SATURDAY, 10AM–5PM. IT IS ADVISABLE TO RING FIRST, IF TRAVELLING A DISTANCE.

It was the flourishing silk industry that made Leek a wealthy, thriving community in the 18th century, and the town is full of fascinating reminders of those days — the cobbled market place, the restored water-powered corn mill by the canal and the Victorian Nicholson Institute. The Institute was founded in 1882 by Joshua Nicholson and his son, Sir Arthur Nicholson, successful mill owners who built the library, museum and technical college for the local residents. It was in the rear garden of Greystones, their gracious late 17th-century house in the heart of Leek, that the Institute was built.

Greystones tearoom is housed in the front parlour of the house where oak beams and leaded light windows create a wonderful setting for morning coffee, lunch and afternoon tea. The Warrillows have created an atmosphere here that makes visitors feel really welcome and relaxed, and they offer a wonderful selection of lunchtime savouries and sought-after homemade cakes and desserts such as the Queen Mother's favourite, melting date and walnut sponge topped with cream, treacle tart, lemon meringue pie, etc.

House Blend, Traditional English, Traditional Afternoon Blend, Assam, Darjeeling, Earl Grey, Lady Grey, Ceylon, Yunnan, Lapsang Souchong, Green, Jasmine, Lemon, Decaffeinated, Organic. Herbal infusions are also offered.

Royal Doulton Visitor Centre

NILE STREET, BURSLEM
STOKE-ON-TRENT
STAFFORDSHIRE ST6 2AJ
TEL: 01782 292434
FAX: 01782 292424
WEB SITE: ROYAL-DOULTON.CO.UK

Leave the M6 at either Junction 15 or 16 and take the A500 towards Stoke-on-Trent. Leave the A500 at the junction with the A527 and follow the brown tourist signs for Royal Doulton in Burslem.

OPEN ALL YEAR EXCEPT CHRISTMAS WEEK.
MONDAY–SATURDAY, 9:30AM–5PM;
SUNDAY, 10:30AM–4:30PM.

The Royal Doulton Visitor Centre is "the home of the Royal Doulton figure" and is located within the Royal Doulton factory. As well as offering refreshment and a relaxing location in which to rest after touring the pottery or watching the skilled demonstrators in the Visitor Centre, the Sir Henry Doulton Gallery restaurant is also the museum of the company's history, with exhibits spanning 180 years. Glass cabinets display nearly 1,500 Doulton figures, early stoneware pieces from the 1830s, Lambeth wares and medal-winning exhibits from international exhibitions — and even has the first china in space.

The menu includes cooked breakfasts, hot meals, light lunches such as soups, toasties, sandwiches and, of course, Staffordshire oatcakes with various savoury fillings. Afternoon tea includes assorted homemade cakes and strawberry scones with dairy cream. Everything is served on Royal Doulton fine bone china.

Assam, Darjeeling, English Breakfast, Ceylon, Earl Grey, Decaffeinated. Herbal infusions are also offered.

Tea-Time Traditions from the North West

CUMBRIA, DERBYSHIRE, LANCASHIRE, STAFFORDSHIRE

As elsewhere in Britain, traditional tea-time and festive foods from the North West included similar gingerbreads, parkins, wakes cakes, fairings and curd cheesecakes. The main ingredients of 18th-century Westmorland pepper cake — rum, spices, brown sugar and molasses — reflect a flourishing trade with the Far East and the West Indies. Originally made for sale at fairgrounds, Grasmere gingerbreads are crumbly biscuits made with fine oatmeal, brown sugar and ginger, and Derbyshire parkin was made to a typical recipe that included oatmeal, treacle, syrup, candied orange peel, lemon and ginger. Parkins and other oatmeal festive cakes once had close associations with pagan gods and their feast days. In Lancashire, they were called Har cakes after the god Har, while in Derbyshire they were known as Thor cakes after the Scandinavian god of thunder.

Several Derbyshire towns produced special recipes of their own, Bakewell pudding being perhaps the most famous of all. Its invention is said to have happened by chance when a customer at the Rutland Arms in Bakewell ordered a strawberry tart and the chef, by mistake, poured an egg mixture over strawberry jam. It was declared so good that the owner of the hotel asked the chef to continue making the pudding in the same way. Other treats from Derbyshire include lemon Derby tarts, pippin pie (eaten with cheese because, as they say in South Derbyshire, "Apple pie without the cheese is like a kiss without the squeeze") and feeberry (gooseberry) loaf, which is actually a pie. Also from the county come Cuddlestone cake with treacle, orange peel, glacé cherries, currants and almonds; Chesterfield buns, strips of flaky pastry tied in knots and sprinkled with chopped nuts; Moorland tarts, a strange mixture of chopped hard-boiled eggs, candied peel, currants, nutmeg, sugar and butter in short-crust pastry; Bolsover cakes made with sherry, raisins and almonds; Carsington pikelets, thin crumpets about five inches in diameter; and Glossop shouters, loaves of bread made with lard, yeast and dried fruit. Wakes cakes, for the holiday week or "wakes" each summer, varied slightly from place to place. In Ashbourne, they used ginger and lemon peel to flavour the round short biscuits, in Melbourne, currants were added instead of ginger, at Langley, it was caraway seeds and lemon, and at Wirksworth, currants, cream and caraway seeds were the preferred additions.

Cumberland is famous for its sweet pie. An early version of mince tarts was a short-crust case filled with a mixture of lamb or mutton, raisins, sultanas, lemon juice and peel, spices, black pepper, salt, eggs and dark rum. Rum is traditionally also beaten with butter, nutmeg and brown sugar to make a Cumberland sweet butter or brown jam that was given to an expectant mother just before the birth of her child, to visitors who called to see the new baby, and served with Christmas pudding and mince pies. Traditional Cumberland cake was flavoured with marmalade, raisins and peel, Cumberland sand cake is a soft lemon cake and Hawkshead cake is yeasted fruit cake with peel; currants and sultanas. Cumberland snaps are ginger oat biscuits, and Cumberland nickies are layers of short-crust pastry sandwiched together with a sticky mixture of currants, rum, nutmeg, butter and demerara sugar, then baked until golden and cut into squares or fingers.

Westmorland teas are a feast of buttermilk scones, cream pancakes and spoon scones made with a thick batter that includes wholemeal flour, cream, sugar and treacle. Lardy Johns from the same county are square currant biscuits.

Lancashire is best known for Eccles cakes, similar and from the same original family as Chorley cakes , which are also from Lancashire, Banbury cakes from Oxfordshire, triangular God cakes from Coventry and Hawkshead cakes from Cumbria. The word eccles originally meant church, and all the variations of the pastry are thought to descend from festive cakes made as offerings for pagan and early Christian celebrations. During the 17th century, religious foods were banned, but these flat round cakes filled with dried fruit, sugar and spices somehow survived. Other specialities from Lancashire include Manchester's own jam-and-brandy-filled tart and Lancaster lemon tart.

Things to See and Do in the North West

CUMBRIA, DERBYSHIRE, LANCASHIRE, STAFFORDSHIRE

Cumbria

Grange-over-Sands, the setting for Hazelmere Café and Bakery, is the perfect centre for visiting any of the attractions in southern Cumbria. Grange itself enjoys the natural beauty of the surrounding countryside and long beaches around Morecombe Bay, and it is within easy reach of the Lake District. Just west of Grange is Cartmel Priory and Village. The Church of St. Mary and St. Michael has recently celebrated its 800th anniversary, and the village is one of the prettiest in Lakeland, with the market square at its heart, a delightful range of old buildings and the glorious surrounding countryside. A little further to the west, Holker Hall and Gardens is a vast property that once belonged to the Dukes of Devonshire and is now home to Lord and Lady Cavendish. Its gardens are classed as "amongst the best in the world" and combine formal design with woodland walks. It is also home to the Lakeland Motor Museum, which includes the Campbell Bluebird Exhibition.

New Village Tea Rooms are in Orton, a village in the heart of Cumbria between Kendal and Penrith. Penrith was once the capital of Cumbria and has been the focus for travellers since Roman days. It is still the main northern gateway to the Lake District and the North Pennines. Its interesting historic buildings include a castle, museum and St. Andrew's Church. The countryside around is full of quaint villages and historic castles and houses. The ruins of 13th-century Brougham Castle sit by the River Eamont, and visitors can climb up to the top of the fortress for splendid panoramic views of the countryside around. At Temple Sowerby, Acorn Bank Garden and Watermill has a spectacular display of shrubs, flowers, herbaceous borders and sheltered orchards that contain traditional fruit trees and a famous herb garden. South to Kendal and visitors can see the surviving walls and tower of the town's early 13th-century castle and learn more about the area at the Kendal

Museum. The Museum of Lakeland Life has a wealth of unusual objects that document the story of social life, the arts and crafts, and spinning and weaving in Lakeland.

Derbyshire

Ashford-in-the-Water was once part of the Duke of Devonshire's Chatsworth Estate, and it is here that the Cottage Tea Room is situated. The village is considered to be the jewel of the Peak District. Five bridges span the River Wye here, and it is a favourite spot for anglers. The Norman church has some fine examples of local coloured marble, and there is a carefully restored 14th-century tithe barn. Chatsworth House is one of the treasures of England, with 26 richly decorated rooms open to the public, and 105 acres of garden with fountains, sculptures, a maze, a farmyard and an adventure playground. Very close to Chatsworth, Haddon Hall is a medieval and Tudor manor house with terraced rose gardens. In Bakewell, a couple of miles from Ashford-in-the-Water, the Old Market Hall houses the tourist information centre and has an exhibition of local products from food producers, craftspeople and artists. Bakewell is also home to the M & C Collection of historic motorcycles, and includes all types from the everyday bike to the exotic sports touring motorcycle. Buxton lies about 10 miles west of Ashford and, as a historic spa town, has plenty of architectural interest, beautiful gardens and Pooles Cavern at Buxton Country Park — a natural limestone cavern with spectacular stalagmites and crystal formations.

Northern Tea Merchants is in Brampton on the outskirts of Chesterfield, famous for the crooked spire of the Church of St. Mary's and All Saints. Dedicated in 1234, this is the largest church in Derbyshire and the 228-foot spire leans nine feet five inches from its true centre. Market Place and the conservation area around it are worth a visit, and next to Market Place is the Peacock Heritage Centre in an early 16th-century timber-framed building. At Old Whittington on the northern side of the town is Revolution House, a 17th-century thatched cottage that was formerly the Cock and Pynot Alehouse, where three local noblemen met to plan their part in the Revolution of 1688. To the southeast of Chesterfield, the National Trust maintains Hardwick Hall and Garden. Built by Bess of Hardwick, this is one of Britain's most important Elizabethan houses and it dominates the surrounding area. The walled courtyards enclose fine gardens, orchards and an herb garden, and the park around contains rare breeds of cattle and sheep. Close by is Stansby Mill, a remarkably complete water-powered flour mill that is in good working order.

Lancashire

Café Caprice is right in the middle of Clitheroe and is an excellent starting point for a visit to the town. Clitheroe Castle sits perched on a rocky limestone crag and possesses what is said to be the second smallest Norman keep in England. In the grounds of the castle are gardens and sports facilities, and Clitheroe Castle Museum, which is housed in an impressive castellated Georgian building and features local history, a print shop, a geology display and a clogger's shop. To the northeast of the town, Browsholme Hall is the ancestral home of the Parker family, Bowbearers of the Forest of Bowland, who have lived there since 1507. Tudor in origin, the house has an Elizabethan façade of warm pink sandstone and inside a collection of portraits, oak furniture, arms and armour, stained glass and unusual antiquities. To the southwest, Stoneyhurst College is open to the public and has chapels, a Great Hall and the table where Cromwell is said to have slept the night before the Battle of Preston in 1648.

Whalley is due south from Clitheroe and is home to the Toby Jug Tea Shop. The village has a rich history, and the spirit of the past is alive for many local people in the grounds of Whalley Abbey. Built by Cistercian monks in 1296, it is today mostly in ruins, but the chapter house is still used for retreats and the abbey is protected as an ancient monument. Whalley also has a magnificent 1852 railway viaduct with 49 arches that has been described as a triumph of Victorian engineering. The town is on the edge of the Pendle Hills and is therefore close to the history of the Pendle witches. From Sabden, just to the east of Whalley, visitors can take the Pendle tour and learn more about the 10 witches who were sent to the scaffold, nine in Lancaster and one in York.

Nostalgia Tearooms is centrally positioned in the elegant 18th-century seaside town of Southport on the Lancashire coast. The town was founded in 1792 when William Sutton opened a hotel at the junction of Lord Street and Duke Street. So, Nostalgia Tearooms is in the oldest part of the town and is close to the Arts Centre, the Atkinson Art Gallery (both in Lord Street), and the Marine Lake with its Model Railway Village, theatre and Floral Hall. Kings Gardens, Princes Park and Victoria Park are all only a short walk away. Each year in August, Victoria Park hosts an annual summer Flower Show and at Churchtown, five minutes from Southport centre, Meols Hall also holds a Spring Gardening Festival each year. For bird lovers, the RSPB's Marshside Nature Reserve is just up Marine Drive from Southport's promenade, and the site has two hides, a viewing screen and public footpaths. For walkers, the Sefton Coastal Footpath links Southport to Crosby down the coast. The paths take you through dunes, farmland and pine woodland, and give impressive views of the sea and the wide beaches.

Staffordshire

Leek, where you will find Greystones 17th Century Tea Room, is surrounded by the peaceful wooded countryside of the Churnet Valley. The Caldon Canal, which runs from Leek to Stoke-on-Trent, was once important for the transportation of coal and limestone, and is used today by pleasure craft. A traditional narrow boat operates from Froghall, offering trips to visitors, and the Churnet steam railway carries passengers down the valley from Cheddleton to Consall, Kingsley and Froghall. There are also two working watermills in the valley — the Brindley Mill in Leek (a corn mill once owned by the great canal builder James Brindley) and at Cheddleton, a mill where flints were once ground to a fine powder for the ceramic industry. Leek is within very easy access of the Staffordshire Moorlands. Walkers and cyclists can enjoy miles of paths and tracks through the dales, beside Rudyard Lake, through the Churnet Valley and in the country parks at Ladderedge on the outskirts of Leek and at Biddulph Grange Garden, a Victorian themed garden with a Chinese temple, Egyptian court, dahlia walk and glen. Leek itself was very important in the 18th and 19th centuries as a silk manufacturing and dyeing centre, and William Morris, founder of the Arts and Crafts movement, visited the town many times. A guided walk through the town tells more of the story and gives visitors a chance to enjoy the antique shops and the converted silk mills, which now hold shops and galleries, and see the work of local craftspeople, including ceramics, wood-carving, painting, hand-thrown stoneware and garden planters. A visit to the Royal Doulton pottery in Stoke-on-Trent is not complete without taking tea at the Royal Doulton Visitor Centre. A tour of the factory allows visitors to see the various stages of production of pottery and china tableware, giftware and figurines, and to watch hand painting, gilding and the intricate manufacture of tiny china flowers. The museum has a collection of representative pieces from various periods, and there is an opportunity to buy Royal Doulton products. Stoke is the British centre for the manufacture of pottery and chinaware, and many other potteries organise guided tours. Outside the town there are other attractions. Ford Green Hall at Smallthorne is a timber-framed 17th-century period garden and farmhouse richly furnished with textiles, ceramics and furniture. Alton Towers is a short drive from Stoke, and at Blyth Bridge to the southeast, Foxfield Steam Railway runs steam trains on Sundays and Bank Holiday Mondays.

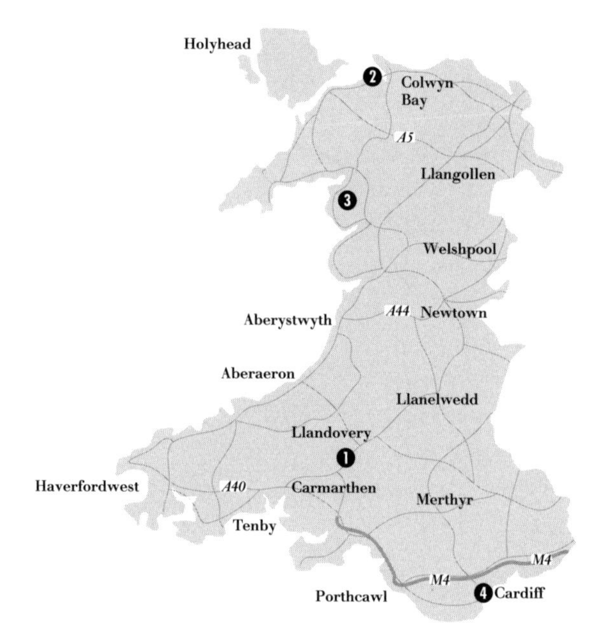
Holyhead
2
Colwyn Bay
A5
Llangollen
3
Welshpool
Aberystwyth
A44
Newtown
Aberaeron
Llanelwedd
Llandovery
1
Haverfordwest
A40
Carmarthen
Merthyr
Tenby
M4
M4
Porthcawl
4
Cardiff

The Welsh Tea Trail

Carmarthenshire

❶ FELIN NEWYDD WATERMILL *p.* 162

Gwynedd

❷ BADGER'S CAFÉ & PATISSERIE *p.* 163

❸ CEMLYN RESTAURANT & TEA SHOP *p.* 164

Glamorgan

❹ GWALIA TEA ROOMS *p.* 165

Felin Newydd Watermill

FELIN NEWYDD
CRUGYBAR, LLANWRDA
CARMARTHENSHIRE SA19 8UE
TEL: 01558 650375
E-MAIL: CMAPLE@NASCR.NET
OWNERS: CHRIS & JO-ANNE MAPLE

Felin Newydd is beside the main A482 Llanwrda to Lampeter road and six miles from the A40. Follow the brown tourist signs as you approach the Watermill.

OPEN FROM GOOD FRIDAY TO END OF OCTOBER.
THURSDAY–MONDAY, 10:30AM–5PM;
CLOSED TUESDAY AND WEDNESDAY.
JULY AND AUGUST: CLOSED ONLY ON WEDNESDAY.

The Grade II-listed mill at Felin Newydd (meaning New Mill) is more than 200 years old and stands on the site of the former Grist Mill thought to have been used to feed Roman soldiers who worked at the nearby gold mines. It was restored in the late 1980s and is still capable of grinding flour today. It is set in the grounds of a 13-acre former smallholding (with tranquil riverside gardens and a wildlife lake) in the beautiful Annell Valley in the foothills of the Cambrian Mountains. This quiet area is renowned for its scenery and wildlife. A renovated byre is now the tea shop, and you can relax in the garden conservatory overlooking the river and pond and browse around the craft area with its selection of Welsh crafts and gifts. Locally commissioned bone china perfectly complements the farmyard theme. The tea shop offers a range of light lunches, homemade cakes and scones, all baked by Jo-Anne on the premises. She tries to make sure that there is something to appeal to all tastes and includes such treats as farmhouse cake, Bakewell tarts, parkin, pecan pie, treacle tart, Dutch apple pie and Welsh cakes on the menu.

House Blend, English Breakfast, Assam, Darjeeling, Afternoon Blend, Earl Grey, Lapsang Souchong, various fruit infusions.

Badger's Café & Patisserie

THE VICTORIA SHOPPING MALL
MOSTYN STREET, LLANDUDNO LL30 2RP
TEL: 01492 871649
FAX: 01492 871974
E-MAIL: MANAGER@BADGERSCAFE.COM
WEB SITE: WWW.BADGERSCAFE.COM
OWNER: BARRY MORTLOCK
MANAGER: DONNA GOODRICH
2000 TEA COUNCIL AWARD OF EXCELLENCE
2001 LES ROUTIERS NEWCOMER OF THE YEAR
2000 WALES TOURIST BOARD AWARDS
2001 INVESTORS IN PEOPLE STANDARD

From the A55, take the A470 Llandudno link road. When you reach the main shopping high street, Badgers is situated in the Victorian Shopping Mall directly opposite Marks & Spencer. There is a multi-storey car park above the shopping mall.

OPEN ALL YEAR. MONDAY–SATURDAY, 9:30AM–5PM; SUNDAY, 11AM–4PM.

Badger's conjures up a Victorian atmosphere with its warm welcome, traditional furniture, tea trolleys, lace curtains and speedy waitresses dressed in neat black dresses, crisp white aprons and white caps. Badgers is often likened to the famous old-fashioned Lyons corner houses because of the girls' "proper" and efficient "nippy" service. The spacious tearoom is elegant and sophisticated inside and relaxingly continental outside, where conservatory-style chairs and tables are surrounded by colourful window boxes.

The menu has a very full and appetising variety of traditional treats — cinnamon toast, buttered crumpets, Welsh bara brith, Welsh rarebit — hot and cold savouries, a delicious range of home-baked morning goods and mouthwatering patisserie are all baked on the premises by resident master bakers (ice mice, dragon eclairs and swan meringues are a must). The traditional Victorian tea is the ultimate treat, offering you a choice of sandwich, bara brith, fresh baked scone and cake — all served on a Victorian tiered cake stand.

English Breakfast, Assam, Darjeeling, Ceylon, Earl Grey, Japanese Sencha, Jasmine, Keemun, Afternoon Pelham Blend and Mango Indica. Flower Tisane is also offered.

Cemlyn Restaurant & Tea Shop

HIGH STREET, HARLECH
GWYNEDD LL46 2YA
TEL/FAX: 01766 780425
E-MAIL: GEOFFREY-COLE@TALKGAS.NET
WEB SITE: WWW.CEMLYNRESTAURANT.CO.UK
OWNERS: JAN & GEOFFREY COLE

Follow signs for Harlech Town Centre. Cemlyn is on the high street between the chemist and the post office. Parking in the high street is restricted, but there is a pay and display car park close by.

EASTER–END OF OCTOBER:
OPEN EVERY DAY, 11AM–4PM;
NOVEMBER–EASTER: SATURDAY AND SUNDAY,
11AM–4PM; OPEN BANK HOLIDAYS.

Cemlyn Tea Shop is just a few yards from Harlech Castle and has wonderful views out over the sea and the Lleyn Peninsula. It was actually the amazing views that attracted the Coles, and it was only after buying the Edwardian terraced building (which was previously a doctor's surgery and a chemist's shop) that they decided to open it as a tearoom. They have created a bright and sunny atmosphere and the yellow, blue, green and orange china adds more colour to the room. Outside in good weather, there's space for customers in the patio garden and on the roof terrace.

Before opening Cemlyn, Jan and Geoff ran a hotel in Llandudno and it is Geoff who does all the baking and cooking. The menu offers such savouries as open sandwiches, the local speciality, Welsh rarebit, homemade wholesome soups and ploughman's lunches. And, of course, a Welsh tearoom can't be without traditional Welsh cakes and bara brith (made with dried fruits that have been soaked in tea), both served with butter. Buttermilk fruited scones are Geoff's speciality, but he also makes delicious chocolate fudge cakes and farmhouse fruit cakes and of course the famous tea cakes.

Assam, Ceylon, Darjeeling, Earl Grey, Lady Grey, Keemun, Lapsang Souchong, Traditional Blend, Blackcurrant, Ginseng and Vanilla, Peppermint, Cranberry, Raspberry and Elderflower, Camomile, Elderflower, Strawberry and Rose, Camomile and Spiced Apple, Lemon and Ginger.

Gwalia Tea Rooms

THE MUSEUM OF WELSH LIFE
ST. FAGANS, CARDIFF CF5 6XB
TEL: 02920 566985
FAX: 02920 566985
OPERATED BY: APPLE CATERING
MEMBER OF A TASTE OF WALES

Take exit 33 off the M4 and follow the signs to the Museum of Welsh Life. The Tea Rooms are situated within the museum grounds.

OPEN ALL YEAR. EVERY DAY, 10AM–4:45PM; OPEN BANK HOLIDAYS; CLOSED CHRISTMAS DAY, BOXING DAY AND NEW YEAR'S DAY. SPECIAL FUNCTIONS (WEDDINGS, CORPORATE ENTERTAINMENT, DINNER PARTIES, ETC) CATERED FOR AT OTHER TIMES.

There is now no entrance charge to the grounds of the museum, so entrance to the tearooms is now free.

Gwalia Tea Rooms are situated on the first floor of Gwalia Stores, a high-class department store that was moved stone by stone from the coal-mining village of Ogmore Vale and meticulously rebuilt within the grounds of the Museum of Welsh Life. The interior, once the corn store, is decorated and furnished in the authentic style of the 1920s, with bentwood chairs, a cut-glass screen at the end of the room and old photographs of the building in its original setting. To get to the tearoom, you have to pass through the old-fashioned ironmongery downstairs, where you can still buy an old tin bath, if you want to. However, you might be more interested in the jams and pickles and other homemade goodies.

The tea-time menu is as traditional as the shop surroundings. All cakes are homemade, using flour from the St. Fagan's mill. Bara brith, Welsh cakes and local specialities, such as Welsh rarebit with homemade dragon chutney, are on the menu daily. On Friday, custard slices are on offer, following a tradition from the days when Mr. Llewellyn, who ran the Gwalia Stores back in Ogmore Vale, baked them himself.

Assam, Darjeeling, Ceylon, Russian, Russian Caravan, Lapsang Souchong, China Oolong, Rose Pouchong, Jasmine, Yunnan, Earl Grey, Kenya, Lemon, Cinnamon-flavoured, Camomile, Rosehip, Peppermint.

Tea-time Traditions from Wales

Welsh traditional cookery shares many dishes with the Scottish and includes oatcakes, honey cakes and breads, and plenty of recipes that use potatoes — potato scones, potato pastry, potato and apple cakes, etc. In Victorian times, potato cakes and potato scones were popular amongst the rural communities. Potato pastry was used to make apple pies and cheese pies, and in the autumn, pastry cases were filled with the pumpkins that grew in Gower. With cinnamon, mace, nutmeg, ginger and raisins, it made a treat at tea or suppertime. The most well-known of Welsh bakestone recipes are pice ar y maen or Welsh cakes — flat round cakes made from a lightly spiced soft dough mixed with currants. Once they are baked to a welcoming and appetising golden colour on both sides, they are dredged with sugar and served to family and visitors at tea time.

As in Scotland, little flat oatcakes were cooked on a bakestone or gridiron and eaten at breakfast, tea and supper. They are descendants of special Beltane oatcakes (bara ceirch), which were prepared for the eve of May Day and eaten traditionally around the Beltane fire, which was lit to welcome the first official day of summer. In Scotland and Wales, the cakes were often made with nine little square knobs, each (as explained in a 1796 manuscript), "dedicated to some particular being, the supposed preserver of their flocks and herds or to some particular animal, the real destroyer of them. Each person turns his face to the fire, breaks off a knob and, flinging it over his shoulder, says, 'This I give to thee, preserve thou my horses: this I give to thee, preserve thou my sheep' and so on."

Laver, the famous Welsh seaweed, is also mixed with oatmeal to make little round, savoury cakes that are often served with bacon. Oatcakes also provided sustenance for farm workers who, at the beginning of spring when the snow had begun to melt on the mountain slopes, would set off uphill to the summer residence or mountain farm where they lived and worked all summer. With them, they carried plenty of curd cheese dishes and a supply of oatcakes (bara ceirch), which they ate with butter and cheese to keep them going through the spring months. At shearing time, they tucked into shearing cake (cacen gneifio) made with butter, brown sugar, caraway seeds, lemon juice, eggs and nutmeg. Harvest workers on arable farms enjoyed harvest cake (teisen blat, which was like a fruit tart but thinner and topped with apples, rhubarb, gooseberries, plums or blueberries), and threshing cake, a fruit bread made with lard or dripping and buttermilk. Welsh lardy cake is similar to the West Country version — the lard coming from the family pig slaughtered at the beginning of winter or in the autumn in order to provide food for the family throughout the dark fallow season. Lard was also used in little yeasted fruit buns made in Pembrokeshire for New Year celebrations.

The Welsh love their food to be spicy, and cinnamon was often traditionally added to honey cakes and puddings. Teisen fêl, a soft honey cake, was served at tea time, but was also a popular dessert drizzled with rum and topped with whipped cream. Welsh gingerbreads have the rich dark flavour of treacle and demerara sugar and the extra texture of candied citrus peel. Bara brith, the Welsh version of the fruit loaf (barm brack in Ireland) is also made with mixed spice and again has the dark flavour of treacle. The dried fruit is often soaked in red wine or cold tea overnight to plump it up before being boiled with sugar, milk, margarine or butter. Flour and eggs are then beaten in and the loaf mixture baked to a lovely moist fruity tea-time bread that is served sliced with butter.

High tea dishes depended on Welsh cheeses to make savoury cheese and fresh herb scones and, of course, Welsh rarebit. Recipes for this favourite tea-time savoury mix grated strong cheese, butter, Worcestershire sauce, dry mustard, flour, beer or ale, a little milk and seasoning. Buck rarebit adds a poached egg and sometimes rashers of bacon to the bubbling golden toasted cheese.

Things to See and Do in Wales

CAMARTHENSHIRE, CONWY, GWYNEDD, GLAMORGAN

Camarthenshire

Felin Newydd Watermill is at Llanwrda in the heart of the Tywi Valley, where tranquil riverside gardens provide a wonderful setting for the tea shop and craft area. Before or after tea, there is plenty to do at the two nearby towns, Llandeilo and Llandovery. Llandeilo is a picturesque town with two castles, Carreg Cennen Castle (Wales' most dramatically situated castle, with its own prehistoric cave) and Dinefwr Castle, and the largest Iron Age hill fort in Wales at Garn Goch. There are also a number of arts and crafts galleries where you can buy locally made gifts, including pottery and paintings. Llandovery, to the northeast of Felyn Newydd, is a pretty market town and an ideal tourist centre from which to explore the rugged scenery of the Brecon Beacons National Park. The chartered town is steeped in myth and legend, and has a castle of Norman origin and a craft centre situated in the Old Meat Market. The Heritage Centre, in a building that dates from the middle of the 18th century, has a number of animated displays featuring the rich history of the town and surrounding areas. The centre is also the National Park and Tourist Information Centre.

Conwy

Guild members Badger's and St. Tudno Hotel are both in Llandudno, a town that combines Victorian style and Edwardian elegance. This stretch of North Wales is famous for its sandy beaches, pier and seaside entertainments, such as Punch-and-Judy shows on the beach, and there are attractions for all the family. Alice Liddell (of *Alice in Wonderland*) spent her childhood summers here and at the Alice in Wonderland Centre, visitors can take a trip down a rabbit hole and relive some of her adventures. Alternatively, take a cable car to the Great Orme, a towering headland at the top of which is a country park, visitor centre and prehistoric copper mines that are open to the public. Llandudno Museum has a child's footprint on a Roman tile and documents the workings of the copper mines. Art lovers will enjoy Oriel Mostyn art gallery, with its exhibits of art, sculpture and photography. Bodafon Farm Park has unusual farm animals, including pot-bellied pigs, alpacas and llamas, and neighbouring Colwyn Bay's Welsh Mountain Zoo has wildlife from all over the world. Colwyn Bay has three miles of golden sands and safe waters and so is a haven for watersport enthusiasts.

Gwynedd

Harlech is home to Cemlyn Restaurant & Tea Shop. A dramatic castle, built by Edward I, dominates the town, and there's a fine beach and some wonderful surrounding countryside. Down the coast, Llanbedr is a quaint village with a narrow stone bridge and impressive houses. A little futher south, Daffryn Ardudwy is a traditional Welsh village close to Cors y Gedol burial chamber, Roman steps and the Dafryn Ardudwy burial chamber. Situated on the edge of Snowdonia, Harlech is a perfect starting point for trips into its amazing countryside and mountain ranges. Serious climbers can enjoy the highest mountains in England and Wales, while ramblers can take gentler walks through the forests and woodlands of Dolgellau and Betwys-Coed, the passes of Talyllyn and Aberglaslyn or along the coastal path. This is also an ideal area for pony-trekking and horse-riding. Agriculture is still the most important industry in the region and there are agricultural shows and countryside events throughout the year.

Glamorgan

Gwalia Tea Rooms at the Museum of Welsh Life is at St. Fagans, just inland from Cardiff. This is one of Europe's largest and most exciting open-air museums, with more than 100 acres containing reconstructions of cottages and buildings from all over Wales. You can discover how people lived and worked, see inside workers' cottages, gardens and outhouses, visit a saddlery, tailor's, bakery, tannery and mill where craftspeople demonstrate their skills. St. Fagans Castle, built here in 1580, is furnished in 19th-century style and has gardens and fishponds. To the south of St. Fagans, Daffryn Gardens is a series of impressive gardens including a rose garden, an arboretum, Pompeiian and theatre garden. From here, it's only a short drive into Cardiff, which has a wealth of museums and interesting historic buildings. Cardiff Castle, guarded by peacocks, is actually three castles in one and spans 2,000 years of history, from Roman times through to Victorian days; andthe National Museum and Gallery contains collections of Impressionist paintings and an award-winning natural history museum; and the extremely modern Cardiff Bay Visitor Centre offers amazing views across the bay and has information about everything to see and do in the town and surrounding area.

John o' Groats
Durness
Balchrick
Thurso
A9
Tongue
Mybster
Ulbster
Unapool
Kinbrace
Lochinver
Lairg
Ullapool
A9
Kincardine
Dornoch
Braemore Junction
Lossiemouth
Fraserburgh
Banff
Achnasheen
A96
Inverness
Craigelliachie
Peterhead
Drumnadrochit
A9
Grantown-on-Spey
A96
A92
Kyle
Inverurie
Invermoriston
Aberdeen
Aviemore
A93
Banchory
Stonehaven
Dalwhinnie
Fort William
Brechin
Pitlochry
A94
Montrose
Aberfeldy
A92
A9
Dundee
Oban
Perth
St Andrews
Callander
Cowdenbeath
Stirling
North Berwick
Dunoon
Glasgow
Edinburgh
Paisley
Motherwell
Peebles
A78
M74
A7
Troon
Kilmarnock
Kelso
Ayr
A68
Moffat
Turnberry
Thornhill
A77
Newton Stewart
Dumfries
Gretna
Stranraer
A75
Kirkcudbright
Drummore

The Scottish Tea Trail

Dumfries

❶ ABBEY COTTAGE TEA ROOMS *p.* 174

Edinburgh

❷ THE CALEDONIAN HILTON HOTEL *p.* 175

❸ THE TEA ROOM *p.* 176

Fife

❹ KIND KYTTOCK'S KITCHEN *p.* 177

Glasgow

❺ MISS CRANSTON'S TEAROOMS *p.* 178

Strathclyde

❻ COACH HOUSE COFFEE SHOP *p.* 179

❼ THE WILLOW TEA ROOMS *p.* 180

❽ WILLOW TEA ROOMS *p.* 181

Abbey Cottage Tea Rooms

26 MAIN STREET, NEW ABBEY
DUMFRIES DG2 8BY
TEL: 01387 850377
FAX: 01848 200536
OWNERS: MORAG MCKIE & KACQUI WILSON
1999 TEA COUNCIL AWARD OF EXCELLENCE
EGON RONAY RECOMMENDED
1998 SCOTTISH THISTLE AWARD
FINALIST "NATURAL COOKING OF SCOTLAND"

Take the A710 from Dumfries to New Abbey (the Solway Coast Road). Abbey Cottage is beside Sweetheart Abbey. The village car park is behind.

OPEN APRIL 1–OCTOBER 31
AND WEEKENDS TO CHRISTMAS.
MONDAY–SUNDAY, 10AM–5PM. TABLE LICENCE.

If you take the Solway Coast Road from Dumfries, you will drive through some wonderful countryside before you find yourself in the quiet village of New Abbey. Here stand the rose-coloured remains of Sweetheart Abbey, built by Lady Devorgilla in the 13th century in memory of her husband, John Balliol, with whom she founded Balliol College, Oxford.

Just across the road from the medieval ruins, 19th-century Abbey Cottage offers a warm welcome and a delicious selection of healthy homemade specialities served in a friendly, caring, non-smoking environment. Morag McKie and her daughter, Jacqui, use high-quality local foods, including locally produced smoked chicken and smoked salmon, and the menu includes low-fat and vegetarian options. Homemade soups, granary breads, Scottish country pâté, and tasty sandwiches or salads are perfect for a light lunch, while the tea-time selection includes Jacqui's excellent carrot or banana cake, and plain, wholemeal or fruit scones served with Morag's homemade jams. In good weather, enjoy your tea in the garden at the back of the pretty cottage, and before leaving visit the craft shop next door to browse amongst the very attractive selection of local pottery, candles and tablewares.

Traditional Blend, Assam, Darjeeling, Ceylon, Earl Grey and Decaffeinated. Fruit-flavoured teas and herbal infusions are also offered.

The Caledonian Hilton Hotel

PRINCES STREET
EDINBURGH EH1 2AB
TEL: 0131 222 8888
FAX: 0131 222 8889
GENERAL MANAGER: DAGMAR MÜHLE
1996, 1999 TEA COUNCIL AWARD OF EXCELLENCE

The Caledonian is situated at the west end of Princes Street, adjoining Lothian Road.

OPEN ALL YEAR.
AFTERNOON TEA IS SERVED FROM 3–5:30PM.

The "Caley" (the locals' affectionate name for the Caledonian Hilton Hotel) occupies a prominent position in one of Scotland's finest streets. The view of Edinburgh Castle from the windows is spectacular, and the setting creates an interesting and relaxing location for informal lunches and gracious afternoon teas between shopping and sightseeing. The menu, which changes regularly, offers a sparkling selection of wonderful sandwiches with truly imaginative fillings such as roast Angus beef with horseradish mayonnaise, and and St. Benoît brie with apple and chutney. The traditional afternoon tea consists of finger sandwiches such as cucumber and crème fraîche, smoked salmon on brown bread, egg mayonnaise on white bread, a selection of warm scones and pancakes with clotted cream and preserves, and a choice of pastries. For a special occasion, choose the celebration tea with its added glass of champagne, or simply enjoy a pot of tea and a traditional Scotch pancake.

Breakfast Blend, Assam, Ceylon, Darjeeling, Earl Grey, Lapsang Souchong, Keemun. Fruit-flavoured teas and herbal infusions are also available.

The Tea Room

158 CANONGATE
ROYAL MILE, EDINBURGH EH8 8DD
TEL: 07771 501 679
OWNERS: TRISH NOON & JOSEPH WINDERS

The Tea Room is situated opposite Canongate Tollbooth on Royal Mile between the castle and Holyrood Palace.

OPEN ALL YEAR.
MONDAY–SUNDAY, 10:30AM–4PM.

In the area around the Tea Room and especially in the Royal Mile, much of Scotland's turbulent history has been enacted. The area is steeped in an extremely colourful history and so the shop is an ideal place to stop and perhaps read a guide book and drink in the atmosphere of this fascinating area of the town.

When Trish and Joseph took over the premises in September 2000, it was already a tea shop, but they spent four months completely refurbishing and restyling the room. They both have five-star hotel experience and had a very clear idea of how their tearoom was to look. It now offers a traditional feel with linen tablecloths and watercolours on show that are for sale by a local artist. The menu lists all sorts of lunchtime dishes — soups, sandwiches, toasted sandwiches, scrumptious home-baked scones and a range of cakes and desserts. Cream teas are available throughout the year, traditional afternoon tea is served during the summer, and on Thursday afternoonsfrom 2 pm to 5pm, there are tea leaf readings over a pot of tea and a shortbread biscuit. So not only can you refresh yourself with tea, but also learn about your future.

English Breakfast, Assam, Earl Grey, Ceylon, Darjeeling, Jasmine, various herbals.

Kind Kyttock's Kitchen

CROSS WYND, FALKLAND

FIFE, KY15 7BE

TEL: 01337 857477

OWNERS: LIZ & BERT DALRYMPLE

1991, 1992, 2000 & 2001 TEA COUNCIL
AWARD OF EXCELLENCE

EGON RONAY RECOMMENDED

1997 WINNER OF THE MACALLAN TASTE
OF SCOTLAND BEST TEA ROOM AWARD

Follow signs from the M90 for Falkland Palace. Cross Wynd joins the high street at the fountain and Mercat Cross.

OPEN ALL YEAR EXCEPT FOR TWO WEEKS FROM CHRISTMAS DAY–JANUARY 5. TUESDAY–SUNDAY, 10:30AM–5:30PM; CLOSED MONDAYS.

Kind Kyttock was the heroine of a poem by William Dunbar, the early Scots poet. "The Ballad of Kind Kyttock" tells how she settled in Falkland and served good food and drink to weary travellers. Liz and Bert Dalrymple, who came here from Glasgow 30 years ago to find a more peaceful life, follow her example and offer tasty traditional Scottish fare in a relaxed atmosphere to thousands of visitors every year from all over the world. In fact, a group of Americans arrived one day with a cutting from the *Los Angeles Times* giving a very positive review of Kind Kyttock's, so news of how good it is has obviously spread far and wide.

The menu has an appealing Scottish flavour — Midlothian oatcakes served with cheddar cheese, Scottish pancakes with cream and homemade apricot jam or fresh fruit, traditional cloutie dumpling with cream, and an irresistible Rob Roy ice cream with butterscotch sauce and petticoat tail shortbread. All these good things are served in two rooms, upstairs and down, where dark furniture, colourful tablecloths ,and an interesting selection of prints and paintings on the walls create a very pleasing, old-fashioned atmosphere.

House Blend, Darjeeling, Earl Grey, China, Ceylon, Assam, Russian, various herbals.

Miss Cranston's Tearooms

33 GORDON STREET
GLASGOW G1 3PF
TEL: 0141 204 1122
FAX: 0141 620 0045
E-MAIL: INFO@MISSCRANSTONS.COM
WEB SITE: WWW.MISSCRANSTONS.COM
OWNER: HUGH BRADFORD
MANAGER: RHENA MCKINNON

From Glasgow Central Railway Station, come out of the main entrance and turn right into Gordon Street. Miss Cranston's is two blocks along on the right-hand side.

OPEN ALL YEAR.
MONDAY–SATURDAY, 8AM–6PM; CLOSED SUNDAY.

Named after Kate Cranston, who at the end of the 19th century opened a chain of very successful tearooms in Glasgow, this charming and artistic venue offers a welcome reminder of bygone days. In much the same way that Kate Cranston commissioned the then-unknown designer Charles Rennie Mackintosh to create the interior and exterior of her shops, the new Miss Cranston's has been developed with similar vision and enthusiasm for local talent. Two young Glasgow designers, Anne Perry and Karen Longmuir, have together created an unusual, stylish and exciting environment.

As you enter the shop, the ground floor is a bakery and patisserie packed full of deliciously mouthwatering cakes, breads and pastries made by the company's own bakers. An elegant staircase leads up to a genteel room decorated with charming etchings on copper panels of old recipes, and tall windows allow in a soft light that creates a very gentle atmosphere.

Using local produce as far as possible, the menu offers a wonderful selection of sandwiches, soups, salads, all sorts of traditional Scottish dishes, delicious scones, pancakes and crumpets, muffins, Danish pastries, continental patisserie, cakes and desserts. Everything is of an extremely high standard, and there is something to satisfy and please absolutely everybody.

Miss Cranston's House Blend, Darjeeling, Assam, Golden Ceylon, China Keemun, Earl Grey, Lapsang Souchong, Gunpowder, Japanese Sencha, China Oolong, Jasmine with Flowers Peppermint, Passion Fruit with Orange, Camomile, Rosehip and Elderberry, Strawberry, Lavender Flower.

Coach House Coffee Shop

LUSS, LOCH LOMOND, ARGYLL
SCOTLAND G83 8NN
TEL: 01436 860341
FAX: 01436 860336
E-MAIL: ENQUIRIES@LOCHLOMONDTRADING.COM
WEB SITE: WWW.LOCHLOMONDTRADING.COM
OWNERS: ROWENA & GARY GROVES

BOOKER EXCELLENCE AWARD
FOR "BEST SPECIALIST CATERER" 2001
2000 WINNER OF TOURIST BOARD
FX AWARD "BEST PLACE TO EAT"

Follow signs to Luss from the A82 (Glasgow to Crianlarich). In Luss, park in the car park and walk towards the centre of the village. The coffee shop is next to the church.

OPEN ALL YEAR EXCEPT CHRISTMAS DAY.
WINTER: EVERY DAY, 10AM–5PM.
SUMMER: EVERY DAY, 10AM–6PM.

The genuine Scottish atmosphere of the Coach House in Luss makes it a really wonderful experience for both locals and tourists. The setting is perfect — a Grade I conservation village, the beautiful countryside around Loch Lomond — and inside the shop, the foyer displays a range of exclusive Scottish merchandise, and the coach house décor includes Harris tweed drapes, hand-painted tartan crockery, an open log fire and a sofa with a warning not to wake guests who may have fallen into a doze after indulging in too many of Rowena's home-baked cakes. With Gary in his kilt and a menu that reflects the locality (with such treats as Skeachan fruit cake, whisky cake and stokies — traditional soft bread rolls — filled with mature Scottish cheddar or egg mayonnaise made with eggs from the Groves' free-range Black Rock hens), the Scottish theme runs throughout. Despite its name, the coffeehouse serves an excellent variety of teas and tea-time traditionals — scones, cinnamon toast, shortbreads, muffins — as well as more robust Scottish lunchtime fillers, including haggis with neeps and tatties.

Famous Edinburgh, Darjeeling, Lapsang Souchong, Earl Grey, Assam, China, Keemun, Gunpowder, Ceylon. Fruit and herbal infusions are also offered.

The Willow Tea Rooms

217 SAUCHIEHALL STREET
GLASGOW G2 3EX
TEL/FAX: 0141 332 0521
E-MAIL: TEA@WILLOWTEAROOMS.CO.UK
WEB SITE: WWW.WILLOWTEAROOMS, CO.UK
OWNER: ANNE MULHERN
EGON RONAY RECOMMENDED

The tearoom is on the first floor above Henderson the jewellers.

OPEN ALL YEAR. MONDAY–SATURDAY, 9:30AM–4:30 PM; SUNDAY, NOON–4PM.

While tea shops often manage to create an impression of past times, the Willow Tea Room is a genuine example of turn-of-the-century design. The Room de Luxe is the only remaining room of Miss Kate Cranston's "tearoom empire," created for her by Charles Rennie Mackintosh and opened on October 29, 1903. His wonderful Arts and Crafts style, which heralded Art Deco, gave his architecture, furniture, lamps and tablewares the strong rectilinear contours and geometric shapes that fascinate the eye. Mackintosh had previously designed the interior for three other Cranston tearooms, but the Willow allowed him to style the exterior and interior of the building. He completely changed the appearance of the original tenement building that became the Willow by adding looped ironwork and clean parallel lines and squares to the façade. Inside, he used a white, pink, grey and silver colour scheme, and designed the now-famous ladder-back chairs and a frieze of leaded coloured glass that ran around the walls.

In 1983, the tearoom was restored by the current owner, Anne Mulherne. The mirror friezes, the gesso panel and the ornate leaded doors had happily survived, and the chairs and tables were reproduced to Mackintosh's original 1904 design. An unhurried atmosphere matches the elegance of the interior and the comprehensive list of teas, favourite tea-time traditionals and cakes makes this a very special experience.

Tearoom Blend, Breakfast Blend, Earl Grey, Lapsang Souchon, Darjeeling, Ceylon, Assam, Rose Petal, Keemun, Jasmine Blossom, Yunnan, Kenya, Rose Pouchong, decaffeinated, various fruit-flavoured teas and herbal infusions.

Willow Tea Rooms

97 BUCHANAN STREET
GLASGOW G1 3HF
TEL: 0141 204 5242
FAX: 0141 204 5242
OWNER: ANNE MULHERN

Buchanan Street is in the city centre, just round the corner from both Queen Street Station and Central Station. Willow Tea Rooms is on the section of Buchanan Street that runs from Argyle Street to St. Vincent Place.

OPEN ALL YEAR. MONDAY–SATURDAY, 9AM–5:30PM; SUNDAY, NOON–5PM.

In July 1997, Anne Mulhern opened this new shop immediately next door to what was once Kate Cranston's original Buchanan Street Tea Rooms. This shop was Charles Rennie Mackintosh's first involvement in Miss Cranston's once-famous chain of tearooms. His work there was limited to wall murals, but he went on to design several other rooms for her. This new property contains re-creations of the White Dining Room, which he created for her Ingram Street shop in 1900, and the intensely blue Chinese Room that he designed for the same premises in 1911. Anybody who enjoys Mackintosh design and architecture will love the style of both rooms, where Anne has lovingly re-created the atmosphere of a bygone age.

The menu has a strong Scottish emphasis. Scottish farmhouse cheddar cheese tops jacket potatoes and drizzles from toasted sandwiches; Scottish smoked salmon fills sandwiches, croissants and bagels, or accompanies scrambled eggs or smoked trout; Arbroath smokies are served with lemon and hot buttered toast, and the cakes and desserts include Scottish shortbread and traditional cloutie dumpling.

Assam, Ceylon, Darjeeling, Earl Grey, English Breakfast, Gunpowder, Jasmine, Keemun, Kenya, Lapsang Souchong, Rose Petal, Russian Caravan, Tea Room Blend. Herbal infusions are also offered.

Tea-time Traditions from Scotland

Many of Scotland's regional specialities result from the plentiful supply of oats and potatoes that was always available in the area. Gingerbreads and parkins, made with treacle or syrup, were given a wonderful nutty texture by the addition of oatmeal (a broonie was originally an oatmeal gingerbread) and sometimes almonds. Recipes varied from town to town — Edinburgh gingerbread contained raisins and almonds, while the Inverness variety was made with lemon peel, green ginger and cream. Flat round oatcakes were a staple at breakfast, tea and supper, and were traditionally baked on the griddle or girdle that was common to the everyday cookery of most Celtic countries. The flat iron utensil was (and still is) a crucial piece of kitchen equipment for baking potato cakes and potato scones, Scottish drop scones (those delicious small soft round pancakes, often made with golden syrup or corn syrup), Scottish pancakes (also called Scots crumpets and a larger version of drop scones, they were wrapped around butter and jam), scones, treacle scones, soda scones and bannocks (yeasted fruit loaves eaten sliced and buttered at tea time). Oatmeal bannocks were a Hallowe'en speciality. Suet tea pancakes straight from the girdle or bakestone were spread with butter and jam and then rolled up and eaten hot.

Scotland is famous too for its shortbreads, which had their origin at Roman wedding feasts, at which it was the custom to break a wheaten cake over the head of the bride. The recipe had to produce a very crumbly cake that would break easily and not hurt the girl as it was broken, and the high fat (or shortening) content led to the name. The buttery, light, biscuit-like cake gradually became a Hogmanay speciality and was made with the very best butter and flour to create something mouthwateringly delicious.

Another Hogmanay treat is black bun — the rich, heavy Scottish version of Christmas cake. Like mince pies, it evolved from dough-crusted raised pies full of spiced meats that were once the traditional Christmas food. A rich cake mixture of brown sugar, dried fruits, spices, chopped almonds and walnuts, lemon juice and brandy is baked inside a pastry case and then stored for at least a week to mature, ready for New Year celebrations. First footers bringing good luck to the house as the new year begins are traditionally offered the first slice of black bun and a glass of whisky or Athole brose — a warming mixture of whisky, honey, water and oatmeal.

There is plenty of heather honey in Scotland and traditional recipes add it to cakes, biscuits and sometimes to drop scones as a more subtle sweetener than sugar or syrup.

Scottish high teas often included potted beef, potted shrimps and Scotch woodcock, made by pounding anchovies with butter and pepper and spreading the mixture on toast before topping it with creamy scrambled eggs. With a rich supply of herring and haddock caught regularly by local fishermen, other high tea favourites included kipper toasts, herring roes on toast, fisherman's pie, Finnan toasts (haddock with gherkins and cream on toast) and creamed Finnan haddie — rather like a Welsh rarebit, but with the addition of smoked haddock to the cheese sauce. When making the traditional rarebit, a spoonful of whisky is often added to the mixture.

Dundee is the home of both marmalade and Dundee cake. The story of the bitter marmalade from the town tells how a Mr. James Keiller bought a large quantity of Seville oranges from a Spanish ship, which took refuge in the harbour during a storm in the early 18th century. He bought them cheaply and expected to make a good profit, but the fruits were so bitter that no one wanted them. His wife Janet had the brilliant idea of turning them into a bitter orange marmalade, which proved very popular. Dundee cake, of course, links with the orange theme with its standard ingredient of fresh grated and candied orange peel.

Whereas English lace makers recognised St. Catherine as their protector, for the Scottish, St. Andrew was considered to be the true patron saint of lace makers, and his day was marked by the drinking of methaglin (rather like mead flavoured with malt and spices) and the eating of Tanders cakes. Very similar to St. Catherine's Cattern cakes, the plain dough was made more exciting for the feast day with extra fat, caraway seeds and sugar.

Things to See and Do in Scotland

DUMFRIES AND GALLOWAY, EDINBURGH, FIFE, STRATHCLYDE

Dumfries and Galloway

Just inland from the Solway Firth lies New Abbey, the location of Abbey Cottage Tea Rooms. Sweetheart Abbey is the splendid remains of a late 13th- and early 14th-century Cistercian abbey founded by Devorgilla, Lady of Galloway, in memory of her husband, John Balliol. The Shambellie House Museum of Costume is in a nearby Victorian country house and has a remarkable collection of period costumes that are on show in the appropriate room settings. New Abbey Corn Mill is a carefully renovated 18th-century water-powered oatmeal mill in full working order. It gives demonstrations in the summer. A short drive north brings you to Dumfries, which has a museum located in the Observatory that documents the history of southwest Scotland. There is also the Dumfries and Galloway Aviation Museum, which charters aviation history since the First World War. In Castle Street, a plaque on the wall marks the site of Grey Friars Monastery where, in 1306, Robert the Bruce is said to have stabbed John, "The Red Comyn," a rival for the throne of Scotland.

Edinburgh

The Caledonian Hilton Hotel is perfectly positioned for visiting Edinburgh's town centre. Dominating the hill above Princes Street is the Castle, an imposing royal fortress that now houses the Scottish crown jewels, the Stone of Destiny and the Scottish National War Museum. The Tea Room is situated in the Royal Mile that runs down from the Castle to Holyroodhouse. Walking from the Castle in the direction of Holyrood, there are countless fascinating buildings and things to see and do. The Tartan Weaving Mill and Exhibition is a working mill that tells the story of tartan and how it gets from the sheep to the kilt, and the outlook tower has a camera obscura. And you can visit Gladstone's land (a 17th-century tenement house that shows how people lived in old Edinburgh), the Museum of Childhood, with everything from teddy bears to castor oil, the Scotch Whisky Heritage Centre, the Writers' Museum and lots more. In the Georgian part of the town is the National Trust Georgian House, with a fascinating collection of furnishings and household items from the 18th century. On the Firth of Forth, north of the main part of the town, visitors can step on board the royal yacht *Britannia*, which is berthed at Leith. There's so much to do in Edinburgh, and the Caledonian and the Tea Room are perfectly placed for refreshing cups of tea in between all the walking and sightseeing. Edinburgh is also host to a series of cultural events that run throughout the year—science, flight, jazz and blues, military tattoo, books, vintage vehicles and film are just some of the subjects that attract visitors from all over the world.

Fife

Kind Kyttock's Kitchen is set in the Royal Burgh of Falkland amidst the rich agricultural land of the valley of the River Eden, known as the Howe of Fife. The Royal Palace of Falkland, now maintained by the National Trust for Scotland, was once the country residence of the Stewart kings and queens, and it was from there that they hunted deer and wild boar in the forests of Fife. It was built between 1501 and 1541 by James V, and the palace has some of the finest architecture of its period. With the Lomond Hills as the backdrop, the town has an appeal all its own, and visitors will enjoy wandering through the narrow streets soaking up the sense of history. The town is full of old weavers' cottages, reminders of the former local industry. Of the three factories, only one, St. John's Works, remains today. Benefactors Margaret and Onesiphorous Tyndall Bruce financed the rebuilding of the parish church in 1826 and erected the Bruce Fountain in the market place. Tyndall Bruce's statue stands outside the church.

Argyll

Coach House Coffee Shop is in Luss, a very attractive community that nestles on the sandy western shore of Loch Lomond. The location is famous as the setting for the television series *High Road*. The contrast between highland

and lowland Scotland is most apparent here. To the south, the landscape is gentle and rolling, while the Arrochar Alps overlook the northern end of the Loch. In Luss itself, are the Thistle Bagpipe Works and the Inverbeg Galleries, which have one of the largest selections in the U.K. of original oil and watercolour paintings by Scottish, European and international artists. At the southern tip of the Loch is Balloch Castle Country Park and also at Balloch, the Lomond Shores and National Park Visitor Centre has just opened. It offers breathtaking views of the landscape, shows films about the area and its history, and has information about the surrounding area.

Strathclyde

Glasgow is home to three Guild tea shops — Miss Cranton's near the main railway station and two Willow Tearooms, one near the railway station and one in the main shopping area of Sauchiehall Street. All three have close links with Charles Rennie Mackintosh, the famous Glasgow-born architect and designer. With its 18th-century merchant city history, its Victorian skyline, its Art Nouveau importance, and contemporary buildings with minimalist glass and titanium, the town offers something for everyone. Buildings of architectural interest include the Glasgow School of Art, Mackintosh's masterpiece and still a working school; the Charles Rennie Mackintosh Society, the only church designed by Mackintosh and with Japanese and Gothic influences and impressive stained glass; the Lighthouse, Scotland's Centre for Architecture; House for an Art Lover, inspired by original designs by Mackintosh and set in beautiful parkland; Mackintosh House, the principal rooms from the Glasgow home of Mackintosh and his wife Margaret, reconstructed in the Hunterian Art Gallery at the University of Glasgow. Other places of interest include the Gallery of Modern Art (which houses four floors of paintings, sculptures and installations from around the world), Glasgow Cathedral (the only Scottish medieval cathedral to have survived the Reformation), the Hunterian Museum (with exhibitions on geology, archaeology, the Romans in Scotland, coins, medals and natural history), the Museum of Piping (the world's foremost museum for the history and music of the highland bagpipe), Glasgow Science Centre (which celebrates scientific innovation and has a 120-seat planetarium) and People's Palace (which tells the story of Glasgow and its impact on the world from 1750 to the present day). On the outskirts of the town, Pollok House is Glasgow's oldest house, dating back to 1471 and with period furniture and a medieval theme garden. In Pollok Country Park, the Burrell Collection has more than 8,000 art objects amassed by shipping magnate Sir William Burrell.

Tea Rooms Around the World

A consumer survey carried out last year found that 60 percent of British holiday-makers miss a decent cup of tea more than anything else when they are travelling abroad. Because many nations around the world are not tea drinkers and do not normally offer it in restaurants, wine bars and cafes, travelling outside the U.K. on holiday or for business can mean having to go without. Because of this, many British holiday-makers actually pack a supply of their favourite tea so that they can at least brew a wake-up cuppa in their hotel room in the morning and another in the evening. But what about during the day when they are out and about sightseeing, shopping or, in the case of business travellers, on their way to meetings? Coffee, beer, wine and soft drinks are easy to find, but oh, for a decent cup of tea!

To help readers find those elusive cups of tea outside the U.K., the Tea Guild is constantly searching for more quality tearooms to promote through the international section of the guidebook. As interest in tea has grown globally in the past 10 years or so, more and more enterprising people have started serving quality tea, and more hotels in some quite unlikely places have started offering comprehensive tea lists as part of their menus. One country where a committed interest in tea over the last few years has meant an exciting increase in the number of excellent tearooms is the United States. So we decided to ask Bruce Richardson, owner of Elmwood Inn, our first American entry to the guide, to recommend other U.S. tearooms for inclusion. He subsequently visited a selection of tea venues around the U.S. on our behalf, and we now have five new honorary members. An already passionate love of tea is still growing in Japan, and the three tearooms run by Barakura English Garden continue to do extremely well, whilst the Mariage Frères shops in Paris are still firm favourites.

As the Guild discovers more high-quality tearooms, tea lounges and tea shops abroad that measure up to our high standards, so this section will grow. We hope by next year to be able to recommend many more shops in Europe and other countries around the world. Tea is, after all, an internationally popular beverage.

Mariage Frères

Mariage Frères has three shops at the following addresses:

MARIAGE FRÈRES LE MARAIS
30 RUE DU BOURG-TIBOURG, 75004 PARIS
TEL: (+33) (1) 42 72 28 11
FAX: (+33) (1) 42 74 51 68

Take the metro to Saint-Paul. Take rue de Rivoli, then turn right into rue du Bourg-Tibourg.

MARIAGE FRÈRES
RIVE GAUCHE
13 RUE DES GRANDS AUGUSTINS 75006 PARIS
TEL: (+33) (1) 40 51 82 50
FAX: (+33) (1) 44 07 07 52

Take the metro to Saint-Michel. Take rue Saint-André des Arts, then turn right into rue des Grands Augustins.

MARIAGE FRÈRES ETOILE
260 RUE DU FAUBOURG-SAINT-HONORÉ 75008 PARIS
TEL: (+33) (1) 46 22 18 54
FAX: (+33) (1) 42 67 18 54

Take the metro to Ternes. Turn left into rue du Faubourg-Saint-Honoré.

OPENING TIMES FOR ALL THREE SHOPS ARE THE SAME. OPEN ALL YEAR. THE SHOPS ARE OPEN MONDAY–SUNDAY, 10:30AM–7:30PM. THE TEAROOMS ARE OPEN NOON–7PM.

Mariage Frère's links with tea began in the mid-17th century, when Nicolas Mariage travelled to the Orient on behalf of Louis XIV and the French East India Company, while his brother Pierre made voyages to Madagascar, also as special envoy for the East India Company. During the 18th century, Jean-François Mariage was still trading teas and spices, a business that was carried on by his sons. The present company was established by Jean-François' grandsons, Henri and Edouard, in 1854 and is today the oldest tea importer in France. Tea lovers can choose from the list of more than 400 teas from all over the world in the three Parisien Mariage Frères *salons de thé*, in several shops in Tokyo, on the fourth floor of Dickens and Jones in London, at T Salon in New York City or by mail order.

Any visitor to Paris should make a special point of taking tea at one of the salons — they are absolutely not to be missed. The original shop in the Marais has a classic colonial feel with elegant palms, calm, relaxing neutral colours and gracious staff who look after guests with impeccable care and attention. The first-floor tearoom in the shop on the Rive Gauche, opened in 1990, and the newest Etoile tearoom, opened in 1997, are both very similar in their period elegance and charm, and serve the same wonderful gateaux, tortes and tartes, and the same selection of fine teas. These are world emporia of tea. You can choose black, green, white, oolong, pu'er, compressed or flavoured teas from India, Sri Lanka, China, Taiwan, Japan, Korea, Bangladesh, Nepal, Indonesia, Vietnam, Russia, Turkey, Iran, Argentina, Brazil, Cameroon, Kenya, Zimbabwe, Rwanda, South Africa and more — in fact, from any of the 30 or so tea-producing areas of the world. The list changes from time to time with the changing quality of teas from different gardens and estates each year, but, for example, if you wish to drink a Darjeeling, you will have a choice of approximately 18 first flush, 20 second flush and several Darjeeling blends. If China black is your preference, there are teas from Yunnan, Anhui, Szechwan and Fujian. If you prefer Earl Grey, Mariage usually offer about 12 different blends, ranging through imperial, silver tip, oolong, green, decaffeinated, English and smoky varieties.

Once you have chosen your particular leaf (with, if necessary, the help and advice of the waiter), a great deal of attention goes into the actual brewing of your tea. It is not simply a question here of putting leaves into a pot, pouring on some boiling water and delivering the pot to the table. At Mariage, the leaves are carefully measured, the brewing time is calculated and timed, and the water temperature is checked before the infused tea is decanted into a clean pot and delivered to your table. So, what each guest enjoys is a perfect liquor in which there are no leaves that can become bitter by over-brewing. To ensure that different flavoured leaves do not contaminate and spoil your tea, scented teas are served in colour-coded pots. Everything is done with such care and style here, and the shops attract tea lovers and connoisseurs from Paris and beyond.

After sampling one of the fabulous teas, don't miss the retail counters in each of the shops. They are almost like museums with unusual teapots and brewing equipment, books, tea caddies, compressed teas, tea jellies and tea-scented candles. The teas themselves are stored in beautiful old-fashioned large black caddies, each sitting in its own niche in the bank of shelves against the wall. How to choose? Take your time and ask for help. All the staff really do know what they are selling and are delighted to explain and offer advice before you buy for yourself or select gifts to take home to friends.

And the shops do in fact each have a little museum, which offer a fascinating insight into the history of tea and tea brewing with their collections of rare brewing equipage, antique caddies, and teapots and teacups of all styles, from ancient Chinese to 20th-century Art Deco. Whatever you do, if you are in Paris, don't miss Mariage Frères. Each shop is an absolute gem.

450 fine loose leaf teas from all world tea regions.

Elmwood Inn

205 EAST FOURTH STREET
PERRYVILLE, KENTUCKY 40468 (USA)
TEL: 859 332 2400
FAX: 859 332 9740
E-MAIL: TEA@ELMWOODINN.COM
WEB SITE: WWW.ELMWOODINN.COM
OWNERS: BRUCE & SHELLY RICHARDSON

Elmwood Inn is located 90 minutes southeast of Louisville and 60 minutes southwest of Lexington.

OPEN ALL YEAR ON THURSDAY, FRIDAY, SATURDAY. SEATING AT 1PM AND 3PM.

Elmwood Inn was built in 1842 for a local merchant by the name of Burton, and the general village store that he ran still stands on the other side of the river. During the Civil War, the house served as a hospice for wounded soldiers from the 1862 Battle of Perryville, then from 1896 until 1924 it became Elmwood Academy. Later, it was turned into a restaurant, and then fell into disrepair and stood totally neglected until the spring of 1990, when the Richardsons bought the derelict building and spent the next few years restoring it to its period charm. Once all the hard work was finished, they initially ran the house as a bed and breakfast as well as a stylish tea venue, but when teas became by far the most important part of their activities, Bruce and Shelly started concentrating totally on that side of the business. At first Shelly baked all the cakes and scones herself, but now employs a skilled and aptly named pastry chef, Debbie Wheat, to create the wonderful selection of sweet and savoury afternoon tea delicacies.

Elmwood has 10 tables in the dining room, library and garden, and it is best to book ahead as available places are rapidly reserved by guests who drive or fly in from California or New England to sample the delicious four-course tea. The menu changes each month and is themed to the season or to a particular festivity. So April brings Shakespeare Tea, with Merchant Tea Sandwich, English Garden Sandwich, Juliet's Sand Bars and Titania's Fairy Cake; in August, guests are served the Sunflower Tea with sunflower wholewheat scones, blueberry bars, summer cake and nectarine sorbet, while the Kentucky Harvest Tea serves you Shaker lemon tarts, traditional chocolate bourbon balls, country ham pâté with corn muffins and Elmwood Inn Woodford Pudding with blackberry brandy sauce. Each menu suggests a suitable tea to complement the sandwiches and desserts, but there is also a comprehensive list of teas to choose from.

Both Shelly and Bruce Richardson hold degrees in music and share a passion for the arts, and have brought an added cultural dimension to Elmwood Inn. Each month they display the work of different Kentucky artists, while the music that plays during afternoon tea is carefully chosen to reflect the time of year, a special event or to enhance the theme of the meal being served. The diary of events also includes live performances by local string quartets, brass bands, pianists or singers, and *plein air* painting with artists working on the lawn. The blend of sensations at Elmwood is really very special. It has been said that "the mixture of tea, beautiful foods, gardens, art and music feeds the soul as well as the body at the Elmwood Inn. You taste first with your eyes at this sanctuary for the spirit" and, in the Richardsons' own words, "Tea is about conversation and taking time for the beautiful things in life — the whole culture of tea is what entices people." The Richardsons have recently started offering training courses for existing and potential tearoom owners and also organise group visits to Britain for American tea lovers.

Elmwood Inn also has two gift shops where visitors can buy packages of tea, homemade lemon or cranberry curd, scone mix, shortbread mix, cookies, gourmet sugar cubes decorated with tiny sugar flowers and teacups, and copies of the three books that the Richardsons have written: *A Year of Teas at the Elmwood Inn*, *A Tea for All Seasons* and *The Great Tea Rooms of Britain*.

Traditional English Breakfast, Darjeeling, Irish Blend, Mayor's Cup, Kentucky Blend, Earl Grey, Lapsang Souchong, Keemun, China Oolong, Gunpowder, Jasmine, Orange and Spice, Raspberry, Apricot, Peach, Rose, Wild Cherry, Blackcurrant.

MacNab's Tea Room

PO BOX 206 BACK RIVER ROAD
BOOTHBAY, MAINE 04537 (USA)
TEL: 207 633 7222; FAX: 207 633 0572
E-MAIL: TEA@MACNABSTEAROOM.COM
WEB SITE: WWW.MACNABSTEAROOM.COM
OWNER: FRANCES ANN BROWNE
MANAGER: LAURIE CARTIER

MacNab's is 60 minutes east of Portland, Maine. Take Route 1 north to Route 27 south to Boothbay centre. Come into Boothbay and at the first junction turn right onto Back River Road. Follow this road for 0.4 mile and MacNab's is on your left.

OPEN JUNE TO SEPTEMBER: TUESDAY–SATURDAY, 10AM–5PM; OCTOBER TO MAY: TUESDAY–SATURDAY, 10AM–4PM; CLOSED SUNDAYS, MONDAYS AND OFFICIAL HOLIDAYS.

MacNab's Tea Room is housed in an 1803 New England-style Cape surrounded by beautiful flower gardens. The theme is Scottish, reflecting Frances's mother's family background and the fact that many Scots settled in this area of Maine. The dining room is furnished with an eclectic variety of antiques and the food is served on antique china from around the world.

The lunch menu includes chef's speciality, highland pie, which is made from real highland beef locally grown in Maine and topped with skirlie. The cock-a-leekie soup is another favourite and in summer, crab salad is added to the menu. At tea time, another hit with the customers is the homemade lemon curd, which is great with scones. Frances offers a wide choice of scones — plain, blueberry, lemon ginger, orange poppy, orange chocolate chip and raisin — which can be eaten with grape preserves, honey, marmalade and other jams. There is a delicious chocolate chai cake, shortbreads, lemon tarts and digestive oatcakes served with cheese.

The gift shop sells a wonderful collection of handmade tea cosies, teapots from all over the world, assorted tea antiques, modern tea accessories, and 80 varieties of tea that are available both retail and wholesale.

More than 50 varieties of tea, including five House Blends, Black and Green teas from China, Japan and India, Chais, Oolongs, Pu-er, Smoky Black Teas and Fruit-flavoured and Flower Teas, Jasmine Pearl, Green Lychee, Green Tea Peonies, Darjeeling Musk Oolong, Darjeeling Whyte served in a Gaiwan cup.

The Fairmont Empress Hotel

THE FAIRMONT EMPRESS
721 GOVERNMENT STREET
VICTORIA, BC, CANADA V8W 1WS
TEL: 250 384 8111
FAX: 250 381 5959
E-MAIL: THEEMPRESS@FAIRMONT.COM
WEB SITE: WWW.FAIRMONT.COM
FOOD AND BEVERAGE MANAGER: AXEL BINNEBOESE
TEA MANAGER: CAROL COWAN

The Fairmont Empress is located in the heart of Victoria's inner harbour. Victoria is easily accessible by plane, boat or ferry. It is just 37 kilometres from the city of Vancouver.

OPEN ALL YEAR. THERE ARE FOUR SITTINGS IN THE TEA LOBBY: 12:30PM, 2PM, 3:30PM, 5PM.

The Fairmont Empress is renowned for its traditional afternoon tea. Each year, more than 100,000 international visitors take tea in the Tea Lobby or Palm Court, with its stained-glass dome, and enjoy what has been a much-loved part of the hotel's activities since 1908. With a portrait of Queen Mary on the wall by the fireside and a magnificent view of Victoria's inner harbour, the Tea Lobby is a charming setting for tea. For those who enjoy taking tea outdoors, the hotel's front veranda also has views over the harbour. In the Lobby and Palm Court, the tables are set with Royal Doulton china, live music plays softly in the background and as guests are asked to observe a smart casual dress code, the atmosphere is one of elegance and refinement. Tea starts with fresh seasonal berries and then a three-tier cake stand brings a selection of sandwiches filled with smoked salmon and cream cheese, egg salad and cucumber, and carrot and ginger, a plateful of fresh scones with homemade strawberry jam and thick Jersey cream and, atop that, a tray of light pastries. The long list of people who have taken tea here include Queen Elizabeth II, Rudyard Kipling, Spencer Tracy, the King and Queen of Siam, and Mel Gibson.

Empress Blend: the Assam (second flush) gives a thick malty and full bodied character; the Kenya (Kiambou region) gives superb fruity and spritely flavour with a lovely finish; Ceylon (Dimbula region) gives an airy almost piquant flavour that opens the blend; and the China (Anhui Provence) gives a burgundy depth with light oaky notes. Truly a great tea!

Farmhouse Tea Shoppe

5455 CHAMBLEE DUNWOODY ROAD
ATLANTA, GEORGIA 30338 (USA)
TEL: 770 673 0099
FAX: 770 673 0055
E-MAIL: BOWLINE99@AOL.COM
OWNERS: VAL SHAVE & LANA QUIBELL

Travelling north on Georgia 400, take exit 5A (Dunwoody/Abernathy). At the second traffic light, turn left onto Mount Vernon Highway. At the third traffic light, turn left onto Chamblee Dunwoody Road. The Farmhouse Tea Shoppe is at the intersection with Mount Vernon Highway. Parking is available behind the house, along the wall near Guardian Bank.

OPEN ALL YEAR. LUNCH SERVED, 11AM-3PM;
TEA SERVED TUESDAY–SATURDAY, 3–5PM;
CLOSED SUNDAY AND SOME PUBLIC HOLIDAYS.

The Farmhouse, which gives this tea shop its name, dates back to 1906 and is now on the national register of historic homes. Fully restored, it sits in half an acre of lawn and gardens where beautiful old pecan trees and antique roses grow. The Dunwoody Preservation Trust owns and maintains the building, and the Dunwoody Arts Association displays and sells the artwork of its members here. The Trust's vision was not that the building should become a museum, but that it should be the literal and figurative heart of Dunwoody, filled with people enjoying it all the time. The Tea Shoppe now occupies several rooms of the house, and the pale yellow walls in all but one rose-coloured room and custom-made drapes lend an air of elegance, while the hand-painted mural in the bathroom is charming and whimsical. As well as serving wonderful afternoon teas with fine loose-leaf tea, assorted tea sandwiches filled with appetisingly imaginative mixtures, traditional sultana scones and delicious cakes (including the signature passion fruit roulade), the Farmhouse organises tea seminars, wine tastings, fashion shows and what they call a Lunch & Learn series at which speakers discuss various issues.

English Breakfast, Decaf English Breakfast, Irish Breakfast, Ceylon, Kenilworth, Earl Grey, Darjeeling, Lapsang Souchong, Apricot , Citron Green, Sencha, various herbal and fruit infusions.

The Tea Room Savannah

7 EAST BROUGHTON STREET
SAVANNAH, GEORGIA 31401 (USA)
TEL: 912 239 9690
FAX: 912 239 9690
WEB SITE: WWW.THETEAROOMSAVANNAH.COM
OWNERS: ELIZABETH RUBY, ANDRÉ BAXTER,
REBECCA WRIGHT, MARJORIE JONES

The Tea Room is a few blocks from the Savannah River. Seven East Broughton Street is between Bull Street and Drayton Street.

OPEN ALL YEAR EXCEPT NEW YEAR'S DAY, ST. PATRICK'S DAY, MEMORIAL DAY, JULY 4TH, LABOR DAY, THANKSGIVING AND CHRISTMAS. MONDAY–SATURDAY, 10AM–6PM; SUNDAY CLOSED.

Located in the National Historic District of a city founded by the British in 1773, the Tea Room is in the heart of Savannah's restored downtown shopping area. Within strolling distance are lovely town squares, ancient oak trees festooned with moss and a plethora of historic house museums. The décor is styled after the Charles Rennie Mackintosh designs for tea establishments in Glasgow. Tables are scattered throughout the main retail section as well as in the library, which has a fireplace, a sofa, wing chairs and antique clocks. This is where tea lectures and private parties often take place.

The luncheon menu includes wonderful soups, salads and quiches, and sandwiches filled with honey-smoked turkey, Lapsang poached chicken salad, or pesto and roast pork with sliced peppers, and delicious cakes and desserts. At tea time, the menu offers everything from light teas to full "royal" afternoon teas; the Tea Room's signature scones with clotted cream and preserves are served with all menus. Some of the loose teas included on the list of more than 60 are available only at the Tea Room. Customers can drink them in the Tea Room or buy some to take home. The shop also sells myriad tea accessories.

Assam, Royal Golden Yunnan, two Keemuns, three Darjeelings, Temi Sikkim, three Oolongs, Mauritius, English Breakfast, French Breakfast, Lapsang Souchong, Morgan's Midday, Riley's Russian Country, Smoky Grey, three Earl Greys, Emperor's Bride, Golden Buddha, Orange Spice, Red Fruits, Vanilla Jasmine, Dragon Pearl Jasmine, Sencha, Lung Ching, Gyokuro, Gunpowder, Pouchong, Soft White Pearls, Mutan Special White, Pai Mu Tan, Madame Butterfly, Citron Green, Green Orchard, White Persian Melon, Chamomile, Rooibos, Honeybush, Gold Tisane, French Verveine.

Dunbar Tea Shop

1 WATER STREET
SANDWICH, MASSACHUSETTS 02563 (USA)
TEL: 508 833 2485
FAX: 508 833 4713
E-MAIL: DUNBAR@CAPECOD.NET
WEB SITE: WWW.DUNBARTEASHOP.COM
OWNER: PAULA & JAMES HEGARTY

Come into Sandwich on Route 6 and take an immediate right onto Route 130. This road leads you into the centre; Dunbar Tea Shop is opposite Dexter Grist Mill.

OPEN ALL YEAR.
MONDAY–SUNDAY, 11AM–5PM; CLOSED CHRISTMAS, NEW YEAR, EASTER AND THANKSGIVING.

Founded in 1637, Sandwich is Cape Cod's oldest town and Dunbar Tea Shop is at the heart of this beautiful heritage community. The shop opened in 1991 and manages to charmingly combine the style of old England with that of New England. Its location is the old carriage house of Dunbar House (built in the early 18th century) and what was once a wood-panelled billiards room and smoking room is now the setting for elegant afternoon teas and delicious lunches. The air is filled with the enticing aroma of baking pies, cakes, shortbreads and scones, and the imaginative menu offers a farmer's lunch with roast beef and mustard, a fisherman's lunch with mackerel and horseradish, a smoked salmon platter and a squire's lunch with pâté. Afternoon teas and cream teas include all the favourite traditional foods, which can be enjoyed in the shady garden or on the patio in summer, and beside a roaring open fire indoors in winter.

The gift shop sells quality teas, British goods and gourmet foods, teapots and tea paraphernalia, and the shop also organises regular special events such as tea tastings, poetry readings and talks on various aspects of tea.

English Breakfast, Decaf English Breakfast, Earl Grey, Decaf Earl Grey, Assam, Darjeeling, Lapsang Souchong, Courtship Blend with Ginger, Formosa Oolong, Gunpowder, Jasmine, Blackcurrant, Hot or Iced Chai, Camomile, Peppermint.

Barakura English Garden

The Japanese company Barakura English Garden has joined forces with three other Japanese companies to establish a chain of extremely attractive traditional English-style shops, gardens and tearooms. The company's Original Teas are being marketed in cooperation with the U.K. Tea Council and St. James's Teas of London.

The philosophy behind the tea concept comes from the president of Barakura English Garden, Eugène Yamada, and the Original Teas are selected from the best tea gardens of the year. Yamada says that this approach will bring about a "tea revolution" in Japan.

The teas served at all the Barakura English Gardens are Assam, Darjeeling and Earl Grey. Camomile, peppermint and lemon grass herbal infusions are also offered on the menus.

Ikspiari Barakura English Garden

MAIHAMA, URAYASU-CITY
CHIBA PREFECTURE, JAPAN
OWNERS: IKSPIARI COMPANY LTD

Ikspiari is in front of Maihama Station on the JR Keiyo-Line. Barakura English Garden is on Museum Lane.

OPEN ALL YEAR. MONDAY–SUNDAY, 10AM–10PM.

Maihama-City is beside Tokyo Bay, which is currently being developed as a resort with hotels and major leisure facilities. Ikspiari is a large shopping centre with the unique theme of a town full of entertainment and history. Barakura English Garden, just one amongst more than a hundred shops, is set out like a classic English manor house and offers a very attractive range of plants, seeds, gardening products, original ladies' clothing and gifts from England. This is Barakura's biggest shop and is run in cooperation with Ikspiari Co. Ltd. The tearoom serves Barakura's original teas, a selection of pastries and traditional British foods from Chatsworth Farm Shop in Derbyshire.

Assam, Darjeeling and Earl Grey. Herbal infusions are also offered.

Tateshiha Heights
Barakura English Garden

5047 KURIDAIRA KITAYAMA
CHINO-CITY
NAGANO PREFECTURE 391-0301 JAPAN
TEL: (+81) (0) 266 77 2019
WEB SITE: WWW.BARAKURA.CO.JP
OWNERS: THE YAMADA FAMILY

The Garden is just off the Chyuo Highway at No 20 Suwa IC. Continue for about 20 minutes along this road, called Venus Line, which leads to Utukushigahara Heights.

OPEN ALL YEAR EXCEPT IN THE SNOW SEASON.
SUMMER: MONDAY–SUNDAY, 9AM–6PM;
WINTER: MONDAY–SUNDAY, 9:30AM–5PM.
PLEASE TELEPHONE TO CONFIRM OPENING TIMES.

The Tateshiha area is famous as one of the most popular resorts in Japan with features not dissimilar from England's Lake District. In the summer, visitors enjoy the beautiful mountains and lakes, and in winter the attractions include hot springs and skiing.

In 1990, the Yamada family of Kowa Creative Art Company Ltd. created Barakura English Garden at Tateshiha Heights. It was the first authentic English-style garden in Japan and had a totally English workforce. Today, both the head gardener and his deputy are English, and when you stand in the midst of the lupins, roses, delphiniums and other typical English plants, you can imagine yourself almost anywhere in England. Miss Kay Yamada, a well-known horticulturalist who has been introducing English culture to the Japanese for 10 years, was responsible for that first garden and for the Japanese boom in interest in English gardens and gardening that followed.

Visitors to Tateshiha Heights can enjoy English afternoon tea, served on traditional English china tablewares, in the conservatory tea room or on the terrace in the garden. The menu offers pastries baked by a French patisserie chef and high-quality contemporary British dishes designed and prepared by English chef Trevor Bryce. Chatsworth Farm Shop foods are also available.

Assam, Darjeeling, Earl Grey, Ceylon, various herbal infusions.

Daimaru Shinsaibashi Barakura English Garden

1-7-1 SHINSAIBASHI-SUJI
OSAKA CITY
OSAKA PREFECTURE 542-8501 JAPAN
TEL: (+81) (0) 6 6271 1231
OWNERS: DAIMARU SHINSAIBASHI COMPANY LTD

The Daimaru Shinsaibashi department store is near Shinsaibashi Station on the subway Midosuji-Line to Nakamozu. The Barakura English Garden is on the rooftop.

OPEN ALL YEAR.
MONDAY–SUNDAY, 10AM–7:30PM.
PLEASE TELEPHONE TO CONFIRM OPENING TIMES.

Osaka has been Japan's second busiest city for 400 years. People in Osaka are well-known as gourmets. On March 25, 2000, the project to create three English gardens, a garden shop and a tea restaurant on the roof of the Daimaru Shinsaibashi department store was realised in cooperation between Barakura English Garden and Daimaru Shinsaibashi Co. Ltd. In response to a request from Daimaru, Mr. Eugene Yamada, president of Barakura, coordinated the details and Robert Adam designed the structure in keeping with the department store's early 20th-century Art Deco style.

The tea restaurant here was the first to serve and sell Barakura's Original Teas. The theme is healthy eating and several of the dishes on the menu are made using British food products.

Assam, Darjeeling and Earl Grey. Herbal infusions are also offered.

350 Years of Tea in Britain

"Tea began as a medicine and grew into a beverage." These are the opening words of the famous Japanese *Book of Tea*, written by Okakura Kakuzo at the beginning of the 20th century. And he was right — the Chinese first drank green tea as a tonic herbal infusion before making it the everyday drink of the people. The Japanese turned it into a ritualised religious experience, and eventually Europe learned of its beneficial properties and drank it both as a cure-all and as a social activity.

The origins of the plant and an understanding of its reviving and refreshing properties are hazy. India claims the earliest evidence of its growth and consumption, and tells how plants were later transplanted from the north of the country to China. The Indian legend claims that the Buddhist monk Boddidharma was in the fifth year of a seven-year sleepless meditation when his eyes began to close in sleep. So, to distract himself, he reached out and plucked some leaves from a near-by bush and chewed them. He quickly found that he was once again wide awake and refreshed and was able to complete his long meditation. The bush was, of course, a wild tea plant. The Chinese legend states that it was as long ago as 2737 BC that the emperor and herbalist Shen Nung discovered tea's beneficial effects. He is said to have been boiling his drinking water in a large pot under a tree one day when by chance a few leaves drifted down into the water. He smelled a wonderful aroma, and when he tasted the brew, he enjoyed the flavour and found that it revived him. So he encouraged the cultivation of the plant and China quickly became a tea-drinking nation, as it still is today.

Buddhist monks are thought to have taken the tea drinking habit to Japan in the eighth century AD. Seeds were planted in the garden of a monastery, and when the emperor tasted the infusion from the new plants, he liked the beverage so much that he instructed plantations to be established near Kyoto — then the capital of Japan. The Japanese adopted the brewing method used by the Chinese at that time whereby powdered green tea was whisked into hot water, and this of course became the focus of the traditional Japanese tea ceremony.

According to the American writer William Ukers, Hajji Mahommed, a Persian merchant, brought the first knowledge of tea to Europe. He claimed that the people of Szechwan "made use of another plant or rather its leaves. This is called Chai Catai and grows in the district of Cathay, which is called Ciacan-fu (Szechwan)."

It was the Portuguese and the Dutch who imported the first shipments of tea to Europe in the late 16th and early 17th centuries. The Dutch started sending regular consignments of China tea from their base on the island of Java (now part of Indonesia) in 1610 and from Japan in 1611. Gradually other European countries became familiar with the herb, but England was behind the rest. The English East India Company had been trading in the area since Queen Elizabeth had granted it a charter in 1600, but was unable to establish a trading base in China. However, a letter from an agent of the company based on the Japanese island of Hirado to a colleague at Macoa proves that the company already knew about tea. He asked for a pot of "the best chaw," but there is no evidence of tea being generally available in England until 1657, when the merchant Thomas Garway claimed he had started to sell both "the leaf and drink." Garway had a shop in Exchange Alley in the City of London (a blue plaque marks the spot today) and in 1660 published a broadsheet extolling the virtues of the beverage and its health-giving properties. In 1658, the London newspaper *Mercurius Politicus* had published the first advertisement for the sale of tea by auction at the Sultaness Head Coffee House in Sweetings Rents, by the Royal Exchange in London, and that too made a point of telling readers that the drink was "by all physicians approved."

So the fashion for drinking tea began in the coffee houses of London — the forerunners of gentlemen's clubs. But these were not places that ladies could go to and so they drank their tea at home, in a small withdrawing room or closet next to or near the bedchamber where the tea and all the necessary tea wares were kept ready for use. Both the tea and the Oriental porcelains were too expensive and valuable to be left with the servants, and so they were displayed as extremely precious items in the lady's private rooms. The popularity of the new beverage increased when the Portuguese princess Catharine of Braganza arrived in London for her marriage to Charles II in

1662. Since the Portuguese had been drinking tea since the early part of the 17th century, she was very fond of the drink and so brought a small chest of loose-leaf tea with her to England. She started brewing it for her friends at court, and awareness and demand amongst the upper classes slowly grew.

As well as being offered to visitors, the beverage was particularly drunk after the main meal of the day to help settle the stomach after the rich and heavy foods that made up the English diet of those days. In the 17th and early 18th centuries, the meal was served in the middle of the day, and after three or four hours of eating and drinking the men would remain around the dining table with their tobacco and alcohol while the ladies withdrew to a closet to talk quietly and brew tea. Later the men would join them, and there would be more tea drinking (often served with thin slices of bread and butter), card playing and music. So the idea of serving tea at some point in the afternoon or early evening was firmly established as part of the day's activities.

From the earliest years of tea drinking in Britain, both black and green teas were being imported from China. Apart from Japan, no other country was involved at this time in the commercial production of tea. When tea was required, a servant would bring all the necessary equipage to the room where tea was to be drunk, but it was then the responsibility of the host or hostess to measure the tea into the pot, pour on the boiling water, and then serve the tea for guests and family. The leaves were brewed in small Chinese stoneware and porcelain teapots and then drunk with sugar. There is little evidence that milk was generally added to the brew until the end of the 17th century, when milk and cream bottles and jugs started to appear.

Throughout the 17th and 18th centuries, tea remained very expensive, due at first to the fact that it was a new and somewhat rare commodity and then because of the heavy taxes imposed by the government. The high prices meant that tea remained an upper-class luxury well into the 18th century. Poorer people had become aware of the drink and wanted their share too, but could not afford it. This inevitably led to a very active black market for smuggled tea that was brought in from Holland and France. It also meant that unscrupulous traders adulterated real tea with the leaves of other trees, or dried and recoloured used tea leaves that had often been sold out of the back door of grand houses by servants who never missed an opportunity to make a little extra money.

It was tea taxes that also led to the serious rift between Britain and her American colonies, and eventually led to the American War of Independence. In 1767, George III's government pushed through an act that gave Britain the power to raise revenue by taxing various goods, including tea, going into America. Since the only official supplier of tea in the colony was the English East India Company, it was almost impossible for the Americans to avoid paying the hated taxes—except by smuggling tea in from other European countries. The Act was repealed in 1773, but almost immediately a new Act gave the East India Company the right to sell tea in America without paying any duties at all. The American merchants were outraged, and when ships carrying 60,000 tons of tea sailed into various American ports, there were hostile demonstrations and in Boston on December 16, 1773, the now famous "tea party." Despite declaring that they would never drink tea again, the Americans did not give it up, and tea drinking continued along very similar lines as in Britain.

By the middle of the 18th century, London's coffee houses had disappeared and the pleasure gardens of London had taken their place as centres of entertainment, social life and tea drinking for all types of people from all social classes, including royalty and the aristocracy. The charge for entrance to such fashionable gardens as Vauxhall, Marylebone and Ranalagh in Chelsea included tea with bread and butter—welcome refreshment after firework displays, concerts, boat rides, promenades, bowling and gambling. But rapid urban growth in the early 1800s led to the closure of the gardens and the only places left serving tea (and coffee) were the inns, taverns and hostelries. Tea now began to play an important role in the temperance movement's battle against the very high levels of alcohol consumption, and tea meetings were held all over Britain in an attempt to convert drinkers and to raise money for the cause. It is possible that the word "teetotaler" has close connections with the beverage.

The first half of the 19th century brought reduced taxation and the wider availability of tea all over the country, and it was at this point that the beverage really became the drink of the British people. In the 1830s, British tea plantations were established in India and the 1870s saw the growth of production in Ceylon, now Sri Lanka. This meant that prices came down even further, consumption continued to increase, and we turned more and more to the stronger flavour of the black tea being produced in our own tea estates — a preference that is still noticeable among British tea drinkers.

Despite ever increasing amounts of tea coming into Britain from the colonies, we were still importing some tea from China, and in the 1840s the first of the sleek and speedy American clipper ships proved that it was possible to bring the teas home much more quickly than previously. In 1850, the first of the British clippers was launched, and soon the ships were racing their cargoes back to the London docks. The annual contest won more publicity for tea than any conventional advertising had ever been able to achieve. But with the opening of the Suez Canal in 1869 and the introduction of steam ships, the clippers were doomed.

As trade increased, packaging and advertising became an important feature as companies fought to keep existing customers and win new ones. Until this point, tea had been sold loose from the chest wrapped in a screw of paper, but in 1826, John Horniman tried to introduce the idea of packaging carefully measured and guaranteed amounts of tea into hygienic, air-tight, foil-lined packets that carried his name. His innovation did not catch on until much later in the century, when all the major companies started to take advantage of the marketing possibilities offered by packeted tea. By the 1870s and 80s, clever publicity ideas included the offer of special blends with fancy and royal names, and free gifts such as teapots, linens, almanacs, pens and even pensions for widows. Eye-catching slogans became important. Lipton advertised their tea as "Direct from the tea garden to the teapot," the United Kingdom Tea Company claimed that their teas were "First hand, Direct From Importer to Consumer," while Lewis's Department store wrote a poem that praised their brand as "A tea strong and savoury, lasting and luscious; A national tea, tea quite nutritious ..."

Until the early 1800s, tea had continued to be taken in the late afternoon or early evening as an after-dinner beverage.

But by this time dinner was served at a much later hour — sometimes at 8 or 8:30pm. To fill the long gap during the day, a new midday meal, luncheon, had been introduced. But this still left a long afternoon without any sustenance, so the tea that had previously been offered after dinner was now served as a perfect afternoon refreshment. It is said that Anna Maria, the seventh Duchess of Bedford, was the first lady to serve afternoon tea to her aristocratic circle of friends in order to stave off what she called "a sinking feeling" at about 5 o'clock. The idea quickly caught on and throughout the Victorian period, tea was adapted to almost all occasions and became a focal point of social life for all classes. High tea, with its filling savoury dishes, home-baked breads, cheeses, cakes and puddings, was the hearty meal that fed hungry working-class families at the end of a long working day in mines, mills, factories and offices, and it was always a large pot of tea that accompanied the food. Because high tea often included a meat dish of some kind, it was also called meat tea or great tea. Afternoon tea, on the other hand, was referred to as little tea or low tea because those taking it sat in low armchairs and sofas and had small tables at their side on which to place cups and saucers. At-home tea receptions gave society ladies the opportunity to receive up to 200 guests at an afternoon tea buffet, with cups of tea handed round by servants. Children at the top of an upper-middle-class or aristocratic home took nursery tea every afternoon with their nanny or governess. Ladies gathered over their sewing or bridge games and always included tea on the agenda. Cheap travel on steam trains allowed town dwellers to escape into the country for a picnic tea by a river or in the corner of a field. Walkers and cyclists stopped at country tearooms for some light refreshment before heading back home. For by now the tearoom and tea shop was a feature of British life. The first had opened in 1884 when the Aerated Bread Company (ABC) had turned a spare back room into a tearoom at their London Bridge branch. When that proved to be an enormous success, other tea shops opened up all over the country. Glasgow became a mecca of tea shops, with Stuart Cranston and his sister, Kate, hitting the headlines with their chain of stylish shops that included the Willow Tea Rooms in the centre of the town.

At the same time, fashion designers were creating breathtakingly beautiful tea gowns of silks and satins, chiffon, lace and velvet, in which fine ladies draped themselves on chaises longues and armchairs and took tea with friends. The idea of these flowing, comfortable but elegant robes was to allow the lady to remove her cripplingly tight corsets, breathe freely and enjoy her tea while still looking incredibly stylish and feminine.

By the end of the 19th century, cookery and etiquette books were instructing ladies and housekeepers as to how and when to serve tea, how to invite guests, the duties of the servants, what foods to offer, how to brew the tea and how to organise different tea events. The simple slices of bread and butter that had always been served with tea were replaced with neat sandwiches (always with the crusts cut off), scones and muffins, buttered toast, biscuits, cakes and pastries. The brewing of the tea was still carried out by the hostess, just as it had always been ever since tea first arrived in the 1650s. A small table was placed close to the hostess with the cups and saucers, the kettle on its burner, one or two teapots for different types of tea, little side plates, sugar and milk or cream and silver teaspoons. She would then pour the tea for her guests, and her daughter or a maid offered the plates of food.

In the early 1900s, newly opened hotels featured afternoon tea in palm courts and lounges where string quartets and palm court trios entertained guests while they relaxed over a cup of Darjeeling or Ceylon. When the tango arrived in London from Argentina in 1910 and a craze for the dance hit fashionable society, these rooms became the venues for afternoon tango tea dances. From 1913 until the 1920s, tea dances were all the rage, but two world wars and later the 1950s coffee boom and fast-food revolution changed British life and pushed tea out of the limelight.

Then in the early 1980s, there was a gradual resurgence of interest in tea. Was it nostalgia or perhaps a feeling that some of us had had enough of plastic tabletops and self-service fast food? Whatever the influence, tea was back in the news. New tea shops opened, retailers started selling a wider range of teas, business meetings were held over tea, charities started using tea as a focus for fund raising, hotels once again organised tea dances, and visitors started arriving from the

U.S. and Japan to sample British tea for themselves. Today, despite a slight decline in the amount of tea drunk in the 1980s and 90s, tea is fighting back against the onslaught of coffee, juices, soft drinks and bottled waters, and is proving itself to still be Britain's favourite drink. Tea is the "power drink" of the 21st century, and some London hotels say that laptop computers are almost as common as handbags in their tea lounges because of the number of businesspeople who not only like to relax over tea, but work over it as well. It seems that people now hold interviews and meetings over tea and even plug into specially installed modems that allow access to Internet and e-mail facilities while they enjoy the more traditional features of afternoon tea. On the more general work front, it seems that some people feel that bringing back the tea lady would increase productivity and team spirit in the workplace because it creates a meeting point where people who are generally isolated at their computer screens and telephones can gather for a chat.

However and wherever we drink it, we import more tea than the whole of Europe and North America combined, and about 75 percent of the British population drinks tea. Each day of the year we consume roughly 165 million cups of tea — that's approximately three cups each. Tea really is still the best drink of the day!

What is Tea?

Although most of us will never taste all of them, the tea-growing regions of the world produce more than 3,000 different teas — and they are all made from the leaves of one plant, an evergreen plant called the *Camellia sinensis*. Part of the same family as the camellias we grow in our gardens, it has shiny evergreen leaves and tiny delicate white flowers and grows slightly differently in different parts of the world.

The characteristics and flavour of the teas that are made from those leaves vary according to the soil, altitude and climatic conditions of the areas in which it is grown. Other contributory factors include the methods of cultivation, the manufacturing process, the blending of teas from different growing areas and whether anything is added to the tea to flavour it.

TEA CULTIVATION

In the wild, tea grows as a large bush or tree that can reach a height of 10 metres or more. Under cultivation, the plant is kept to bush size — approximately 1.5 metres high — and planted in rows roughly 1.5 metres apart. Bushes are trained to grow in a "fan shape," with a flat or rounded surface known as the plucking plateau or table. Leaves are only picked from that plucking table, and for the finest tea only one new bud and two leaves are nipped off by hand and deposited in the basket carried by the pickers. In some hot countries the tea bush grows all year long, while in others it lies dormant during the winter months and starts pushing out new shoots in the spring.

TEA MANUFACTURE

Tea is divided into six categories — white, compressed, green, black, oolong and flavoured. White teas are rare and very expensive and the majority are produced in China. Compressed teas also come mainly from China and are made by compacting processed tea into little cakes, balls or slabs.

The process was developed in the seventh and eighth centuries AD in order to make it easier to transport and store tea. The other four categories are familiar to all of us now, and a wide selection of each is now generally available.

Green tea is made by pan-frying or steaming the freshly gathered leaves to remove the enzymes that would cause them to deteriorate. Then they are rolled and twisted, by hand or by machine, to give each type its individual shape and appearance. For example, Gunpowder tea comes as tightly rolled grey-green pellets that look like lead shot; Chunmee is called Precious Eyebrows because each dried leaf is curved to look exactly like that; Lung Ching leaves are flat and yellowy green. In Japan, machines steam the leaves and then cut them and roll them flat into shiny dark green needles. Green teas usually give a pale yellow-green liquor with a slightly pungent, herby or sappy flavour that is best without milk.

Black tea makes up the largest percentage of all the tea produced worldwide. There are five basic stages to its manufacture.

1. Withering. The plucked leaf is taken to the factory, spread out on trays and left in temperatures of 25–30 degrees Centigrade for between 10 and 16 hours in order to reduce the water content. In some factories, the time is shortened with the help of warm-air fans.

2. Rolling or cutting. The withered leaves are fed into machines that twist and break the surface, thus releasing the enzymes or leaf juices. For "orthodox" manufacture, the machine rolls and gently twists the leaf, and in China and Taiwan, this is sometimes still done by hand. For CTC (Cut Tear and Curl) teas, the machine cuts the leaves down into small particles.

3. Oxidation (fermentation). The twisted or broken leaves are laid on trays or placed in troughs in a cool and humid atmosphere for between three and five hours, during which time it is gently turned at regular intervals. The juices that have been released by the rolling and cutting process now come into contact with oxygen in the air, and the leaf begins to oxidise (or ferment, as the trade still terms it). At the end of this stage, the green pieces of leaf have turned a golden russet colour.

4. Drying (firing). The oxidised tea is fed on to a conveyor belt that passes slowly through a hot air chamber, so

evaporating the remaining leaf moisture and turning the leaf to a dark brown or black.

5. Grading (sorting). After drying, the black tea is fed through a series of sieves, which sort or grade the tea into different particle sizes. The different grades are then packed into bags or chests ready for their onward journey to tea auction centres, merchants and packers all over the world. Wooden chests are generally only used today for the expensive large leaf varieties, while small leafed teas go into foil-lined paper sacks that are more environmentally friendly and easier to handle.

Oolong tea is a semi-oxidised (semi-fermented) tea produced in China's Fujian Province and in Taiwan. After withering (often in direct sunlight), the leaves are shaken in bamboo baskets to bruise the leaf edges. Then they are alternately shaken and spread out in cool air until the veins and bruised edges turn a reddish colour while the rest of the leaf remains green. Sometimes the bruising process is carried out with the leaves wrapped inside cloth bags that are gently rolled by hand or in a special machine. The oxidation period is stopped by firing the leaves at a higher temperature than for black teas, and the finished leaf is often a pale reddish-brown colour. The infusion is pale golden or amber in colour and has a soft, subtle, sometimes peachy flavour that is best without milk.

Flavoured teas are made by adding fruits, nuts, flowers, spices or herbs to green, oolong or black teas after the manufacturing process is finished. Flower-flavoured teas such as jasmine, orange blossom, orchid or rose are mixed with actual flower petals; fruit-flavoured teas such as apple, lemon, lime, peach, etc, are blended with the essential oils of the fruit or with small pieces of dried peel or fruit flesh; spiced teas often contain such flavourings as pieces of vanilla pod or cinnamon bark; while herb teas, such as mint tea or sage tea, are mixed with dried leaves or stems from the particular herb. The huge variety of flavoured teas is becoming increasingly popular and accounts for 2 percent of today's tea market.

Flavoured teas should not be confused with herbal infusions and tisanes, which are not made with leaves from the *Camellia sinensis* but with plant parts of the specific herbs. They are often believed to have medicinal properties and the most popular are camomile, a calming soothing herb; peppermint, which is good for the digestion; and lemon verbena, which calms the stomach and aids the digestion. Fruit infusions, similarly, do not contain any actual tea. They are made instead with pieces of peel or fruit blossoms blended with dried hibiscus leaves to produce a refreshing fruit-flavoured infusion. Some people believe that herbals are overtaking regular tea and it is a fast-growing section of the market, but the amount of herbals drunk in the U.K. is still very small compared to the gallons of tea that we consume.

Decaffeinated tea is now widely available for those tea drinkers who are worried about caffeine. Three methods of decaffeinating are now used in different countries (using carbon dioxide, methylene chloride or ethyl acetate), and research is still going on in order to produce better-quality products. Scientists are also working to develop modified tea plants that do not contain caffeine. Researchers at Glasgow University have cloned one of the genes responsible for caffeine production in tea plants, and this could lead to the production of caffeine-free plants.

TEA GRADES

The word grade is used by the tea trade to describe the size of a leaf particle after the manufacturing process is finished. There are two main grade divisions — leaf (or pekoe) and broken. Pekoe is a corruption of the old Chinese word describing the downy white hairs on the back of a young leaf or bud. A leaf or pekoe grade (P) is virtually a whole leaf, and the largest is orange pekoe, with orange having nothing to do with flavour but more probably signifying "royal," from a reference the Dutch House of Orange (the Dutch were, of course, the first to ship fine teas into Europe). Broken pekoe grades range from the largest pieces of broken orange pekoe to the very fine pekoe fannings or dust, which are further classified PF1, PF2, PF3, etc, to denote decreasing particle size.

BLENDING

Some connoisseur tea drinkers enjoy the subtle differences offered by speciality teas from named estates each season. Like wine drinkers, they appreciate the effects that seasonal variations make on the final character of the tea. Others prefer a standard flavour every time they buy their favourite tea from their regular retailer. So each packing company employs a team of tea tasters who carefully select a range of teas from around the world that will give that predictable character every single time the customer opens the packet. Since tea flavours vary all the time, the recipe that goes into a blend is always slightly different. A blend, either loose in a packet or in tea bags, can contain between 15 and 35 different teas from any of the world's producing areas.

Tea tasters train for five years, and most of them will tell you that they go on learning the art throughout their working lives. Tasters assess the quality and flavour of a tea by examining the colour and appearance of the dry leaf, the smell and appearance of the wet infused leaf, and the smell and flavour of the liquor. Tasters often taste between 200 and 1,000 teas every day in order to adjust the recipe to suit customers' requirements.

Some of the World's Best Teas

As well as offering everyday blends of tea, usually in tea bags, most retailers also now stock a good range of speciality teas. Blends account for 90 percent of tea consumed in Britain, while the speciality sector makes up the other 10 percent.

SPECIALITY TEAS ARE:

- Teas that take their name from the plantation on which they are grown (these are often referred to as single-estate or single-source teas).
- Teas from a particular area or country.
- Teas that are blended for a particular time of day or occasion.
- A blend of teas to which fruit, flower, spice or herb flavourings have been added.

Teas from China

GUNPOWDER

A green tea that is steamed and rolled into small pellets without breaking the veins or leaf surface. These are then dried and, when brewed in hot water, produce a very light, refreshing, pale-coloured tea that has a slightly grassy taste. The name is said to have been given to the tea because the little pellets look like gunshot or gunpowder of years gone by. Drink without milk.

CHUN MEE

A green tea whose leaves are delicately curved to look like the "precious eyebrows" that its name means. The tea is processed with skill and patience, and the long, twisty pieces of leaf give a pale yellow infusion that should have a smooth, subtle, slightly plummy taste. Drink without milk.

LUNG CHING

A green tea also known as Dragon's Well. Processing demands very careful handling and an understanding of how the temperature of the pan in which the leaves are dried can affect the final quality and flavour. The flat yellow-green leaves give a wonderful mellow aroma and flavour. The very finest is made from one bud and one leaf. Drink without milk.

JASMINE

Green tea that has been mixed with jasmine flowers. The blooms are picked during the day but stored in a cool place until nighttime, when they open to release their powerful fragrance. Sometimes the flowers are placed in piles next to piles of tea so that the leaves absorb the flowers' perfume. Ordinary grades are perfumed two or three times. The very best are scented seven times. Sometimes the blossoms are layered with the tea in tea chests. The flowers mixed in with the tea in the packet are not the blossoms that were used for scenting. They are often added later just to give the tea an attractive appearance.

KEEMUN

A black tea from Anhui Province. The Chinese refer to all black teas as red teas, and this is to them the "king of red teas." The processing is skilled and each tight black strip is an entire leaf. The infusion is a clear rich amber colour and the aroma and taste are delicately scented with sometimes a hint of rose or orchid. Drink without milk.

LAPSANG SOUCHONG

A large leaf black tea distinguished by its smoky aroma and flavour. The story goes that when the Chinese first discovered tea, they used to dry it in the sun, and Chinese legend claims that the smoking process was developed by accident. One night an army decided to camp in a tea factory that was full of drying leaves awaiting processing, and they held up the normal working routine. When the soldiers left, the workers needed to prepare the leaves for market as quickly as possible, so they lit open fires of pinewood to speed the drying. The tea reached market on time and a new flavour had been created. Today, the tea is withered over pine fires, then stuffed into wooden barrels, covered with a cloth and left to oxidise. Then it is rolled and pan-fried and finally spread out in bamboo baskets and left to dry over smoking pine fires. The infusion is a rich red colour and is better drunk without milk.

YUNNAN

A black tea from Yunnan Province in the southwest of China, where tea is first thought to have grown. The plants that grow in the area produce fat sturdy buds and shoots, and the leaves are thick and fleshy. Yunnan teas are very similar in appearance to Assam teas, having plenty of little golden flecks amongst the black pieces of leaf. The fairly strong, slightly peppery flavour is also similar, and it is the only China tea that drinks well with a little milk.

OOLONG

China oolongs are mostly made in Fujian Province, although some other districts now also produce them. The leaves are often quite twisted and crinkly in appearance and are usually much lighter brown than Chinese black teas. When brewed in boiling water, the leaves gradually unfurl and reveal a wonderful mixture of pink-red markings mixed with the greens and browns of the semi-oxidised tea. The best known of China's oolongs is Ti Kwan Yin (Tea of the Iron Goddess of Mercy), Wuyi Shui Hsien, Dahongpao (Scarlet Robe) and Fonghwang Tan-Chung. But these are not often found in Britain and most blends are marketed simply as China Oolong. Drink without milk.

POUCHONG

Lightly oxidised China tea whose name means "the wrapped kind" from the fact that the tea is wrapped in paper made from cotton while it oxidises. The oxidation time is shorter than for oolongs and it gives a pale golden yellow infusion with a very mild, smooth flavour. It is often used as a base for jasmine teas. Drink without milk.

ROSE CONGOU

A large-leafed China black tea flavoured with dried rose petals. Congou is a derivation of the Chinese word gongfu meaning "demanding skill." The leaves have to be very carefully handled, and the temperature control and timing of each part of the process is crucial to the final quality. The Chinese also flavour their teas with magnolia, orchid and lychee. All should be drunk without milk.

Teas from Taiwan

FORMOSA OOLONG

When farmers from China's Fujian Province emigrated to the island of Formosa (now Taiwan) in the 1850s, they took with them their traditional methods of manufacturing tea. The best of Taiwan's oolongs are produced on the slopes of Mount Dung Ding. The infusion is orangey-green and the taste is light and smooth. Drink without milk.

Teas from Japan

SENCHA

The most common and popular of Japan's green teas. The freshly picked leaves are first steamed and then fluffed by hot air, and rolled, dried and polished to become flat, dark-green, needle-like leaves. They brew quickly to give a pale yellow, very clear infusion that has a soft herbal taste. Drink without milk.

GYOKURO

The very best of Japan's green teas. The bushes are covered for about 20 days before being plucked with canvas or reed mats to reduce the amount of light reaching the bushes as they grow. The leaves therefore produce more chlorophyll and have a much more concentrated sweet flavour than Sencha. It is this tea that is ground down to a fine powder to make "matcha," which is whisked into hot water and drunk during the Japanese tea ceremony. Drink without milk.

HOUJICHA

A roasted tea that turns lower-grade green leaves into light brown, wedge-like pieces that give a pale, slightly sweet infusion. Drink without milk.

GENMAICHA

Lower-grade green tea that is mixed with popped rice and corn that has been boiled and dried. The addition of the grains gives the light brown brew an interesting and gently sweet flavour. Drink without milk.

Teas from India

ASSAM

Black teas grown in the hot and steamy conditions of the Brahmaputra River valley in Assam in northeast India give a full-bodied, rich, dark liquor that has a smooth, malty flavour. It is ideal as the first cup of the day and as a breakfast tea. Single-source teas from named estates often give a more subtle flavour than the blends of Assam that are more readily available. Drink with or without milk.

DARJEELING

Known as "the champagne of teas," Darjeeling is grown several thousand feet above sea level in the foothills of the Himalayan mountains. The cold days of winter and the chilly mornings and extremely hot days of summer give a concentrated, slightly astringent flavour that is prized all over the world. Drink without milk.

NILGIRI

The black teas from the Nilgiri hills in the south of India are bright, fruity and flavoursome and are often blended with lighter teas to add strength and interest.

Teas from Sri Lanka (Ceylon)

DIMBULA

Grown at 5,000 feet above sea level, Dimbula black teas give a light, bright infusion and a crisp strong flavour. Dimbula was one of the first areas of the island to be planted with tea after the demise of the coffee estates in the 1860s. Drink with or without milk.

NUWARA ELIYA

Black teas from the hill country in the centre of the island are Sri Lanka's finest. The even pieces of brown leaf give a rich golden liquor that has a lightly perfumed brisk flavour.

UVA

A fine-flavoured black tea from the eastern slopes of the central mountains of Sri Lanka, where the dry wind has a marked effect on the quality and character of the teas. Uva teas are bright in colour and have a dry, crisp taste. Drink with or without milk.

Teas from Kenya

Kenya's black CTC teas give a strong rich tea. The infusion is dark and coppery and the flavour is brisk and full. In Britain, we buy approximately 50 percent of our teas from Kenya and they are ideal for the blends that go into everyday teabags. Drink with milk.

Tea from South Africa

ZULU TEA

A black CTC tea from Kwazulu—the only South African tea to be exported for international consumption. The flavour is lively and strong and is best drunk with milk.

Teas from Indonesia

Indonesian black teas are light and flavoursome. Most are sold for blending purposes as this produces good financial rewards in terms of foreign currency for the country. It is possible to buy some single estate Indonesian teas, and these are very refreshing drunk without milk and perhaps with a slice of lemon.

Tea blends

ENGLISH BREAKFAST

This is traditionally a blend of Assam and Ceylon teas that gives pungency, strength and flavour to complement a traditional English breakfast and give a good brisk start to the day. Today, many breakfast blends contain teas from African countries such as Malawi, Tanzania, Zimbabwe and Kenya, which give the tea a coppery colour and strength of flavour.

AFTERNOON BLEND

This is traditionally a blend of delicate Darjeeling teas and high-grown Ceylon teas to produce a refreshing light tea, which makes an ideal companion to cucumber sandwiches, cream pastries and fruit cakes.

EARL GREY

Traditionally, a blend of black China teas treated with the natural oil of the bergamot fruit which gives the blend a perfumed citrus flavour. Earl Grey is said to have been originally blended for the second Earl Grey when he was British prime minister in the 19th century. Today it is the most popular of all speciality teas.

HOUSE BLEND

A house blend may be a standard blend already offered by local suppliers, but it may have been specially created for a particular tea shop by its tea supplier in order to give a quality and taste that suits the local water, local customers and the menu offered.

Buying, Storing and Brewing Tea

When you buy packaged tea, make sure that packets and tins are undamaged and that any wrapping is intact. It is important that the tea has been kept in air-tight conditions in order to preserve flavour and quality.

When buying loose-leaf tea, it is worth remembering that tea keeps best at the retailers' shop when stored in large canisters that have air-tight lids with a strong seal. Tea should not be stored in glass and is best in dry, cool conditions.

The leaf should look dry and even, and all the pieces of leaf should be approximately the same size. An uneven blend that has leaves of varying particle size can cause problems when brewing since the different-sized pieces of leaf will release their flavour and colour at different rates, therefore giving an unbalanced overall flavour and quality.

At home, always store leaf and bagged tea in an air-tight container with a tightly fitting lid and keep in a cool dry place away from other strong flavours and smells since tea easily absorbs other flavours.

TEA	COUNTRY OF ORIGIN
Darjeeling	India
Assam	India
Ceylon Blend	Sri Lanka
Kenya	Kenya
Earl Grey	China or India
Lapsang Souchong	China or Taiwan
China Oolong	China or Taiwan

Brewing a Good Cup of Tea

- Always use good-quality loose-leaf or bagged tea.
- Always fill the kettle with freshly drawn cold water.
- When brewing black and oolong teas, allow the water to reach boiling point before pouring on to the leaves.
- When brewing green tea, boil the water and then allow it to cool slightly before pouring on to the leaves.
- Measure the tea carefully into the pot: use one tea bag or one rounded teaspoon of loose tea for each cup to be served.
- Allow the tea to brew for the correct number of minutes. Small-leafed black tea normally needs 2–3 minutes; larger leafed black tea needs 3–5 minutes; oolong teas need 5–7 minutes; green teas need 1–3 minutes. Where possible, follow instructions on packets or test each tea to find the number of minutes that suits.

MILK/BLACK/LEMON*	CHARACTERISTICS
Black or milk	Delicate, slightly astringent flavour
Black or milk	Full-bodied with a rich, smooth, malty flavour
Black or milk	Brisk, full flavour with a bright colour
Black or milk	A strong tea with a brisk flavour
Black or lemon	Flavoured with the natural oil of the citrus fruit bergamot
Black	Smoky aroma and flavour
Black	Subtle, delicate, lightly flavoured tea

**The addition of lemon is a matter of personal choice.*

Index of Best Tea Places

Cornwall

CHARLOTTE'S TEA-HOUSE *p.* 10

MAD HATTER'S *p.* 11

THE OLD RECTORY FARM TEAROOMS *p.* 12

THE PLANTATION CAFÉ *p.* 13

TRENANCE COTTAGE TEA ROOM & GARDENS *p.* 14

Devon

COURT BARN COUNTRY HOUSE HOTEL *p.* 15

THE CLOCK TOWER TEAROOMS *p.* 16

THE COMMODORE HOTEL *p.* 17

THE COSY TEAPOT *p.* 18

TILLY'S TEA ROOM *p.* 19

Somerset

LEWIS'S TEA-ROOMS *p.* 20

SALLY LUNN'S HOUSE & MUSEUM *p.* 21

THE PUMP ROOM *p.* 22

Wiltshire

POLLY TEA ROOMS *p.* 23

THE BRIDGE TEA ROOMS *p.* 24

Berkshire

CROOKED HOUSE TEA ROOMS *p.* 38

East Sussex

CLARA'S *p.* 39

PAVILION TEA ROOMS *p.* 40

THE TEA TREE *p.* 41

Hampshire

GILBERT WHITE'S TEA PARLOUR *p.* 42

Kent

CLARIS'S *p.* 43

Surrey

HASKETTS TEA & COFFEE SHOP *p.* 44

West Sussex

SHEPHERDS TEAROOMS *p.* 45

London

THE LOUNGE, FOUR SEASONS HOTEL *p.* 56

GEORGIAN RESTAURANT, HARRODS *p.* 57

PALM COURT, LE MERIDIEN WALDORF *p.* 58

OAK ROOM LOUNGE, LE MERIDIEN PICCADILLY *p.* 59

CAVALRY BAR AND PALACE LOUNGE,
THE RUBENS HOTEL *p.* 60

THE CONSERVATORY, THE CHESTERFIELD *p.* 61

THE CONSERVATORY, THE LANESBOROUGH *p.* 62

THE PROMENADE, THE DORCHESTER *p.* 63

THE LANDMARK HOTEL *p.* 64

THE MILESTONE HOTEL *p.* 65

THE MONTAGUE ON THE GARDENS *p.* 66

Essex

POPPYS TEA ROOM *p.* 78

SQUIRES *p.* 79

TEA ON THE GREEN *p.* 80

TRINITY HOUSE TEAROOM & GARDEN *p.* 81

Norfolk

MARGARET'S TEA ROOMS *p.* 82

NORWICH TEA & COFFEE SHOP *p.* 83

Suffolk

FLYING FIFTEENS *p.* 84

THE SWAN *p.* 85

Gloucestershire

THE BAY TREE *p.* 96

THE BLACK CAT *p.* 97

TETBURY GALLERY TEA ROOM *p.* 98

TWO TOADS *p.* 99

Nottinghamshire

OLDE SCHOOL TEAROOM *p.* 100

OLLERTON MILL TEA SHOP *p.* 101

THE LOCK HOUSE TEA ROOMS *p.* 102

Oxfordshire

ANNIE'S TEA ROOMS *p.* 103

Shropshire

ANN BOLEYN TEA ROOM *p.* 104

BIRD ON THE ROCK TEAROOM *p.* 105

DE GREYS *p.* 106

THE MARSHMALLOW *p.* 107

County Durham

THE MARKET PLACE TEASHOP *p.* 120

Northumberland

THE COPPER KETTLE TEA ROOMS *p.* 121

Yorkshire

BETTYS CAFÉ TEA ROOMS, HARROGATE *p.* 122

BETTYS CAFÉ TEA ROOMS, ILKLEY *p.* 123

BETTYS CAFÉ TEA ROOMS, NORTHALLERTON *p.* 124

BETTYS CAFÉ TEA ROOMS, YORK *p.* 125

BULLIVANT OF YORK *p.* 126

CLARK'S OF EASINGWOLD *p.* 127

CLARK'S TEAROOMS *p.* 128

ELIZABETH MOTHAM & SONS *p.* 129

LITTLE BETTYS *p.* 130

THE MAD HATTER TEA SHOP *p.* 131

THE PRIEST'S HOUSE *p.* 132

Cumbria

THE HAZELMERE CAFÉ & BAKERY *p.* 144

NEW VILLAGE TEA ROOMS *p.* 145

Derbyshire

THE COTTAGE TEA ROOM *p.* 146

NORTHERN TEA MERCHANTS *p.* 147

Lancashire

CAFÉ CAPRICE *p.* 148

NOSTALGIA TEAROOMS *p.* 149

THE TOBY JUG TEA SHOP *p.* 150

Staffordshire

GREYSTONES 17TH CENTURY TEA ROOM *p.* 151

ROYAL DOULTON VISITOR CENTRE *p.* 152

Carmarthenshire

FELIN NEWYDD WATERMILL *p.* 162

Gwynedd

BADGER'S CAFÉ & PATISSERIE *p.* 163

CEMLYN RESTAURANT & TEA SHOP *p.* 164

Glamorgan

GWALIA TEA ROOMS *p.* 165

Dumfries

ABBEY COTTAGE TEA ROOMS *p.* 174

Edinburgh

THE CALEDONIAN HILTON HOTEL *p.* 175

THE TEA ROOM *p.* 176

Fife

KIND KYTTOCK'S KITCHEN *p.* 177

Glasgow

MISS CRANSTON'S TEAROOMS *p.* 178

Strathclyde

COACH HOUSE COFFEE SHOP *p.* 179

THE WILLOW TEA ROOMS *p.* 180

WILLOW TEA ROOMS *p.* 181

Tea Rooms Around the World

MARIAGE FRÈRES (*France*) *p.* 190

ELMWOOD INN (*United States of America*) *p.* 193

MACNAB'S TEA ROOM (*United States of America*) *p.* 195

THE FAIRMONT EMPRESS HOTEL (*Canada*) *p.* 196

FARMHOUSE TEA SHOPPE
(*United States of America*) *p.* 197

THE TEA ROOM SAVANNAH
(*United States of America*) *p.* 198

DUNBAR TEA SHOP (*United States of America*) *p.* 199

IKSPIARI BARAKURA ENGLISH GARDEN (*Japan*) *p.* 200

TATESHIHA HEIGHTS
BARAKURA ENGLISH GARDEN (*Japan*) *p.* 201

DAIMARU SHINSAIBASHI
BARAKURA ENGLISH GARDEN (*Japan*) *p.* 202

Notes

Notes

Notes

Notes

Notes

Notes

Notes

Notes